# Fair Sex

# Fair Sex

*Family size and structure, 1900–39*

Diana Gittins

Hutchinson

London  Melbourne  Sydney  Auckland  Johannesburg

Hutchinson & Co. (Publishers) Ltd
An imprint of the Hutchinson Publishing Group
17–21 Conway Street, London W1P 6JD

Hutchinson Group (Australia) Pty Ltd
30–32 Cremorne Street, Richmond South, Victoria 3121
PO Box 151, Broadway, New South Wales 2007

Hutchinson Group (NZ) Ltd
32–34 View Road, PO Box 40–086, Glenfield, Auckland 10

Hutchinson Group (SA) (Pty) Ltd
PO Box 337, Bergvlei 2012, South Africa

First published 1982

Set in Times

Printed in Great Britain by The Anchor Press Ltd
and bound by Wm Brendon & Son Ltd
both of Tiptree, Essex

**British Library Cataloguing in Publication Data**

Gittins, Diana
  Fair sex.
  1. Family – Great Britain
  I. Title
  306.8'0941      HQ614

ISBN   0 09 145490 5 cased
       0 09 145491 3 paper

*For Emily and Sydney*

# Contents

# Preface

The principal aim of this book is to analyse the dramatic decline in family size which occurred among the working classes in England and Wales between 1900 and 1939. Not much interest has been taken in this phenomenon, partly because it is often assumed that working-class behaviour and ideals are simply an imitation of earlier middle-class ideals and practices: a result of 'diffusion'. This assumption seems far too simplistic and unsatisfactory, so much of this book is concerned with seeking out alternative explanations. The problem of fertility and family size is, however, extremely complex and, rather than starting with one particular theoretical framework, I have been primarily concerned with looking at the question in an exploratory way.

Most research on fertility and family size has concentrated either on demographic and economic change at a 'macro' level, or has examined the family unit alone without reference to its wider socio-economic context. I have tried to consider both the macro and the micro aspects of social change and family structure, as it seems misleading to divorce the two. In past studies too little attention has been paid, in particular, to the potential influence of social norms, values and power relationships on reproductive behaviour; this book deliberately pays a quite substantial amount of attention to the interpretive dimension to the problem. Moreover, most research has classified families in terms of the husband's social class and occupation, taking little account of the potential relevance of women's occupational experience and relation to the economic system. This book considers women's occupational experience as a crucial factor, a previously missing link, in understanding reproductive behaviour and family organization.

The research has thus been of a highly cross-disciplinary nature, and will hopefully be of interest to sociologists, social historians, demographers and those involved in women's studies. No doubt its very diversity will render it liable to criticism, but I hope readers will bear in mind that it is very much an exploratory study, in terms of approach, methods and data. Many of the ideas are speculative and provide ample scope for further research.

I have received a great deal of help and criticism from various sources, for which I am very grateful. I would first like to thank the Social Science Research Council for financing the research and the University of Essex for providing the facilities in which to carry it out. I owe an enormous amount to Joan Busfield, who first kindled my interest in this field, and who, as supervisor for my Ph.D, consistently helped, encouraged and criticized my work. I owe a great deal to Leonore Davidoff for her encouragement, support and useful comments throughout. My thanks are also due to Kenneth MacDonald, David Robertson and Phil Holden for all their help with the statistical analysis, to Brenda Corti for her help in coding the census, to Thea Vigne and Paul Thompson for help and advice on interviewing and the research generally, to David Lockwood, Howard Newby, Joe Banks, Geoffrey Hawthorn for reading and criticizing the thesis, to Mary Girling for all her moral support, and to all those who helped to type the manuscript.

I am greatly indebted to the women who allowed me to interview them, and without whom this research would have been impossible. I would also like to thank the Family Planning Association for letting me use their records from the Manchester and Salford Mothers' Clinic. I alone, of course, remain responsible for all the mistakes and imperfections which still remain.

# 1 Theories of fertility and the family

Fertility has declined dramatically over the past 100 years. During the same period there have been numerous and wide-ranging changes and developments in the social, economic and political spheres. As a result the small family has become widely recognized as an essential factor in the industrialization process,[1]* and has been accepted as an integral part of advanced industrial society. The dynamics of population change and social change are inextricably linked, yet for all that there are considerable gaps in our knowledge and understanding of why and how family structure and size change and vary, or exactly how industrialization is related to these changes.

Demographers have generally studied population change at a macro level, ignoring to a great extent the institution in which population dynamics are generated: the family. Sociologists have studied the family in relation to social change, but have seldom considered the question of family size and demographic change. Others have studied marriage and reproduction within the context of the family unit alone, paying little attention to the wider social, economic and political systems in which families are situated and with which their members interact. While a strong inverse correlation between women working and fertility has been noted for some time, few have considered the changing position of women in society as a potentially important factor in understanding the relation between social change and family structure. Studying fertility and family structure involves analysing demographic, sociological, economic and political variables. By and large, the majority of relevant theories on the subject are demographic, socio-economic or sociological. Let us first consider demographic theories.

*Superior figures refer to the Notes and references on pages 207–17.

**Demographic theories**

Few demographers have attempted to explain population changes solely in terms of demographic factors. Many, however, have given them primary concern, while acknowledging that they can be affected by other (usually economic) variables.[2] Few have considered the potential impact of social or cultural factors. Demographers tend to regard their subject as a science concerned primarily with quantitative measurement and statistical analysis. They leave little room for the less easily quantifiable realm of norms, ideals and values.

Demographic variables cannot, however, be ignored in any analysis of fertility. To understand changing patterns of fertility it is essential to examine variables relating to birth rates, death rates and migration. The age structure and sex ratio of a population are also crucial, for they in turn affect patterns of marriage and fertility rates. The older a woman is, the less fecund she is and the less she is exposed to the risk of pregnancy; age at marriage also affects the patterning of childbearing. If a given population manifests a high age at marriage for women and a low level of fertility, it can be assumed that there is a strong causal link between the two. Such explanations, however, tell us nothing as to why there was a high age at marriage in the first place; the answer to this often relates to the realms of sociology and economics rather than to demography.

Hajnal,[3] for instance, attributed the decline of fertility among the working classes between the wars to a temporary phase of postponed marriage. This he interpreted as a reaction to the economic depression. While there can be little doubt that many working-class couples did defer marriage, exactly how and by what process was this related to the economy? Was it only those working-class couples who were suffering most from the depression who postponed marriage? In other words, how did individuals' *perceptions* of their situation change and vary, and how did this affect beliefs and behaviour concerning marriage and family size? Demographic theories give no consideration to the problem at an individual level, to the actual dynamics of decision-making within the context of the family. Nor do they give attention to values, norms and beliefs as potential determinants of reproductive behaviour.

Economic variables do not operate in a mechanistic way on

demographic variables, but are interpreted, perceived, internalized by individuals before they directly affect patterns of marriage and family size. Certainly demographic factors must be considered, but they should not necessarily be regarded as causal explanations in themselves. Low age at marriage does not necessarily result in high fertility;[4] marriage involves interaction between two individuals with their own sets of values and norms, which are in turn related to, and affected by, the broader socio-economic, political and cultural systems. As Parkin says: 'values are generally not imposed on men in any crudely mechanistic way. Men also impose their will by selecting, as it were, from the range of values which any complex society generates. At the same time, individuals do not construct their social worlds in terms of a wholly personal vision'.[5] Demographic explanations take no account of the availability of choice at an individual level, and thus ignore an important dimension to problems of fertility, family size and population change generally.

## Economic and socio-economic theories of fertility

Malthus explained the problem of population in terms of resources. There are two basic premises to his theory; first, that while a population will grow exponentially, material resources cannot: 'the power of population is indefinitely greater than the power in the earth to produce a subsistence for man'.[6] Second, he argued that if a population grows beyond a limit at which resources can support it, population growth may be 'checked' in either, or both, of two ways. First, by what he called 'positive checks': war, famine, disease and mortality generally. Second, and preferably, by 'preventive checks' or 'moral restraint' – either by delaying marriage (Malthus's hope) or by birth control (the neo-Malthusian strategy).

Central to his theory is the idea that population and the economic system are causally linked, so that patterns of family size, fertility and mortality are held to be responses to the changing availability of resources. Yet in pre-industrial society disease was capable of decimating a population which was not, relatively, lacking in adequate means of subsistence. The same was often true with war. Clearly famine was linked to resources, but with the increasing improvements in transportation and agriculture during the eighteenth century, famine had become a rare occurrence. Resources, therefore, were not linked in a causal way to population change in the way Malthus proposed (although Wrigley has argued that Malthus's theory fits the pre-industrial, if not industrial, period reasonably well).

Also implicit in Malthus's theory is the concept of an ideal balance between population and resources (an 'optimum population' as it has been called). This notion, however, pays inadequate attention to the question of *distribution* of resources – Marx's criticism of Malthus. It ignores the relevance of the economic and social systems through which resources must flow. To some extent, Malthus was aware of this. He assumed, however, that the social order was 'natural', and that there would always be uneven distribution of resources; as poverty could never be cured, it could only be alleviated through 'moral restraint'. Needless to say, Marx also attacked Malthus on this point: for Marx, population was only a problem relevant to the capitalist mode of production, when an excess population forms a reserve army of labour necessary for capitalists to keep wages down and profits up.

There are, therefore, two criticisms of Malthusian theory. First, there is little substantiation that resources and population are causally linked in the way he suggested. Second, little account is taken of the influence of the socio-economic system on distribution of resources or of the ways in which patterns of fertility and childbearing might change and vary. While Marx rightly drew attention to the importance of economic distribution, he, no more than Malthus, provided sufficient evidence of a direct link between the economic system and changes in population and fertility. As Eversley comments: 'the failure which the Marxist school shares with many of the neo-classical economists lies in their omission of any explanation of the mechanism which translates this theoretical demand for labour into marriages and children, or alternatively, turns an excessive labour force into a smaller one'.[7]

Neither Malthus nor Marx showed much interest in the family as the institution within which population dynamics are generated, or its relation to the broader socio-economic, political and cultural systems. Engels, however, did consider the relation between the socio-economic system, the family and the position of women. He saw the subordinate position of women in society and their relegation to unpaid domestic work as a direct result of the institution of private property and the resultant system of inheritance through the male:

thus on the one hand, in proportion as wealth increased it made the man's position in the family more important than the woman's, and on the other hand created an impulse to exploit this strengthened position in order to overthrow, in favour of his children, the traditional order of inheritance. This . . . was impossible as long as descent was reckoned according to mother right.[8]

Engels's work is important because it draws attention to the broad material factors affecting the relations between the socio-economic system and family organization. He does not, however, give adequate consideration to the problem of women's relation to the socio-economic system through *reproduction*:

families perpetuated themselves through time by the inheritance of property. Thus changes took place in the definition of children. From new members of a societal group, they became either private heirs or subordinate, dependent workers . . . women's reproductive labor, like their productive work, also underwent a transformation from social to private. People and property became intertwined, and each became part of the definition of the other.[9]

Engels's analysis stopped short in considering woman's role as reproducer of labour; recently feminists have examined this question (see the discussion on pages 23–4).

Contemporary socio-economic theories of fertility have concentrated on the family as the unit of analysis. In many ways, however, they have remained Malthusian in their approach, giving prime consideration to the question of resources, albeit on a micro level, by assuming a direct causal relationship between resources and family size. Few have analysed the problem in broader materialist terms seeking to explain the relationship between the socio-economic system, the position of women and the changing structure of the family. They have drawn extensively from the Malthusian heritage, while, it would seem, ignoring some of the important factors to which Engels drew attention.

Theorists such as Becker,[10] Leibenstein[11] and Okun[12] have concentrated primarily on the relationship between income and family size. Essentially, they postulate that parents will only have as many children as they can afford, and that decision-making on family size is similar to the decision-making process couples make about consumer goods. The analogy made between children and consumer goods has been criticized from several sources.[13] Refinements to these theories have included variables relating to education, time, contraceptive technology, employment opportunities and occupation, infant mortality and migration.[14]

Some recent socio-economic theories have been paying more attention to the implications of the correlation between women working and fertility. Essentially, they maintain that the 'opportunity cost' of children increases when women give up earning in order to have and look after children:

This opportunity cost is measured in relation to potential rather than actual earnings, so that the cost of children to women increases as women obtain an education, whether or not they actually work. The cost of children rises for a particular mother, too, if the demand for female labour pushes up women's wages, again regardless of whether she works or not.[15]

Research has shown, for instance, that fertility is directly proportional to a husband's income and inversely proportional to a wife's income.[16] These studies, however, by no means explain the relationship between women working and fertility satisfactorily. As Birdsall points out, fertility in the 1950s rose during a period of high female participation in the labour force. Lower fertility has occurred in some countries with high female employment, yet not in others, although some of this can be attributed to rural–urban differentials and the type of work in which women are employed. These refinements to the economic model of fertility, and, in particular, the increasing attention paid to women's work, are important developments. Nevertheless, there are certain assumptions inherent in all these theories which need to be considered critically.

Parents are assumed to act together rationally – as equals – in their decision-making on family size. Children are regarded, to a greater or lesser extent, as equivalent to consumer products, the utility of which can be weighed in terms of their costs, benefits and so on. The essential premises of these theories are that parents always act rationally as a family unit; it is usually implicit that they will always *agree*, and that in their decision-making on family size, children are evaluated in terms of costs and utilities (whether purely financial, or, as later theorists have suggested, in terms also of time and 'quality'): 'cultural and other impedimenta which might thwart this process, or even render such decision-making highly unlikely in the first place, are thrust aside'.[17] Many also assume that parents possess perfect control over childbearing.

It is these general assumptions, rather than individual theories, which I propose to criticize. First, there is little substantiation for the notion that couples necessarily act rationally in their decision-making on family size. If, indeed, they did, the rational answer to questions of cost and utility could be, not 'How many children should we have?', but 'Should we have children at all?' To which a rational answer might frequently be 'No'. No consideration is given to the *normative* constraints on parents regarding children and family size.

Second, it is assumed that all married adults desire children as part of a natural order; there is no attempt to consider questions relating to why people marry and why they want children in the first place. As Macintyre says:

though sex, marriage and reproduction may be linked empirically in a particular society and its dominant ideology, we still need to enquire into the process leading to them and the meanings attributed to them. We cannot assume *a priori* that people have babies because they are married, or marry in order to have babies; nor that people have babies because they have had sex, or that they have sex in order to produce babies.[18]

Third, there is little substantiation for the idea that couples will agree in their decision-making. No account is taken of the internal dynamics and organization of family life, of the possible relevance of role-relationships and relationships of dominance and subordination within the family. There is no consideration of the role of norms and social and ideological pressures exerted on individuals concerning marriage and childbearing; they assume decision-making occurs within some sort of social vacuum. Futher, there is little scope in these theories for any adequate explanations of *change* – did medieval couples sit by their turf fire calculating a cost-benefit analysis of producing another child? If not, when did the current pattern emerge? Is it universal, or does it vary? Socio-economic theorists have never tackled these questions adequately.

## Sociological theories of fertility

There have been attempts to formulate more comprehensive sociological theories of fertility which take greater account of social factors than those discussed above. Banks, for instance,[19] draws attention to the possible influence of social values, norms and beliefs on family size.

In seeking to explain the decline of family size which began among the middle classes about 1870,[20] Banks suggests that this represented a response to what the middle classes *perceived* as a potential threat to their standard of living, and that the very concept of a standard of living was a recent phenomenon of great importance to the middle classes:

if we are to take notice of the material provided by the population controversy, we cannot avoid the conclusion that during the first thirty years or so of the nineteenth century, the middle class, as a class, became quite definitely conscious of the standard of living as something at which one aimed. . . . It had now become a moral issue, a part of the code of life, to consider the standard of living.[21]

He regards this desire to maintain a certain standard of living as an attempt to retain a measure of differentiation, linked to which was the growing need for middle-class parents to provide a 'good' (and expensive) education for their children as a means of entry to the professions. Further, the period which he was examining was 'felt' to be one of economic depression by the middle class, and he maintains that family limitation was one response to this.

There are, however, certain problems with Banks's theory. First, the theory still assumes rational decision-making by parents, which is questionable. Second, no account is taken of internal family dynamics and, in particular, power relations and role relationships. Banks's theory, therefore, has certain similar drawbacks to economic theories, despite the fact that it does introduce the important factor of social norms and values.

It is necessary at this point to consider the idea of diffusion. While there are no specific theories of diffusion, the concept has often been implicit in a number of sociological, socio-economic and historical works. Young and Wilmott, for instance, in *The Symmetrical Family*, illustrate their so-called 'Principle of Stratified Diffusion' thus:

the image we are trying to suggest is that of a marching column with the people at the head of it usually being the first to wheel in a new direction. The last rank keeps its distance from the first, and the distance between them does not lessen. But as the column advances, the last rank does eventually reach and pass the point which the first rank had passed some time before.[22]

Banks introduced the idea in the context of family size, arguing that the new values and norms regarding family size among the middle classes in the 1870s spread outwards and downwards to the working class and to rural areas through such a process.[23] It has also been suggested that the low fertility of domestic servants in the nineteenth century was a direct result of the diffusion of middle-class ideals and practices between mistress and servant. Domestic servants at this time, however, married very late, and this, rather than any direct 'diffusion', is a more probable explanation of their low fertility.

While there has been little interest in attempting to test this idea, the work that has been done suggests that it is not valid. Carlsson, for instance, carried out research on the decline of fertility in Sweden and concludes that: 'the decline seems to have started at about the same time in Stockholm as in other parts of the country, even including rural areas, but once under way the change proceeded at a quicker pace in the capital',[24] and 'if the spread of birth control and the resultant decline in fertility were to take place with marked lags between regions, one would expect this to show up as a strong increase in regional variation as fertility starts to decline. Of this effect . . . there is little sign'.[25]

With regard to England and Wales, Wrigley's work on Colyton[26] indicates the strong likelihood of the practice of birth control in pre-industrial England. Abortion would seem to have been a common practice among the industrial working classes in the early nineteenth century in Lancashire; the fertility of textile workers has been very low since the nineteenth century. Clerical workers, who would presumably qualify as being several ranks behind the 'head of the marching column', manifested lower levels of fertility than those in the professional and commercial sectors in the early part of this century. It is my argument that when the working classes did alter their patterns of family organization and family size it was not a result of their copying the middle classes, but rather a result of their changing relations to the socio-economic system. The idea of diffusion does, however, rightly draw attention to the importance of ideals and values as determinants of behaviour.

Lee Rainwater provides a more comprehensive approach in his study of American fertility, *Family Design*.[27] It is more comprehensive because it considers both how couples are influenced by social pressures from outside marriage and how internal family dynamics affect the decision-making process within marriage. His studies have been strongly oriented towards exploring the *attitudes* of individuals within marriage: 'With respect to family size preferences, a couple's problem is essentially that of coming to some successful resolution of (1) each individual's desires with those of the partner, and (2) their joint desires with their perception of the society's norms about family size.'[28] The most important factor affecting the decision-making process and desired and achieved family size, is the type of role-relationship organization between husband and wife. This association appears to apply to *all* social classes: 'over 80 per cent of those who want small or medium-size families have jointly organised conjugal relationships, while about 60 per cent of those who want large families have more segregated conjugal relationships'.[29]

Rainwater's theory was influenced by sociological theories of the family, in particular, that of Elizabeth Bott. Neither Bott nor Rainwater, however, offers a cogent explanation as to why conjugal role-relationships should vary across categories of social class, or whether and why they changed over time. Bott relates variation in role-relationships to the degree of 'network-connectedness' of a couple within their community:

the degree of segregation of conjugal roles is related to the degree of connectedness in the total network of the family. Those families that had a high degree of segregation in the role-relationship of husband and wife had a close-knit network.... Families that had a relatively joint role-relationship between husband and wife had a loose-knit network.[30]

While the concept of network-connectedness is important, one wants to know what determines it in the first place. Turner suggests five variables which could affect network-connectedness[31] and, in turn, conjugal role-relationships: occupation, geographical mobility, education, stage of developmental cycle, and cosmopolitan or local orientations.

### Sociological theories of the family

Sociological theories of the family have for a long time been dominated by functionalism. Many have concentrated on the supposed relation between industrialization and the changing 'functions' of the family, seeing the family as a wholly dependent variable. Industrialization is considered to have changed the family from an 'extended' to a 'nuclear' unit, losing its productive and many of its educational functions in the process. Parsons, in developing a general macro theory of modern society, regarded the family as the crucial institution linking – and integrating – the personality system, the cultural system and the social system, the primary result of which was social cohesion.[32]

There are many problems with functionalist theories of the family. First, they never adequately explain *how* the family changed in the ways stated; it is assumed that these changes occurred organically, in a Durkheimian sense, and that the individual actor, or group of actors, was irrelevant. There is no scope for notions of choice, interaction or power relations. Second, there is an implicit assumption that *the* family is universal, and little allowance is made for the considerable variations occuring in family structure and organization between social sectors, across time, and between different cultures.[33] Anthropologists as well as historians and sociologists have demonstrated beyond doubt that the extended family was definitely not universal prior to industrialization, just as it has not been universally nuclear subsequent to industrialization.[34] Moreover, functionalist theories imply that psychological and personality factors had been absent prior to industrialization, which is highly questionable.[35]

Parsons and Bales, in particular, discuss the division of labour within the family in terms of 'natural' differentiation and performance, ascribing to women the 'natural' role of the focus of gratification, security and comfort, based on 'the division of organisms into lactating and non-lactating classes'.[36] While the division of labour and consequent power relations within families are crucial factors to be considered, they cannot be described as 'natural' and 'organic' in the way Parsons and Bales do, for there has not always been a strict division of labour within all families, and family organization has not been identical through time or across social strata.

Goode[37] and others have focused more specifically on the relations between the family, society and the economy in an historical context. He rightly draws attention to the importance of inheritance as a determinant of family organization and attitudes to children. Nonetheless, he assumes that those who lack property therefore have no control over their children. Probably parents among the lower strata did have less power over their children than those in the upper strata; historically, however, it has seldom been the case that working-class children entering the labour market could earn sufficient wages to live independently of their parents.[38] They were still dependent on them until they earned full wages; their parents expected them to contribute some – or often all – of their wages to them in return for board and lodging. So that, while economic relations between parents and children differed according to social strata and also according to the sex of the children, they were still important, in different ways, and still implied power relationships between parents and children, which did not *necessarily* result in a more conjugal family form among the lower strata. Goode emphasizes the importance of the relation of each individual family member to the economic system as a determinant of family organization. He does not, however, discuss the possible relevance of these factors to ideals of family size and processes of decision-making within the family. Further, he neglects sexual divisions and concentrates on generational divisions only.

Harris constructs a more complex and convincing argument regarding the relationship between the economy, industrialization and the family:

In some cases the ideological changes and in others the economic changes precede industrialisation itself. Indeed, they may be a precondition of autonomous industrial growth. Hence one may find the 'conjugal' family before industrialisation .... The *next stage* of industrialisation demanding *a more exact fit between work skills and job demands* will result in the need to act in accordance with the values of universalism and achievement ... [but] there will still be large areas of industrial society (mainly service industries) where both level of skill and job differentiation are low, and the adoption of such values may not be required .... Whichever phase of industrialisation the society is in therefore, we may expect to find great variation between different occupational areas in terms of the degree of skill required and in the extent of job differentiation. Correspondingly we should expect to find wide differences in family form between different occupational categories.[39]

His emphasis on the possible correlation between different occupational categories and family structure is important, although he does not specify how such a relation might actually operate. Is there, for instance, a direct causal link between the occupational structure and family organization? Exactly how, and why, would there be a link between them? Further, could variations according to occupation be in any way directly related to different patterns of family size, and if they are, why?

Few sociologists of the family have given adequate attention to questions of power relations and their development within the family. Harris and Goode have touched on these questions, but their prime interest has been in considering the problem at a much wider societal level. While Bott draws attention to the importance of role relationships, she does not give adequate consideration to power relations within the family or how and why family organization developed and varied as it did. Power is as essential a dimension to family structure as it is to society itself. Questions relating to who controls the economic basis, who earns the money, who decides how it is to be distributed and spent, who makes which decisions, all affect, indeed, determine, the relations of dominance, subordination and deference within families.

In recent years an increasing amount of attention has been paid to the above problems, while the long-standing dominance of functionalist theories has been seriously challenged. Two of the first important attacks on 'traditional' (i.e., functionalist) sociological theories of the family came from Laing and Cooper[40] who both drew attention to the destructive, negative and violent aspects of family life, and implicitly, the importance of power relationships within families. Their primary focus, however, was on the family unit itself and its effects on individuals, rather than its economic, political and social context; their analyses were thereby weakened by inadequate consideration to the dynamics of variation according to social class and through time. Moreover, their main interest was in the power relationships between parents and children, with little consideration to the equally important power relationships between husbands and wives.

Certainly the greatest challenge to traditional functionalist assumptions and theories of the family has come from feminist historians and sociologists, although demographic work on the pre-industrial family[41] has also contributed to refuting these assumptions. While the feminist debates have been numerous and varied, at a very general level the central question to which they have addressed themselves is the origin and nature of women's oppression in society and, more precisely, in the family. Related to this is the problem of how to adequately account for women in the social stratification system: a complex theoretical problem which poses a serious challenge to classical sociological theories of stratification.[42]

The situation of women within the family as daughters, wives and mothers has been the main focus of the debate. Marxists initially tried to argue that the family was a unit where use value alone was produced in contrast with the production of surplus value in the labour market.[43] Other theories attempted to explain the connection between the family and the capitalist mode of production by proposing that the essential role of unpaid domestic labour by women was through their maintenance and reproduction of labour power, i.e., that they were directly contributing thereby to the production of surplus value.[44] As Gardiner points out, however, Marx never actually considered housework in his theories, and she argues that female domestic labour is a source of surplus value for both capitalists *and* wage labour.[45] It has also been suggested that unpaid domestic labour is more akin to slave labour under feudalism:

While the wage labourer depends on the market ... the married woman depends on one individual. While the wage labourer sells his labour power, the married woman gives hers away; exclusivity and non-payment are intimately connected.... To supply upaid labour within the framework of a universal and personal relationship (marriage) constitutes precisely a relation of slavery.[46]

Others have argued that since exploitation and oppression of women long pre-dates capitalism – and also flourishes in socialist societies – it is patriarchal ideology, instilled through socialization and based on biological differences (and not, as most Marxists would argue, simply part of the superstructure), which is at the root of women's oppression in all societies. More recently it has been proposed that it is misleading to view women as totally passive in their oppression by men; that, while oppressed in certain ways, women also can and do create their own 'space' through social networks with other women. These networks are, and have been, important in that they provide a certain degree of power to women in their relations with men, with society generally and also in their control over reproduction.[47] Probably the most important contribution of feminists to studying families has been their determined effort to destroy the notion of 'the family' as an isolated private unit, and to show how the gender system is reproduced and maintained, both within families and in the wider 'public' spheres.

Most women have been involved in the economy both through the labour market (or in unpaid production) as well as performing unpaid domestic labour; the period 1900–39 was therefore most unusual given the very low proportion of married women who were active in the labour market. It is also an interesting period because, while the standard of living of many was increasing, other trends were serving to destroy, or weaken, many of women's traditional social networks and power bases, and in many ways women were becoming increasingly dependent on their husbands within the context of the family. The effects of these developments on family life, attitudes to family size and power relationships within marriage are one of the main areas with which this book is concerned.

## The foundations of the research

As none of the above theories is in itself considered adequate as a framework for the subject of this research, the emphasis has been primarily on the generation of new ideas and insights. Nevertheless, certain assumptions are inherent in the study and it is necessary at this point to consider why and how specific variables were selected for analysis.

Several criteria have been used. First, some variables were chosen as a result of problems and ideas raised by an earlier project.[48] Second, I decided to concentrate on variables which had generally been neglected in other studies, and to pay less attention to those which had already been given ample consideration. Last, but not least, was the problem of data availability.

The earlier project focused on the decline of family size in Essex in the 1930s using in-depth interviews. The interviews provided valuable material and led me to the tentative conclusion that: 'one of the crucial determinants of differential family ideals ... is the degree of knowledge and awareness obtained by women prior to marriage ... the degree of knowledge was directly related to (the nature of) their work experience'.[49]

The association between women working and fertility was discussed earlier. It became obvious that research on this question has tended to be formulated within the economic and socio-economic models of fertility, which for various reasons are considered unsatisfactory. The nature of the association, and the reasons for it, have not yet been adequately explained. My earlier work had suggested one possible reason for the association. It was equally possible, of course, that other variables were affecting the association: demographic factors, subfecundity, social and economic factors of one sort or another. To explore in greater depth the association between women working, fertility and family size therefore became a central aim of the research. The possibility that the association was the result of other intervening variables was real; the nature of the data used in other research was often of an aggregate nature. Associations deduced through the use of aggregate data can, of course, be very misleading.[50] While I did not intend to ignore aggregate data, I planned to match it, wherever possible, with individual data.

The essence of the problem lay at an individual level; did women who worked have different ideals of family size than those who stayed at home? Were they able to achieve their ideals more efficiently? And why would variations – if variations there were – exist according to their participation in the labour market? Further, were there any differentials according to the *type* and *nature* of their work? The problem was even more complex, however, because women's work, unlike that of men, is seldom continuous. Often it is interrupted, or stopped altogether, through marriage and/or reproduction. Thus women's work would have to be considered in terms of marital status and the stage of their reproductive cycle. Further, many women work on a part-time basis after marriage and childbearing, and this phenomenon is often not recorded in data sources such as the census.

To explore the nature of the relationship between the broader socio-economic and political systems and the family, it is essential to consider how social phenomena are interpreted by actors, and how interpretations in turn influence behaviour. Aggregate data are useless for the exploration of this type of factor; detailed individual data are needed. I decided, therefore, to examine the question of women's work at two levels; first, at an aggregate level, to see if, when other factors were taken into account, there was still an association between women's work and fertility. Second, to examine what working and different types of work *meant* to women as individuals, in particular, how their interpretations of their social world and phenomena relating to marriage, children and family size were influenced by the nature of their relationship to the economic system through work and work experience.

It may be said that I pay too little attention in this research to men and to their relation to the socio-economic system and their interpretations of it. I do not deny that these relationships are important, and for this reason variables relating to men's employment and occupations are considered at an aggregate level. They have not, however, been examined in much detail at an individual level; ideally, they would have been. Women have been given greater consideration here, first, because, although they have been interviewed in other studies, they have generally been *classified* according to their husband's social class, occupation and income. I intend to classify them here according to their own relations to the socio-economic system. Second, though men are equally involved in processes of courtship, marriage and family dynamics, they are not as involved in pregnancy, childbirth or lactation, and seldom equally involved in childrearing.

One of the main aims of the research then, is to examine in detail the relationship between the *nature* of women's work, fertility and family structure. Occupation was therefore chosen as one of the main variables for further analysis. There are marked differentials in fertility between occupational groups, and occupation often appears to be more closely related to fertility than social class; for example, while textile workers and miners would be classified as 'skilled working class', textile workers have manifested a relatively low level of fertility since the middle of the nineteenth century, while just the reverse was the case with miners. Work, if classified in terms of social class, offers little insight into the nature or location of the work situation itself, i.e., whether it is isolated or involves interaction with large numbers of other people, whether it occurs at home, in someone else's home, in a factory or other premises distinctly separate from the home.

Occupations vary widely in terms of structure, organization and locale, and these differences occasion different meanings and beliefs not only about work itself, but also about other social phenomena, including family life, marriage and children. As Caplow puts it:

the few thorough studies of occupational milieus which extend to family life and social participation ... provide us with an understanding of certain social mechanisms which no studies of the general class structure are likely to distinguish .... In all of them, the shaping of extra-occupational life by occupational influences appears to be extensive and complex .... First, there are the customs and folkways which arise out of the nature of the occupation, or out of the traditions of the occupational group. Second, there are the standards of conduct which are enforced because of the real or supposed effects which their violation would have on the performance of the job.[51]

Studying occupation rather than social class, can create problems for generalization. The examination of occupation, however, does not necessarily mean listing every occupation in existence from road sweepers to waitresses to tax inspectors. Rather, there are

certain characteristics of occupations, and groups of occupations
which may be grouped along various dimensions. These include:
isolation from/integration with other individuals during the
performance of a job; the locale of the workplace (for example,
home-centred, office-centred, factory-centred, etc.); the organization
of the occupation (hierarchical versus egalitarian); repetitiveness
or diversity of the work; sexual, chronological and marital
organization of the occupation, that is, whether it is predominantly
or entirely a one-sex occupation or whether it is relatively mixed,
whether it is restricted by marital status (for women) or by age,
and so on. Occupation is given prime consideration here because
it provides more detailed information as to the socio-economic
and cultural context within which individuals interact and interpret
their situations.

Power is another factor that should be considered, although the
actual definition and measurement of power is notoriously difficult.[52]
It is important for two reasons; first, it is important to see how one
dominant group or groups can alter the relations of subordinate
groups to the socio-economic and political systems (for example,
by legislation forbidding women or children to enter certain types
of occupation, by enforcing the dependency of children through
compulsory education, etc.). Any changes will tend to produce
different meanings and belief-systems among those groups affected,
and these can, in turn, influence and change behaviour patterns.
Power can be exerted in any number of ways, primarily through
control of social, economic, political and ideological institutions,
and, in the last resort, through superior control of force.

Second, power will be considered within the context of the
family. This is one of the most important factors to which feminist
historians and sociologists have recently drawn attention, and can
no longer be ignored in any study of families or family structure.
Actually pinpointing power is not easy; within the family it will be
analysed primarily in terms of the relations of husband and wife as
individuals to the economic system. Power within marriage will be
assessed according to whether both partners worked, or only one;
what differences in pay and status existed if both worked; how
non-participation of one partner in the labour market affected
power relations within marriage, and so on. Power, as defined by
relation to the economic system is, of course, only one aspect of
the problem. There will also be social pressures and norms which
'define' the power relationship within marriage; psychological and

personality factors also affect the distribution of power. Knowledge – and withholding knowledge – from a partner or child is also a form of power and can influence patterns of decision-making within the family.

To some extent, power can also be equated with responsibility. That person held responsible for a certain task or area will also tend to have greater power over the way with which such a task is dealt. For the purpose of this research the main area of power which will be considered is power over decision-making and responsibility for children, family size and use of birth control. Another area of power relationships to be considered is the nature and importance of social networks.

Inherent in concepts of power is the notion of communication: communication of ideals, norms, values. Power is dependent, to a large extent, on the ability of one group (or individual) to communicate expectations of behaviour to another group, groups or individual. Communication, or its absence, is also important in a work situation or community context, for it determines the degree of interaction and exchange of information, ideas and norms. Communication in this context may, to a great extent, determine the degree of 'ideological integration' of an individual into a particular social group. Integration, or non-integration, will in turn influence patterns of beliefs and behaviour in other situations.

Similarly, communication in the family is an important variable to consider. The extent, degree and substance of communication between husband and wife will affect their role-relationship and family organization, as well as the definition of responsibility for decision-making generally, and that concerning family size and the use of birth control specifically.

In sum, if we are to explain the relation between the socio-economic, political and cultural systems and family organization and size, the principal variables to consider are: first, the occupational structure of the society and the relation of both men and women to the socio-economic system. Second, the individual's occupational experience at various stages in his or her life-cycle. Third, the power of one group in society to alter the relations of subordinate groups to the socio-economic and political systems, and the precise nature of these changes. Fourth, power relations within marriage, the family and the community and their effects on decision-making concerning family size. Fifth, and finally, communication of ideals, norms and values at a societal, community and individual level. In addition, variables related to the demographic, economic and social structures will be considered.

Methodologically this has meant looking at a variety of types of data and employing different means of analysis. The quest for ideas has meant that relatively little time has been spent on verification or 'testing'. It is an attempt to see the problem at both an aggregate and an individual level, an exploration of both the subjective and the more objective aspects of the problem.

Three principal sources were used for this study: first, census data for 1911 and 1931 used in conjunction with the Registrar-General's Annual Abstracts for those years; second, 500 individual case records for the Manchester and Salford Mothers' Clinic for the years 1928–33; third, thirty in-depth interviews with women from Essex, Lancashire and South Wales.

Census data were used because they provide a breakdown of women's and men's occupations by geographical area and give details of the demographic structure of each area. By correlating these data with data from the annual abstracts (births and deaths) for the same areas, it was possible to test the strength of associations between occupational and demographic variables, in particular, between whether women work, the nature of their work, and patterns of fertility.[53]

The demographic variables from the annual abstracts were for the years 1911 and 1931 only. Trend data were not used, partly because of the problem of 'lagging', and partly because it was felt that the size of the areas analysed would to a great extent counteract the problem of fluctuations.

The second main source consisted of 500 individual case records for married women attending the Manchester and Salford Mothers' Clinic between 1928 and 1933. Birth control clinics at this time were still few and far between,[54] and overwhelmingly urban institutions. The Manchester set of records was the only one which could be located, the rest apparently having been lost or destroyed. The most important information these data provided was how women found out about the clinic and from whom, previous use of birth control, and information on family size, age at marriage and husbands' occupations. Unfortunately, there was no information on the women's previous occupations.

One of the main problems with these records was establishing to what extent they might have been representative of the population as a whole. The data were compared with the 1931 Census and with some of Lewis-Faning's material for the Family Census; comparison was only possible on certain questions (see Appendix 2). The results suggest that while the proportions using birth control among the different social classes and between the two samples correspond roughly, the women from the clinic were characterized by a higher degree of motivation to control family size than was necessarily typical of their social class.

The aim of the third source of data – the interviews – was to gain insight into individuals' values and beliefs relating to work, marriage, children and family size. They also provide useful information on occupational histories, age at marriage, and so on. Data of this type raise various methodological problems, in particular, those of selection, representativeness, reliability, comparability and recollection.[55]

As I wanted to explore the relationship between women's work and family size, I decided it would be useful to select groups of a contrasting nature that might elicit useful comparisons. The census indicated a strong inverse correlation between the proportion of men and women working in textiles, and a strong positive correlation between the proportion of men working in mining and fertility. I therefore decided to interview ten women who worked as textile workers after marriage and childbirth, ten who did not work after marriage and were married to miners, and a further ten from the South East of England as a group for comparison with the others. Respondents were further selected by occupation prior to marriage, by age, and having given birth to at least one child. The idea was to interview women from two 'extreme' groups, compare them with one another as well as with the 'control group', and see whether any of the results could provide possible explanations or insights into the statistical associations revealed in the census data.

The interviews were analysed in two ways. First, what respondents said about various topics, and how they said it. This provided information of a general nature on meanings and beliefs. Second, a fairly simple form was filled in for each respondent, from which I constructed tables on role-relationships etc., which are presented in later chapters. Given that only thirty respondents were involved, these tables cannot be regarded as having any statistical significance, but have been used and presented as a means of suggesting *possible* trends and relationships.

Thus the nature and scope of this research has been deliberately broad. Consequently the sources and methods are diverse and often general, and the theoretical propositions are the end product rather than the starting point. There is, of course, no reason why they should not be a starting point for further research. Before discussing the data, however, it is useful first to consider briefly the general historical background to the period.

# 2 A period of contradictions, 1900-39

The period between 1900 and 1939 was one of contradictions. People living in areas of high unemployment experienced crushing financial strains, often poverty, while the standard of living of the majority of the population was rising gradually. The staple 'old' heavy industries on which Victorian prosperity had been built were declining rapidly and severely, bringing mass unemployment and poverty to those once thriving areas. On the other hand, the new light industries, concentrated in the South-East and Midlands, were growing steadily, although slowly, and these areas were becoming the new centres of prosperity and affluence.

Both fertility and mortality had been declining from the middle of the nineteenth century. The decline of family size[1] in late Victorian times was by and large a middle-class phenomenon, while the rapid decline during the early part of this century was most marked among the working classes. Of all marriages taking place about 1860, 20 per cent had two children or less, while the figure for marriages taking place in 1925 was 67 per cent.[2] The decline among the working classes is often assumed to have been simply a result of the diffusion of both ideals of family size and the knowledge and availability of birth control from the middle classes,[3] but this has never been satisfactorily proved or disproved.

During this period birth control was a particularly controversial issue, and it received a great deal of publicity in the rapidly expanding media. It was also at this time that birth control clinics were first established,[4] and when both church and state gave official sanction to the use of birth control. Nevertheless, there was no 'contraception revolution' as there was in the 1960s; family limitation was still achieved primarily by non-mechanical methods. Although the use of mechanical methods was increasing, it was much more common among the middle classes. The decline of working-class family size was achieved in the main by non-mechanical means of birth control.

A number of developments took place which had important effects on the position of women in society. The most obvious was their enfranchisement after the First World War. Arguably more important was the changing nature of women's work. Fewer women took up residential domestic service (although service still employed the majority of women in the labour force), many more women were doing clerical jobs; more single women were working, but fewer married women did so.[5] While the Liberal reforms laid the foundations for a welfare state, most of the benefits went to men and children; married women, unless employed on a full-time basis, were generally excluded. Indeed, contemporary social surveys[6] showed repeatedly that married women were the group worst hit by the effects of unemployment and poverty. At a time when mortality generally and infant mortality specifically were plummeting, maternal mortality actually rose. It rose slightly but persistently from the end of the war until 1934, when it reached a rate of 4.66 per thousand live births.[7]

Community structure was radically altered in many areas, partly as a result of the rapid growth of bus and tram services throughout the country, and partly because of the large-scale development of suburbia. For many working-class families there was an increasingly large distance developing between home and work.

The period was also important politically. After the First World War there was a dramatic increase in the scale and power of central government, parallel with the abandonment of a *laissez-faire* policy in economic and social matters. Moreover, the Labour Party became assimilated into the political system and, despite various labour crises, generally ceased to be seen as a threat to parliamentary government. Institutions that could be used as a means of social control increased and extended into the realms of welfare, education, housing, health and, of course, the control of the newly emergent mass media.

The First World War provided a catalyst to change in all spheres of society. It precipitated the need for a more centralized government and for closer co-operation between the trade unions and the government. It was also the occasion for many women not only to experience greater independence, but also to be accepted (albeit reluctantly and temporarily) in occupations previously denied them. Disillusionment after the war almost certainly contributed to the decline in the importance of the church and religion both socially and ideologically. The Boer War, but particularly the First World War, made the government and the middle classes more aware of the poor quality of health prevalent among the working classes, which led to new policies to improve public health, hygiene, housing and welfare.

Obviously a number of important changes were occurring, and it is important to examine them in more detail. It is also crucial to remember, however, that there was a great deal of variation in terms of the type of, and impact of, social and economic changes, particularly according to geographical area as well as social class.

From the middle of the eighteenth century there had been dramatic changes in the population structure specifically; it was the start of a period of rapid growth (see Table 1). These demographic changes were not, however, unique to Britain, but were general (with certain variations) in Western Europe, and cannot therefore be taken as direct effects of the industrial revolution.

The period of most rapid growth occurred between about 1780 and 1870; thereafter the rate of growth began to slacken, and it fell dramatically between 1911 and 1939. The decline was a result of changing patterns of fertility, mortality and migration.

Mortality declined from the second half of the nineteenth century, although it varied significantly according to age group and social class. Mortality rates among those aged between 5 and 34 years began to decline from the 1840s or earlier; those among the age group 35–44 started to decline from the mid 1870s; those for the age group between 45 and 74 not until the 1890s. Infant mortality did not begin to decline continuously until the beginning of the twentieth century (see Appendix 1). The decline of mortality meant a marked increase in life expectancy,[8] which had important effects on attitudes to life, death, work, marriage and children generally.

**Table 1**   *The population of England and Wales, 1695–1939*

| Date | Population ('000,000s) |
|------|------------------------|
| 1695 | 5.2 |
| 1751 | 6.5 |
| 1801 | 9.2 |
| 1851 | 17.9 |
| 1901 | 32.5 |
| 1939 | 41.5 |

*Source*: Tranter (1973), p. 41

While the national birth rate did not begin to decline until the 1860s, fertility varied greatly by class, and among the upper classes had started to decline much earlier.[9] In the latter part of the nineteenth century fertility contracted considerably among the middle classes. The largest families occurred among miners and agricultural labourers, although the family size of textile workers had been low for much of the nineteenth century. By the twentieth century, while differentials still remained between social classes and occupational groups, they had been substantially reduced as the result of a rapid contraction of family size among most sectors of the working class.

Migration rates varied considerably, both nationally and locally. Between 1871 and 1931 there was a consistent net loss nationally by migration. The majority of these migrants were young and male, which reduced the proportion of the economically active to the dependent population and resulted in a higher ratio of women to men in the population. While this had important effects on marriage patterns at a local level, in England and Wales as a whole there were surprisingly few changes in the marriage rates between 1841 and 1931, fluctuating from just over 15 to just over 17 (see Appendix 1). The age at marriage has fluctuated somewhat more; Table 2 shows the proportion of certain generations who had married. While part of the early decline in the fertility rate can be explained by a smaller proportion married in the 20–24 age group from 1881, the trend towards younger marriage after 1911 was not

**Table 2**   *Proportion of the population who had married in the quinquennial age group, 20–24*

| Period of birth of generation | Date at which occupied 20–24 age group | Proportion married at 20–24 (%) |
|---|---|---|
| 1826–31 | 1851 | 25 |
| 1836–41 | 1861 | 27 |
| 1846–51 | 1871 | 28 |
| 1856–61 | 1881 | 27 |
| 1866–71 | 1891 | 24 |
| 1876–81 | 1901 | 22 |
| 1886–91 | 1911 | 19 |
| 1896–1901 | 1921 | 22 |
| 1906–11 | 1931 | 20 |

*Source*: Royal Commission on Population (1949), p. 22

paralleled by an increase in fertility rates. On the contrary, the marital fertility rate continued to decline. This indicates that fertility was being controlled within marriage to a greater extent, particularly as all evidence available indicates that subfecundity was likely to have *decreased* from 1870, mainly as a result of a reduction in the frequency of venereal disease and the incidence of rickets (which often caused pelvic deformities).[10] Marriage patterns, however, varied quite considerably between geographical areas and social classes.

Between 1871 and 1931 the national age structure changed quite noticeably (see Appendix 1). The proportion of the population aged 0–14 years declined markedly; part of the reason for this can be explained in terms of the higher proportion of women to men during the childbearing years, which would reduce fertility to some extent. Up until 1911 this unbalanced sex ratio was mostly a result of outward migration by young males; in 1921 and 1931 the gap was even more pronounced and was primarily a result of the heavy losses of young males during the First World War. The decreasing ratio of 0–14 year-olds to the adult population can also be seen as a result of the general decline in mortality; longevity was increasing noticeably during this period. Thus the dependency ratio was 66.3 in 1871, but only 46.0 in 1931. The youth dependency ratio (those aged 14 and under) was 59.6 in 1871 and 34.3 in 1931, while the aged dependency ratio (those aged 65 and over) had increased from 6.7 to 11.7.

In the economic sphere, despite the enormity of Britain's empire and vast overseas investments, she had not developed close links between the state and industry or a true 'monopoly capitalism' as there was in Germany, Japan or the USA:

the very scale of Britain's original industrial dominance had produced its own gravedigger; a banking sector which siphoned away funds for reinvestment, distorted the pattern of industrial demand and by its opposition to tariffs created conditions which meant that only industries with the highest degree of concentration could make monopoly profits. The whole economy was held in a state of suspended animation, unable to move forward to the higher monopoly stage, and increasingly out of place in a world now dominated by the 'modern imperialism' of rival powers.[11]

Nevertheless, the period witnessed the growth of several giant concerns: EMI, Unilever, Courtaulds, ICI, Shell, and these firms were becoming increasingly larger and employing greater numbers of workers. By 1935, 55 per cent of the country's labour force was employed in business units with 500 or more employees each.[12] It was also during this time that chain stores such as Sainsbury, Woolworth and Marks and Spencer took off.

The decline of Britain's export trade was a result of the adverse terms of trade for primary products, the stagnation of world trade in manufactures, and the increasingly rapid industrialization of other countries. These trends were greatly exacerbated by the First World War: 'the war accelerated the adverse forces at work. It encouraged other countries to supply for themselves both more goods and more services, and forced some realisation of overseas assets, which reduced the income from abroad'.[13] Moreover, technological changes affected not only industrial development and capital investment, but also had far-reaching effects on patterns of transportation, commuting, and suburbanization.

Thus, before 1914 approximately 75 per cent of all Britain's exports consisted of coal, cotton, iron and steel, and machinery; they accounted for half of the national product and employed almost a quarter of the working population. By 1922 exports of cotton were less than half the pre-war figure, exports of coal were down by one-third, and during the twenties the numbers of coal miners and shipbuilders both fell by some 20 per cent. The Wall Street Crash of 1929 made the situation even worse: output of steel was halved between 1929 and 1931, as were outputs for cotton and shipbuilding. Coal was not so badly affected, but still declined appreciably.[14] It is hardly surprising that the worst unemployment was concentrated in the old industrial areas, with rates in some areas two or three times higher than those in London and the Midlands, as shown in Table 3. Certain towns were literally paralysed by unemployment: in 1934, 74 per cent of all male

**Table 3** *Percentage unemployed, by areas, 1923 and 1930*

| Area | 1923 (%) | 1930 (%) |
|------|------|------|
| London | 9.0 | 9.8 |
| Midlands | 9.4 | 18.6 |
| North-East | 11.7 | 24.5 |
| North-West | 12.7 | 29.3 |
| Wales | 5.6 | 31.2 |

*Source*: Mowat (1968), p. 275

workers in Brynmawr were unemployed, 73 per cent in Dowlais, and 68 per cent in Jarrow.[15] Areas with wide-scale primary unemployment also experienced secondary unemployment in local distributive trades: hotels, pubs, restaurants and so on. Moreover, unemployment in the depressed areas was usually long-term unemployment, in contrast with other areas.

One important result of these changes was that, as the new industries were primarily centred in the south-east of England, there was a swing of population to the South-East, and a decline in the areas dominated by heavy industry (South Wales, the North-East and the North-West):

the concentration of population in a half-dozen conurbations continued, and among these Greater London was growing most of all. In these sprawling built-up areas – London, South-East Lancashire, Merseyside, W. Midlands, W. Yorkshire and Tyneside – 41 per cent of the population of England and Wales lived in 1911. By 1931 when the proportion in all the conurbations was still 41 per cent, more than half of these people were in Greater London.[16]

Up until 1911 heavy in-migration into South Wales, and to a lesser extent the Midlands, was characterized by young male migrants seeking employment in the mines or in industry. The result of this in South Wales was to create a highly unbalanced sex ratio (a much higher proportion of males to females) in the younger age groups, a phenomenon tending to lead to early age at marriage, high marriage rates, and consequently also higher fertility rates.

On the other hand, a large proportion of the migrants into London up until 1911 were young unmarried women seeking work as domestic servants. The results of this were just the opposite to those in South Wales, that is, it created an unbalanced sex ratio with a much higher proportion of women to men. This resulted in a lower marriage rate, a higher age at marriage and a lower level of fertility. Migration patterns from 1911 to 1931, although concentrated in the South-East, were not on such a large scale as before, and while migrants were predominantly young, were not so marked in terms of sex as they had been earlier.

The effects of heavy out-migration from rural areas, and between the wars from the depressed areas, were also important on local population structures. Areas with a high proportion of out-migration were left with an unusually high percentage of the old and the very young.

**Table 4**   *Permanent houses built in five year periods, 1919–39,*
            *England and Wales*

| Years | Local authority | Private builders | Total |
|-------|-----------------|------------------|-------|
| 1919–24 | 176,914 | 221,543 | 398,457 |
| 1925–9 | 326,353 | 673,344 | 999,697 |
| 1930–4 | 286,350 | 804,251 | 1,090,601 |
| 1935–9 | 346,840 | 1,269,912 | 1,616,752 |

*Source*: Halsey (1972), p. 89

Concomitant with the expansion of the South-East during the early twentieth century was an increasing amount of suburbanization. The development of the petrol bus, tram, and the boom in the building trade made it possible for more working-class families to live in suburban housing estates. The social structure of suburbia, however, was very different to that of traditional working-class communities. Suburbanites lived in greater isolation with a higher standard of housing, but without traditional amenities such as the corner shop (and 'tick' facilities), a choice of local pubs or clubs, much less a well-established network of friends, neighbours or kin. Employment opportunities for women were usually very poor, although the opportunities for their husbands to earn higher wages were generally greater – at least in the South-East and Midlands.

Council houses were often too expensive for the less secure sectors and the unemployed; housing conditions for many remained generally very poor. Overcrowding had certainly declined, but was still common among the poor, with sometimes as many as ten people sleeping in one room.[17] Many houses were verminous, and many were still without water or toilet facilities. When families lived in such squalor, the men and older children at least were out of the house a good deal of the day, while the wives were confined to these conditions on a permanent basis. The more squalid the dwelling the worse was the burden of housework for the woman. Thus, while local authorities had built more than a million houses by 1939, and claimed to have rehoused about four-fifths of all slum dwellers,[18] the increase of separate families was still greater than the increase in houses, so that between 1921 and 1931 housing shortage in fact increased[19].

For the majority of the population there was a slow but steady increase in the standard of living. The electrical industry grew very rapidly, particularly in the 1930s; output of electricity quadrupled between 1925 and 1939, and by 1939 two-thirds of all houses were wired.[20] For the better-off, electrical appliances such as refrigerators, vacuum cleaners and cookers eased the burden of housework; for the poorest sectors, the drudgery remained as burdensome as ever. Clothing and furniture had become cheaper with mass production, and accessible to many more through the expansion of hire purchase facilities. Tinned food was much more widely available, and the consumption of fruit, vegetables and eggs rose considerably:

the *average* rise in living standards for the bulk of the population meant that most families were able to spend more on food and obtain a greater variety than in the past. The annual consumption of food per head between 1909–13 and 1934 showed some remarkable increases: fruit up by 88 per cent; vegetables, 64 per cent; butter and margarine, 50 per cent; eggs, 46 per cent.[21]

School milk and school dinners improved the diets and health of the country's children.

Again, however, in the poorest sectors it was almost invariably the wife who bore the greatest burden:

when the child is old enough to go to school he comes under the protection of the School Medical Service with its medical and nursing supervision, and treatment of certain disabling ailments and defects; he also has the advantages of school meals and milk, physical education, special schools and so forth; eventually he comes under the National Health Insurance Act .... The mother, on the other hand, remains within the purview of the official organisation only so long as she is a 'nursing mother', that is, in general terms, until her child is one year old. After that, unless and until she again becomes pregnant, she is not eligible for advice, treatment or social assistance under the Maternity and Child Welfare Act, and unless she is an employed insured woman, which the majority of married women are not, the State is not officially concerned with her physical condition or with the provision of any remedies which may possibly be needed.[22]

In 1930 a report was issued by the Government Actuary which showed that

the sickness and disablement experience of a group of approved societies during 1921–7 had been of a very disturbing character. Within these six years sickness benefit claims, measured by weeks of sickness, had risen for men by 41 per cent, for unmarried women by 60 per cent, and for married women by no less than 106 per cent. Disablement claims for unmarried women had doubled, while for married women they had jumped by 150 per cent.[23]

An investigation carried out by the Women's Health Enquiry Committee in the 1930s, which interviewed 1250 women (almost entirely working-class) in various parts of the country, revealed a very depressing picture of the situation for many working-class wives.[24] Their general health was on the whole poor or indifferent, they were fighting an endless battle against dirt and poverty and were on their feet on average for twelve hours a day. Few of them had had any health training whatsoever and, interestingly, the information they did receive came primarily through the recently established welfare services (note the low proportion receiving any information from a private doctor):

these and the remainder have learnt anything they know from Welfare Centres and Ante-Natal Clinics (591 women cite these), the Health Visitor and/or District Nurse (245 cases); Daily Press, magazines, wireless, lectures at Clubs, Church Socials, etc. (217 cases), and their own doctor (67 cases). Eleven women have been nurses or midwives and have had some special training.[25]

Other sources also reveal a conspiracy of silence between most doctors and working-class women concerning their own health generally and reproduction and birth control specifically.[26]

The growth of the home market resulted in an increasing amount of advertising and commercialization. Most of this was concentrated on the family and, in particular, women and children within the home. The family as an economic unit of consumption was the main object of these developments. To expand consumer industry in the home market it was essential to promote ideals of domesticity, home improvement, family life and so on, and an integral part of this ideology was the concept of woman as housewife and mother.[27] In many ways, married women were now more useful (or seen to be more useful) to the economy as unemployed consumers than as active producers. This ideology was evident not only in advertising and the efflorescence of women's magazines which occurred at the time, but was also promoted by the state through such institutions as ante-natal clinics, schools for mothers, and the infant and child welfare movement generally.

An interesting example of the state actively promoting these ideals was in Liverpool, where in 1937 the Unemployment Assistance Board set up what they called 'reconditioning courses' for single unemployed women. These were quite explicitly institutions to teach working-class girls domestic skills and domestic ideology with a view to their finding work as domestic servants (and also, one presumes, eventually making 'good wives'):

the Reconditioning Course was planned to give those attending it a complete change of surroundings and of company, good food and the discipline of some simple domestic studies, with a view primarily to reconditioning them so that they could return to their own type of employment, and secondarily to fitting them for residential or non-residential domestic service.[28]

All unemployed girls between the ages of 14 and 18 were obliged to attend the Junior Instruction Centres in Liverpool for thirteen weeks. They were taught English, arithmetic, geography, drawing, embroidery, sewing, cooking and 'drill'. Although it was a day institution, they were obliged to stay overnight on occasion to 'learn the duties of a residential maid and at the same time acquire the experience of being away from home and seeing what residential service is like'.[29] This certainly presents a good example of a well-organized attempt to 'diffuse' domestic ideology to working-class women, although what impact it had is not known. Certainly these ideals must have reached virtually all women at the time in one way or another; whether or not they put them into practice, whether they believed them, was more likely to depend on their own particular situation. This will be discussed at greater length in Chapter 5.

As mentioned earlier, one of the most important factors affecting the working class during the early part of this century must have been the rapid development and widespread availability of cheap transportation facilities; for more and more working-class families there was a distinct separation of home from work. While this applied particularly to suburban development, it also meant that for many living in traditional urban communities, they could seek employment much further afield within the conurbation itself. Roberts, in *The Classic Slum* describes the effects of these developments vividly:

the electric tramcar enabled more working-class people than ever before to find and keep a job beyond their immediate neighbourhood, to visit relatives and friends, to go to parks, libraries, theatres, concerts, cinemas, museums, schools and technical colleges. Except for war itself, this revolutionary new form of transport contributed more than anything else to breaking down that ingrained parochialism which had beset millions in the industrial slums of pre-1914 England.[30]

**Table 5**   *Major occupational groups as a percentage of total occupied population, Great Britain, 1911, 1921 and 1931*

| Major occupational groups | 1911 (%) | 1921 (%) | 1931 (%) |
|---|---|---|---|
| 1   Employers and proprietors | 6.7 | 6.8 | 6.7 |
| 2   White-collar workers | 18.7 | 21.2 | 23.0 |
|    (a) Managers and administrators | 3.4 | 3.6 | 3.7 |
|    (b) higher professionals | 1.0 | 1.0 | 1.1 |
|    (c) lower professionals and technicians | 3.1 | 3.5 | 3.5 |
|    (d) foremen and inspectors | 1.3 | 1.4 | 1.5 |
|    (e) clerks | 4.5 | 6.5 | 6.7 |
|    (f) salesmen and shop assistants | 5.4 | 5.1 | 6.5 |
| 3   Manual workers | 74.6 | 72.0 | 70.3 |
|    (a) skilled | 30.5 | 28.8 | 26.7 |
|    (b) semi-skilled | 34.4 | 29.0 | 28.7 |
|    (c) unskilled | 9.6 | 14.2 | 14.8 |

*Source*: Halsey (1972), p. 113

These changes undoubtedly weakened traditional ties with the local community and may have resulted in a greater home-centredness and family orientation.

There were also a number of important changes in the occupational structure as a result of economic changes. Centralization, the development of large-scale businesses and the decline of heavy industry resulted on the one hand in an increase in the white-collar sector, and on the other hand in a decrease in the manual sector, specifically a decrease in skilled and semi-skilled occupations and an increase in unskilled occupations, as illustrated in Table 5.

Parallel with these developments was a decline in union membership from 1920. The unions, moreover, were becoming increasingly centralized and bureaucratized at the same time as the Labour Party was becoming established as an integral part of the political system (see Table 6). The unions' traditional power base – in the areas of heavy industry – was substantially weakened because of the depression, and a new power base in the areas of the new industries had not yet developed: 'the General Strike marked the end, and not the beginning of a time of unrest and possible revolution'.[31] The coal miners suffered total defeat, and ended up working longer hours for lower wages. All these developments tended to lead to an atomization of the working class, a retreat from open political and economic struggle into a more individual world, with more emphasis on home and family.

Women were affected in a number of ways by changes in the occupational structure. First, fewer women were working as residential domestic servants, although service still remained the largest occupational group for women. Second, there was a rapid and dramatic increase in the proportion of women employed in non-manual occupations, especially in the clerical sector; of the increase in non-manual occupations between 1911 and 1931, 40 per cent was comprised of women.[32] Third, while the proportion of women occupied in the textile and dressmaking trades decreased, there was an increase in women's employment in unskilled jobs in the 'new' industries. Women's wages, however, were seldom more than half those of men, even for similar work, and women employed as shop assistants sometimes earned no more than 10s. a week.[33]

The growth of the clerical sector was an urban phenomenon, and was particularly marked in the Greater London area; similarly, the expansion of job opportunities for women as unskilled workers in light industry was concentrated in the South-East. The decline of domestic service was also concentrated in the major conurbations. Further, the tendency was for more single, and fewer married, women to work; the percentage of all women working in 1901 was 29.1 per cent, in 1931 29.7 per cent, while the percentage of married women working was 6.3 per cent in 1901 and 4.8 per cent in 1931.

**Table 6**  *Density of union membership in the UK by sex, 1900–35 (by five-year periods)*

| Year | Density of membership males (%) | Density of Membership females (%) |
|------|--------------------------------|-----------------------------------|
| 1900 | 16.7 | 3.2 |
| 1905 | 15.5 | 3.6 |
| 1910 | 18.6 | 5.3 |
| 1915 | 30.7 | 9.0 |
| 1920 | 54.5 | 23.9 |
| 1925 | 37.0 | 14.8 |
| 1930 | 30.8 | 13.4 |
| 1935 | 30.6 | 12.4 |

*Source*: Halsey (1972), pp. 123-4

Moreover, the changing nature of the occupational structure meant that more single women were in occupations where they could gain ready access to other women and probably also more information on reproduction and birth control. The isolated position of the residential domestic servant in a one or two servant household, where virtually no opportunities for communication and information from other women existed, was being replaced by the position of single girls in offices, factories or shops with other girls and women, a more egalitarian structure, and greater possibility of access to information, new values and ideals. Even girls who worked as 'dailies' had more freedom and chance to associate with other women in their spare time than did their residential counterparts. Thus, partly as a result of different job opportunities, more working-class women would be entering marriage with a greater amount of information and knowledge of what it actually entailed, and also, no doubt, a clearer idea of what they expected and wanted to get from it.

Again, however, these trends do not seem to have had much effect on women in the poorest sectors: 'only 29 women (out of 1250) ... seem to be aware that too many or too frequent pregnancies may be the cause of, or contribute to, their unfitness, lassitude, or definite illnesses'.[34] It was also among these sectors that there was least evidence of the dramatic decline in family size occurring among other groups at the time. Marjorie Spring Rice found that the average *admitted* number of pregnancies among the women in her sample was nearly five, while 221 of them admitted to eight or more.[35]

For those who remained in traditional working-class communities, social networks probably continued as an important factor affecting women's knowledge and marital relationships. Nevertheless, the changing occupational structure would also mean that some women would be gaining more information prior to marriage than hitherto, and this may have weakened the strength and importance of social networks after marriage. For instance, a woman's work experience in a factory, office or shop may have resulted in a definition of marital values and norms to the effect that marriage *should* be of a joint rather than segregated, nature, and that therefore the woman (and also the man) may have deliberately sought isolation from a social group, even if one was ready at hand. Futher, the tendency for men to work further afield even in urban areas, would lead to a weakening of *his* local social network with other men. In other

**Table 7** *Numbers employed by the Civil Service*

| Year | All grades of Civil Service | Higher Civil Servants | Executive and clerical grades |
|------|------------------------------|------------------------|-------------------------------|
| 1914 | 57,706 | 1,077 | 33,329 |
| 1923 | 116,241 | 1,596 | – |
| 1930 | 120,418 | 1,708 | 82,900 |

*Source*: Mowat (1968), pp. 15 and 16

words, even in a traditional working-class community, socio-economic changes and different patterns of work experience meant than many working-class men and women probably *wanted* a more joint type of role-relationship and may well have deliberately chosen to isolate themselves, to some extent at least, from the rest of the community. While their relation to the socio-economic system as wage-earner/housewife had changed little, the *nature* of that relationship had changed and resulted in a weakening of ties with, and allegiance to, the community, and a strengthening of marital and domestic ties.

Many of these trends were encouraged, sometimes directly and sometimes indirectly, by state institutions. The economic problems thrown up by the First World War (the munitions crisis, labour difficulties, inflation of government expenditure, difficulties in obtaining imports) had resulted in a dramatic increase in the power and control of the central state. Certainly centralized government had been growing and extending its power and influence since the sixteenth century, but not until the twentieth century had it reached so many areas of the socio-economic system. The First World War precipitated these developments, but once the war was over, the state continued to grow and develop further centralized agencies of control. For example, the numbers employed by the Civil Service grew, as Table 7 illustrates. Between 1916 and 1920 the following ministries were established: Health, Labour, Transport, Pensions, Air, the Forestry Commission, the Medical Research Council and the Department of Scientific and Industrial Research.

Matters once left to the individual, the family, the community or the local authority were now becoming more and more matters concerning the state and its institutions:

the exaltation of the State was of course, the result not only of the war, but of the attitude towards it which the war encouraged ... the State had intervened, more pryingly than before, in such matters as conditions of employment, industrial hygiene, housing, the daily bread. The individual looked to the State to help satisfy his needs, to promote social equality, as a means of completing his political liberty.[36]

Not only was the state in effect changing the relation of many individuals to the socio-economic system, but it was also determining and defining their life-style and the nature of their communities. Council housing and the development of New Towns, for example, invariably separated residential areas quite distinctly from industrial areas. Compulsory education up to the age of 14 imposed a lengthy period of children's dependence on all social sectors, while at the same time the institution of old age pensions relieved many families of dependants at this end of the age-scale. Married women working was further discouraged, in some cases – such as teachers – forbidden.

To a great extent, although perhaps inadvertently, the state was actually *defining* what family structure and home life should be; the *size* of council houses, for instance, betrayed what the government felt to be the normative, the 'right', size of family.[37] The government made it more difficult economically and geographically for married women *not* to have their place in the home. There is no doubt that the government was increasingly concerned with 'the family', and parallel to this, with a man's obligation to work and support his family:

the fear that the family was threatened . . . arose partly from an exaggerated respect for the protection which it offered its members against the hazards of life. In general, social policy never managed clearly to define the family which was so often the focus of concern, nor to decide whether the main task lay in ensuring the observance of ties which were in danger of neglect, or in supplementing an effective net of kinship and help . . . . By comparison, legislation unequivocally stated the obligation to work.[38]

Increased interest in the welfare of infants and children had developed during the nineteenth century, but was related more to children's employment generally than to health specifically. As McCleary comments, it witnessed

an increasing public concern in the protection of children from various kinds of evils, arising chiefly in the course of industrial employment. During the nineteenth century some hundred Acts of Parliament were passed for this purpose. Child labour in factories, mines, and theatres, and in chimney sweeping was either abolished or subjected to increasingly stringent regulation. Free elementary education was provided, and with the Prevention of Cruelty to Children Act, 1889, a new code of child protection was introduced. When the century ended the principle had been established that the community as a whole had become responsible for the welfare of its children.[39]

Nineteenth-century legislation thus enforced a lengthier period of children's dependence, which meant in practice an increase in married women's dependence who, more than 'the community as a whole', were seen as primarily responsible for their care.

Concern for children's health had not really become a salient issue until the turn of the century. This was a result of several factors: the infant mortality rate was still very high, and reached a particularly high peak in 1899; there was a growing concern with the falling birth rate; the Boer War had brought attention to the poor state of health in which the majority of the population lived. Initial attempts at combating infant mortality were made by voluntary organizations and then later taken over by municipalities.

Inherent in the early infant welfare movement were the ideas of the importance of personal hygiene (parallel with, yet distinct from, public sanitation), and the importance of 'educating' women to be 'good' mothers. These concepts were very much part of middle-class domestic ideology, implicit in which were the notions that not only was a woman's place most definitely in the home, but also that her most important role and duty was as a mother. Pioneers in health visiting not only gave instructions on cleanliness and hygiene, but also on thrift, temperance and religion. Here is direct evidence of a middle-class attempt to diffuse their own values and ideology concerning children and the family. The direct impact of these attempts, however, was almost certainly slight, as they were very localized, *except* in the way in which they influenced later governmental policy and action. This, of course, had far greater and more widespread impact.

While an increasing number of municipal authorities adopted measures for infant and maternal welfare (health visiting, provision of cheap or free meals for nursing mothers, etc.) during the first decade of the century, the central state began to show interest in the infant welfare movement and several important Acts of Parliament were passed just before the First World War. The Midwives Act of 1902 came into full operation in 1910, by which all midwives were legally obliged to be certified medically before practising. The National Insurance Act of 1911 also provided a maternity benefit, and from 1914 the Local Government Board started making grants to develop the infant welfare movement. It was the First World War, however, which precipitated much more action by the central government, for it was only then truly realized by the government in what a poor state of health a large proportion of the population actually lived: 'in a Circular dated July 29, 1915 the Local Government Board urged upon local authorities the importance of putting into operation all their powers for promoting maternal and child welfare, pointing out that the war had intensified the need for that work'.[40] Whether from these efforts or, more probably, from medical developments and a rising standard of living, the rate of infant mortality began to decline after 1900, and thereafter declined very rapidly indeed (see Appendix 1). Local variations still remained very marked; McNally, for instance, found that in 1933 the infant mortality rate in Oxford was 32, while in St Helen's it stood at 116.[41]

Other measures were introduced by the government at this time relating to children's health and hygiene, and these were operated through the education system. In 1907 medical inspection was imposed upon local authorities as a duty, although it was some time before it became truly comprehensive. School meals, facilities for eye examinations, the provision of spectacles, and general instruction about health and hygiene must have affected the attitudes of both parents and future parents at the time. As Lowndes notes:

there is no doubt that the school medical service made its own distinctive contribution to the *education* of the people. It taught the country to look upn the child, not as a unit, for statistical record of clinical data, but as an individual to be trained in a hygienic way of life, preserved in health where he possessed it or restored to health where he did not. It taught the parents of the first generation of children to be subjected to school medical inspection and that ailments could not with impunity be treated as trifling in an urbanised population. It created in that generation, when they became parents in their turn, a health conscience which abolished the 'Mother Gamp' of the slums and endowed the young mother of the 1930s with a fund of common sense and a readiness to seek advice which her prototype of forty years before rarely possessed.[42]

The education system was certainly providing a greater amount of information on, and a certain access to, health and hygiene. This information almost certainly influenced, directly or indirectly, attitudes to the home, the family and children generally. On the other hand, the ability to put these principles into practice in the future was very much a factor depending on the economic future of the individual. A 'health conscience' is all very well if the material resources are there to back it up, but in the 1920s and 1930s neither women nor children were covered by national insurance, and therefore it might be said that among the poorest sectors 'Mother Gamp' was still alive and well.

Pregnancy, childbirth and childcare had traditionally been dealt with exclusively by women within the family, kin and community on a basis of 'self-help' in working-class areas. The state and the medical profession (often working hand in hand, and both, of course, male-dominated) had increasingly taken control of these matters.[43] Beds available in maternity hospitals increased from 210 in 1891 to 10,029 in 1938. Child welfare clinics increased from a total of 2054 in 1920 (1061 run by local authorities, 993 by voluntary organizations) to 4585 in 1938 (2752 run by local authorities).[44] Government expenditure on the social services increased from £25 million in 1890 to £500 million in 1940.[45] The government also imposed strict control on midwifery; any complications during childbirth were to be dealt with by doctors.

Thus the development of the infant and child welfare movement greatly eroded the traditional power base of women's social networks and mutual support system through the local community making them more dependent both on the immediate family (or more specifically, their husbands) and on state agencies and the medical profession. Moreover, as mentioned earlier, welfare was quite specifically concerned with the health and well-being of *children*, and not with (and indeed, often at the expense of) *women*. The only time when women were given any significant help from the state was when they were pregnant; over and over both the government and the medical profession emphasized the importance of women *as mothers* and their 'natural' duty to their children; married women working was discouraged, often prohibited, as a danger to the health and welfare of their children. This emphasis on women's natural duty to their children and their dependence was reinforced by many of the changes discussed earlier: suburbanization, isolation, the weakening of local social groups and networks, and so on.

Economic, political, demographic and ideological changes resulted in a very different position, status and meaning attached to the family and children in the early twentieth century. Children were now much more of an economic burden than an asset to working-class families. A prolonged period of dependence and compulsory schooling meant that the time during which a child could actually contribute to the family income was less than before. Through government legislation, the media and the education system, however, the importance of women bearing and rearing healthy children as their one essential role in society was emphasized in one way or another continuously. Successful womanhood was becoming virtually synonymous with successful motherhood.

Economic factors must certainly have affected attitudes to, and ideals of, family structure and family size, yet they were by no means the *only* important factors; the situation in reality was far more complex. Relative isolation for many women, for example, meant that childminding once performed by kin or neighbours was more difficult to obtain, thus making the possibility of full-time or even part-time work for married women more difficult, even where there may have been appropriate job opportunities. More important, however, was that greater isolation from social networks for both men and women would lead to a greater home-centredness and privatization of the family. This, in conjunction with a more elaborate domestic ideology defining the woman's role as mother and housewife rather than producer, the influence of welfare state institutions and the education system, resulted in a greater emphasis being put on the role of children *within* the home and family, as an enhancement of domestic and family ideals, than on their potential as future wage-earners.

Further, the reduction in infant mortality meant that for the first time most couples could assume that all their children would reach maturity: 'for the whole of human history up to the turn of the present century, simple physical survival has been the dominant issue in child upbringing: a question not of "How shall I rear my child?" but of "*Will* I rear him?" '.[46] Concern with methods of childrearing was fostered not only by the welfare movement, but also by the popularization of psychological theories on child development. The importance of forming strong emotional bonds with one's children, of leisure pursuits with the whole family, of play, and so on all contributed towards the image of an 'ideal type' of family as being a small one. In a sense, where the traditional urban working-class family of a few decades earlier had been very much part of a broader community life, where women had their social groups and networks, men had theirs, and children also had theirs, the weakening of the community and the declining importance of local social networks meant that many working-class families were becoming more groups unto themselves, with a greater participation in family life from *all* members of the family, a greater interest in children as an integral part of family life and leisure, and in particular a growing emphasis on the importance of child *quality* rather than child *quantity*.

Another important development influencing ideals of family size, at least for the more prosperous sectors of the working class, was the increased possibility for children to become socially mobile through the education system (perhaps in itself a result of a trend towards atomization; a few decades earlier such families might have thought more in terms of *group* mobility through political action). While primary education had been established in the nineteenth century, the first provision for secondary education was not made until 1902, when legislation was passed to provide national secondary schools. Then in 1907 the 'Free Place System' was initiated. In 1895 no more than three to six children out of every thousand leaving elementary school passed on to endowed grammar schools, while by 1934 the proportion had increased to 119 per thousand.[47] Although this undoubtedly represents a significant expansion of educational opportunities, it must also be remembered that between those years there was also a sizeable expansion of the middle income groups, in other words, while there were better chances for the gifted working-class child to go on to secondary education, it was still overwhelmingly the preserve of the middle classes. During the 1930s, not more than 14 per cent of all 11 year-olds went on to secondary schools, and of that number no more than 7 per cent went free. Nevertheless, the *possibility* of further education existed, which had not been the case a few decades earlier.

Even if a child did gain a free place at secondary school, considerable financial strain was still put on the parents, as it lengthened the child's period of dependence and shortened the period during which he or she could contribute to the family budget. For working-class parents who did have strong aspirations for their children's education, this seems to have been an important motive for restricting family size quite drastically. Further, these aspirations spread quite markedly, partly as a result of the gradual increase in the standard of living for those in secure employment, and also as the occupational structure changed. As greater opportunities developed within the white-collar sector, so the possibility of secure opportunities within the skilled manual sector contracted. Table 8 shows how the proportion of children going to grammar schools increased during the period. Of course the proportion of working-class children in secondary schools was still extremely low, yet the increase in their places is significant both as a measure of the increasing importance attached not only to education, but also to children themselves, both by the government and by working-class parents.

There were also a number of other important changes and developments occurring during this period which could have affected attitudes to children, the home, the family and family size. The first four decades of the century witnessed the development and efflorescence of the cinema and cinema-going as a leisure pursuit. In 1914 there were 3500 cinemas open; by 1939 the number was 4800.[48] Virtually every town in Britain had at least one cinema, and the revolutionization of public transport meant that they were available to the vast majority of the population.

It is, of course, impossible to ascertain the effect which films and cinema-going had on people's beliefs and values; whether they served as an 'ideal' for a higher standard of living, or whether they simply served as an escape for many – all that really can be said is that they must at least have broadened the horizons of many within the working classes, which, in a subtle sort of way, could have contributed to the weakening of community social networks. Cinema-going was (and is) a relatively isolated pastime; it was not a social group activity involving social interaction and discourse, but a passive activity usually involving a couple, an individual or a small single-sex group. It coincided with, and some said was a

**Table 8**  *Social origin of boys and girls going to grammar schools*

| Father's occupational group | Percentage obtaining secondary education in grammar and independent schools | | |
|---|---|---|---|
| | born pre–1910 (%) | born 1910–19 (%) | born 1920–9 (%) |
| professional/managerial | 37 | 47 | 52 |
| Other non-manual and skilled manual | 7 | 13 | 16 |
| semi-skilled and unskilled | 1 | 4 | 7 |

*Source*: Halsey (1972), p. 182

cause of, a decline in pub attendance and drinking – the group activity *par excellence*, and one very much tied to the local community. Further, there was a gradual increase in the practice of couples going for a drink together, where previously pub attendance had been predominantly a male-dominated, single sex, activity. Between 1900 and 1935 the percentage of consumer expenditure on alcohol declined from 20.8 per cent to 7.0 per cent.[49]

Another important development during this time was the founding of the BBC in 1922, and a rapid increase in ownership of radios; by 1939, 75 per cent of all families owned a radio. The radio, probably more than the cinema, offered the possibility of broadening people's awareness of the world beyond the immediate community, as well as being a centralized means for the state to inform and influence the populace. As Mowat comments: 'one thing the new technology could do was to spread ideas, news, falsehoods, entertainment more rapidly and to more people than had ever been possible before'.[50] While the radio would in *content* tend to orient individuals more towards the country as a whole and divert attention from the importance of the local community, as an *activity* it was virtually entirely home-based and isolated, and contributed to an increasing emphasis on home and family (both in terms of programme content and by its very nature). The new leisure pursuits of cinema and radio were thus essentially centralized and national activities, emphasizing the importance of the country itself, rather than the local community, as an individual's prime focal point in terms of *content*, while as *activities* emphasizing the importance of the home, the family and leisure pursuits shared between family members within that context.

Further, the inter-war years witnessed the first period in history where universal literacy prevailed. This was almost entirely a result of compulsory primary education; its effect was to create a much wider reading public. This was evident not only in the dramatic expansion of the press which occurred at the time, but also in the use and extension of public library facilities and the publication and purchase of books (see Table 9). Reading, of course, is an entirely atomized activity and regardless of what was actually being read, certainly indicated the growth of home-centred, individuated leisure activities at this time.

Interestingly, it would seem that the 'boom' in reading as a leisure pursuit was experienced most by women. Women's magazines during this period expanded dramatically in both quantity and

**Table 9**  *Number of book issues in public library service, Great Britain and Northern Ireland, for selected years, 1896–1939*

| Date | Number of issues |
|------|------------------|
| 1896 | 26,225 |
| 1911 | 54,256 |
| 1924 | 85,668 |
| 1935 | 207,982 |
| 1939 | 247,335 |

*Source*: Halsey (1972), p. 564

readership, while their content also changed: 'almost without exception, the new periodicals dedicated themselves to upholding the traditional sphere of feminine interests and were united in recommending a purely domestic role for women'.[51] Between 1922 and 1939 no fewer than nine new monthlies were established; *Good Housekeeping*, 1922; *Modern Woman*, 1925; *Woman and Home*, 1926; *My Home and Modern Home*, 1928; *Wife and Home*, 1929; *Everywoman*, 1934; *Mother*, 1936; *Woman and Beauty*, 1939. Among many new weeklies, three were to become the first of the mass circulation weeklies: *Woman's Own*, 1932; *Woman's Illustrated*, 1936; and *Woman*, 1937. While these magazines were primarily aimed at middle-class women, they were also probably read by a great many working-class women. They tended to contain a mixture of entertainment and information; advice was given on budgeting, housekeeping, childbearing, and, in the 1930s, a certain amount on sex and birth control. Undoubtedly these magazines were a valuable source of information to women, and may have affected attitudes to the family, although it is impossible to gauge whether they were a response to, or a reflection of, an existing ideology, or whether they actually helped to create one. Most probably they served to *elaborate* an existing ideology of domesticity.

Parallel with the boom in women's magazines directed mainly at the middle-class market was a rapid development of publications aimed at the working-class woman: *Peg's Paper*, 1919; *Woman's Friend*, 1924; *Woman's Companion*, 1927; *Red Star*, 1929; *Secrets*, 1932; *Oracle*, 1933; *Lucky Star*, 1935; *Miracle*, 1935; *Glamour*, 1938. In these, interestingly, there is virtually no emphasis put on home, family or children, but instead on romance and excitement:

Their chief ingredients were romance, glamour, sensation, mystery and revenge, showing the deep need of hard-worked poorly-paid girls and women to escape from their drab surroundings into a colourful, action-packed dream world, where love and riches were for once within reach. Despite the lurid illustration and inferior writing, the values projected were always moral, if sometimes naive in their assumption that in this life the good always triumphs over the bad.[52]

The lack of a domestic ideology in these magazines apparently aimed at the working class is interesting and somewhat puzzling; perhaps it was because it was automatically assumed that women who *worked* would not be *married*, and sought only escapism. To a certain extent this is confirmed by the fact that a great emphasis was put on romance *leading* to marriage. The division of these two types of magazine into 'working-class' and 'middle-class' may be misleading; it may have been that they were aimed at two different groups of women divided by marital status. Whatever the case, it is obvious that more and more people, in particular among the working class, were reading material of one sort or another, and that this in turn was indicative of a growing tendency to pursue leisure activities within the home or with one's partner and/or children, instead of with members of a single-sex group rooted in the local community.

One further leisure activity which expanded greatly at this time and deserves mention is that of betting. Opportunities increased for betting on horse racing, greyhound racing, and, in the 1930s, the football pools; and betting on all these activities become one of the most popular forms of entertainment among the working class. In 1928 the totalizator was introduced in England. While many undoubtedly attended the races or matches on which they were betting, many did not, and betting itself was basically an individuated pursuit; people were just as apt to seek 'tips' from the press as from friends, neighbours or work colleagues. While it was not necessarily an anti-social pursuit (as reading was), neither was it really a social pursuit. It might also be pointed out that betting is, to some extent, indicative of a belief in 'luck', chance, fate; in a way, such beliefs could be said to conflict with notions of progress, solidarity, and religious faith, and could be taken in a broad sense as indicative of a *Weltanschauung* resulting from individuation, atomization or anomie.

In any case, there can be little doubt that the general trend of leisure pursuits among the working class was changing during this time, and, in particular, the tendency was increasingly towards fewer group-oriented, single-sex activities, and more towards individual or family-based home-centred activities and entertainment: 'the public house . . . came to have a good deal of competition. If still the poor man's club, it was not necessarily his resort. The wireless might keep him at home. Sporting interest might send him to the dogs. A hunger for romance or for excitement might take him to the cinema'.[53] Similarly, the urban working-class woman tended to gravitate less to the street and its social group, and more to home-based activities either on her own or with her husband and/or children. Children, too, were affected by these changes; the wireless, the cinema, libraries and magazines, not to mention the rapid growth of youth movements such as the Scouts and Guides, all tended to take children increasingly away from the traditional 'street' culture and more into the home or specific leisure institutions.

Were these developments in leisure pursuits a result of increased leisure time? There was a certain reduction in working hours; in the 1870s the average working week had been of fifty-four or fifty-four and a half hours, and 'in common practice there was little change until 1914, though rather shorter weeks – 48 to 53 hours – were gradually spreading, especially in engineering. For coal-miners a statutory daily maximum of 8 hours underground was fixed in 1908'.[54] After the First World War a working week of forty-seven and a half or forty-eight hours became standard in most organized industries, though it was longer in the less organized ones. Week-ends now started from midday on Saturday.[55] Further, the decline in residential domestic service and outwork meant that more young girls and women had a greater amount of leisure time than a few decades earlier. Working hours were, in the main, shorter, and 'the general shortening of hours in 1919–20 was the unions' last major victory in these decades'.[56] They did not change again appreciably until after 1940.

It is doubtful, however, that the shortening of working hours by itself was in any way really influential in changing patterns of leisure; for one thing, many more people were travelling further to work, and this itself nullified any gain in leisure time. Changing patterns of leisure were more a result of changes in the socio-economic structure generally, the increasing influence of state institutions, suburbanization, education, and the growing tendency for social groups based in the community to become less important factors in working-class life. Most important for many married women was that less time was being spent in childbirth and childcare; smaller families meant more leisure time for women, and that leisure time tended to be spent primarily within the context of the family. Spending leisure time with the family was partly a necessity, given the increased length of dependence but was also a result of other changes. It was not that couples necessarily decided to have small families so as to have more leisure time, but rather that the various socio-economic, demographic, political and ideological changes which were occurring resulted in a greater emphasis on the home and the family as a unit more unto itself, with a greater importance ascribed to the emotional gains to be had from parenthood and shared leisure activities within the family. These ideals essentially precluded large families, for large families generally meant overcrowding, discomfort, overwork for women, and the inability to share leisure together or to develop strong emotional bonds with their children.

In other words, the changing relations of *all* members of working-class families to the socio-economic system, in conjunction with the spread of welfare institutions and the social services generally tended not only to weaken the traditional importance of the working-class community, its social groups and networks, but also strengthened the importance of the family as a more isolated, and also more self-sufficient, unit within the community. Where the man was in secure employment, the wife and children usually remained complete dependants. The woman's position as dependent housewife and mother led to an increasing glorification of both home and family; inherent in this ideology was the ideal of a close-knit, small family. The strength of this ideology and the ability to achieve it did, of course, vary greatly according to economic circumstances, occupational experience, marital role-relationships and knowledge and use of birth control. Generally, however, broader work experience and a greater exposure to other women, other information, values and ideals prior to marriage meant more working-class women had a greater knowledge of reproduction and the possibility of controlling it, and meant that they had less need of communication networks with other women *after* marriage. With more men working further from home, their local social networks also became less important, and they tended to spend more time in the home. This fact alone may have made many men more aware of the problems of childcare and housework, and may have made them feel more directly concerned with, and affected by, the issue of decision-making concerning family size.

On a much more general level, the First World War and the popularization of psychological ideas were affecting the values and ideals of all social sectors in a number of ways; these trends were reinforced by advances made in science and medicine. As McGregor notes: 'the power of religious faiths to command intellectual loyalties and regular public observance had weakened. . . . The evangelical faith which had once sustained the family code was perishing in an atmosphere of scepticism and indifference'.[57] Where the dominant concern of the middle class concerning the working class in the past century had been to educate them to lead a more 'moral' and religious life, their principal preoccupation during this period was to elevate the social conditions of the working class (mostly through state institutions), in particular, with regard to the health and hygiene of the next generation. While these concerns were temporal, the 'Evangelical concern to eradicate the devil in the child finds many echoes in the hygienist movement which dominated the 1920s and 1930s of our own century'.[58]

This shift in ideological emphasis from spiritual well-being to physical and psychological welfare had important effects on working-class family structure and ideology. In the nineteenth century, religious dogma and church attendance were not easily enforced on the working classes, but the establishment of compulsory education and other measures which altered the relations of working-class children, in particular, to the socio-economic system paved the way for establishing a more subtle and temporal ideology of domesticity, maternal and child welfare, health and hygiene. Preservation of health and life itself are ideals which few people reject, while spiritual welfare is a far more nebulous and often irrelevant concept to those who are ill and hungry. The ideology of domesticity was founded on the essential importance of woman as guardian of her children's health and welfare, and as such her prime role was that of dependent reproducer rather than independent producer. Further, spiritual welfare is a concept, and church-going a practice, which form an integral part of notions of community, while the new ideals of health and welfare were basically ideals to be constructed within the individuated and private world of the nuclear family.

Thus, during the first four decades of this century an increasingly centralized and more powerful state was, by means of various policies, considerably altering the position of working-class individuals within society, the community and the family. This, in combination with changes in occupational experience, leisure pursuits, residential and community patterns, was resulting in a weakening of working-class communities as primary sources of recreation, solidarity, information and assistance. The political implications of these trends were to weaken the working-class movement and to strengthen the central state.

The impact of these changes on different areas, groups and families depended on local variations in individuals' relations to the socio-economic system. Where women were still crucial to the family economy (and this was now very rare), or in areas where massive unemployment occurred, the situation was frequently very different, and it is at this point worth considering some of these variations.

Unemployment, of course, was the crucial variable dividing society between the prosperous – or relatively prosperous – and the poverty-stricken. As mentioned before, unemployment on a massive scale was located in the regions of the old staple industries: South Wales, the North-East and the North-West, although pockets of unemployment existed in the prosperous areas as well.

Unemployment affected different areas in different ways. Mining areas, for instance, had previously been quite prosperous, the trade unions were strong, and the local labour market was over-whelmingly male-dominated. Unemployment was on such a massive scale in mining towns that it was often regarded as a community problem with residents making communal efforts of various sorts to help alleviate it. Due to their recognition as 'Special Areas' there was also some amount of government help available, and according to the Pilgrim Trust's report[59] most mining areas were able to maintain a relatively high standard of living compared to other areas of high unemployment.

Nevertheless, there can be no doubt that unemployment in these areas meant considerable hardship and often terrible poverty for many families. Hutt, for example, when discussing conditions in South Wales observed that:

in 1929 the medical officer of health in Merthyr was reporting that there was no advance in housing; that there were in the town no fewer than 834 houses which required entire rebuilding to make them habitable; and that 118 cellar-dwellings, many of which had previously been closed, were now each occupied by a separate family, owing to lack of suitable accomo-dation.[60]

Mortality remained very high, often as much as 50 per cent higher than towns in the South-East. Again, if any one group in these areas suffered more than most it would seem to have been married women: maternal mortality in South Wales and other depressed areas was approximately twice as high as in the South-East. The Pilgrim Trust found that men and children suffered the effects of malnutrition and ill-health considerably less than did the women in these areas.

Unemployment in mining towns was of course an overwhelmingly male phenomenon. While a few miners' wives were able to find some part-time work to supplement the dole, the majority remained at home as before, but with less income to maintain the home and family. Miners' traditional leisure pursuits of drinking and betting were undoubtedly severely curtailed, although local institutions such as the WEA, political parties, chapels, choirs and brass bands continued to thrive. Certainly a much larger proportion of miners spent more time at home than before, and this, coupled with their loss of economic power, may have resulted in a shift in power relations within the family. More emphasis was put on family life and family leisure pursuits. Certainly in Wales there was traditionally a strong belief in the importance of education as a means for children's social mobility, and this seems to have increased during the inter-war period.

It is interesting to note that the Rhondda experienced a dramatic decrease in fertility between 1911 and 1931 (which was typical of most mining areas): from a marital fertility rate of 235.0 to 109.0 – a decrease of 53.7 per cent (the equivalent for England and Wales was 38 per cent). While the proportion of women married between the ages of 20 and 24 increased in England and Wales by 9 per cent between 1911 and 1931, the proportion in the Rhondda *decreased* by 28 per cent. Couples, it seems, were restricting fertility both by deferring marriage and by increased use of birth control once married.

Unemployment in the Lancashire textile towns was different in many ways to that in mining towns. Wages were lower than in mining, and both men and women had worked in the industry since its beginning. Unemployment therefore affected both men and women directly. If the husband became unemployed, the chances were that the wife, and often a child or children, would continue to earn, and although this resulted in a general decline in earnings, it did not mean such a drastic change as occurred in mining areas, nor was it by any means always the case that the husband was the one who was unemployed:

where unemployment most affects families as a whole, in the Special Areas and in Liverpool, dependence on Unemployment Assistance is greatest. It is least in Blackburn, where the practice of both man and wife working often means that, when one is unemployed, the other is not . . . . In Blackburn there was a higher proportion of earners in the household, and corresponding to this, a smaller proportion living actually 'in poverty'.[61]

Fertility in Lancashire had long been low relative to other working-class areas; nevertheless, it declined quite markedly between 1911 and 1931. In Burnley, which was typical of the weaving towns, it declined from a marital fertility rate of 151.0 to 80.0, a decline of 46 per cent. There was only an insignificant decline in the proportion of women married between the ages of 20 and 24 (1 per cent). Unlike the Rhondda, it seems that the decline was achieved almost entirely through exercise of birth control within marriage.

Lancashire textile towns were in no way as male-dominated as were mining areas. Single and married women had been active in the labour market for a long time, and since the late nineteenth century there had been a tradition of women's active participation in, and organization of, political activities:

several years before 'suffragette' became a household word, the cotton workers of Lancashire were debating the controversial issue of votes for women . . . . The speakers who addressed the crowds were not educated middle class ladies, but local women who had come to the suffrage movement through their experience of factory work and of organizing working women.[62]

Despite these differences, Lancashire textile towns experienced a high degree of poverty during the inter-war period. For instance

in Burnley Dr. Lamont reports the existence of 2,140 back-to-back and single houses, of which 1,748 were 'unfit for human habitation or dangerous'. Details of sanitary inspection of over 600 Burnley houses in 1931 indicate the large number of small rooms, the frequency of dampness in bedrooms, the vast number of defects of all kinds – windows that would not open, floors and walls out of repair, rooms without fireplaces. Of all these houses only seven had baths, and a mere handful had pantries.[63]

The infant mortality rate in the poorest wards of Burnley stood at over 100 in 1931, compared with 39 in Bath for the same year. Maternal mortality was also high.

Other areas characterized by high unemployment rates also varied, variations arising in the main from their previous occupational and class structures. Liverpool, for instance, had a range of industries besides her most important ones of shipbuilding and dockwork, and by and large had been characterized by low wages, a high degree of casual labour, weak unionization and a large proportion of Irish immigrants. In other words, before the depression a large sector of the working class there would already have been used to conditions of uncertainty and insecurity in employment. Regional unemployment statistics also disguise the existence of enclaves of high unemployment within generally prosperous areas – for example, fishing, shipbuilding and farming communities in Essex.

Despite the general decline in the birth rate there were also marked variations in fertility between geographical areas and occupational groups. To illustrate just how marked differences were, I have selected ten areas for comparative purposes. Hampstead as representing an area dominated by the middle classes; Bethnal Green as a predominantly working-class area of London; Middlesex as a typical middle-class suburban area; Edmonton as a predominantly working-class suburban area; Montgomeryshire as a rural area dominated by smallholdings; Lincolnshire as a rural

**Table 10** *Marital fertility rates for ten 'key' areas, 1911 and 1931*

|  | 1911 (%) | 1931 (%) | Decrease (%) |
|---|---|---|---|
| Hampstead | 117.0 | 76.0 | 35.0 |
| Burnley | 151.0 | 80.0 | 46.0 |
| Middlesex | 157.0 | 96.0 | 38.9 |
| Montgomeryshire | 175.0 | 131.0 | 27.7 |
| Lincolnshire | 187.0 | 121.0 | 35.0 |
| Edmonton | 193.0 | 111.0 | 45.0 |
| Stoke-on-Trent | 203.0 | 119.0 | 43.0 |
| Gateshead | 204.0 | 135.0 | 33.5 |
| Bethnal Green | 221.0 | 120.0 | 45.7 |
| Rhondda UD* | 235.0 | 109.0 | 53.7 |
| Mean (England and Wales) | 167.0 | 103.0 | |

*Source*: Census (1911 and 1931)

*UD stands for Urban District.

area dominated by wage labour; Burnley as typical of a Lancashire weaving town; Rhondda UD as a typical Welsh mining town; Stoke-on-Trent as an example of a town with a variety of industries, although dominated by the pottery industry; Gateshead as a typical area of shipbuilding.

The marital fertility rates of these ten areas varied widely as Table 10 shows. Looking first at the rates for 1911, there is a marked contrast between the ten areas, Hampstead having the lowest, and the Rhondda having the highest. Only Hampstead, Burnley and Middlesex are below the national mean.

Quite a different pattern emerges when the marital fertility rates for the same areas in 1931 are examined. Although Hampstead, Burnley and Middlesex are still the only three below the national mean, all of the areas are now much more clustered around the mean, while Bethnal Green and the Rhondda have declined very markedly indeed; the Rhondda in fact manifested the fourth lowest marital fertility rate of all ten areas. Considering the percentage decrease in the marital fertility rate, the most marked declines occurred in the predominantly working-class areas (with the exception of Gateshead); this does, of course, correspond with national data on class trends.

Much of the variation in fertility between the different areas can be explained by their demographic structures. There was, for instance, a close correlation between the marital fertility rate and the area's sex ratio, with areas manifesting the highest ratio of women to men also manifesting the lowest fertility, and vice-versa (see Table 11). All areas experienced an increase in the ratio of women to men between 1911 and 1931, except for Hampstead. The sex ratio, taken for all age groups can, however, be deceptive. The crucial point to consider is the sex ratio of the various age groups; if there is an unbalanced sex ratio from the age of 49 upwards, this will have no effect on fertility patterns. If, however, a marked imbalance occurs during the childbearing years for women, it will tend to affect both marriage patterns and the fertility of an area. The most markedly unbalanced sex ratio during the child-bearing years of the ten areas is that of Hampstead. Burnley, on the other hand, is relatively evenly balanced throughout all age groups, and yet the fertility of that area was lower than all others except Hampstead. Conversely, the sex ratio of Bethnal Green was also fairly evenly balanced (although the proportion of women was below the national mean and lower than that of Burnley), yet

**Table 11**    *Ratio of females to males in the ten 'key' areas, 1911 and 1931*

|  | 1911 (%) | 1931 (%) |
|---|---|---|
| Rhondda UD | 83.0 | 92.0 |
| Lincolnshire | 97.0 | 98.0 |
| Edmonton | 100.0 | 105.0 |
| Gateshead | 102.0 | 104.0 |
| Stoke-on-Trent | 104.0 | 107.0 |
| Bethnal Green | 105.0 | 107.0 |
| Montgomeryshire | 106.0 | 108.0 |
| Middlesex | 112.0 | 116.0 |
| Burnley | 117.0 | 119.0 |
| Hampstead | 161.0 | 155.0 |
| Mean (England and Wales) | 108.0 | 109.0 |

*Source*: Census (1911 and 1931)

manifested a high level of fertility. Clearly the sex ratio is an important factor to consider, correlating strongly with fertility, but it is still necessary to know exactly *how* it affected fertility and why it varied so much between different areas.

The most obvious way in which the sex ratio affected fertility was through its effect on age at marriage and rates of marriage. There was a very strong correlation between the marital fertility rate and the proportion of women married in the age group 20–24,[64] and areas with the highest ratio of women to men tended to be areas with the lowest proportion of women married in the younger age groups. This correlation, however, was less marked in 1931, which could indicate that age at marriage had become rather less important as a means of restricting fertility, and that fertility was being controlled increasingly within marriage itself.

One of the strongest correlations with the marital fertility rate in 1931, which was relatively weak in 1911, was the proportion of women married in the 30–34 age group. Areas with high fertility also tended to be areas with a high proportion of women married in this age group. Although the evidence is not conclusive, it does suggest that in such areas the high fertility may have been at least partly a result of the older marriage cohorts continuing to reproduce with relatively little control exercised within marriage, rather than a result of high fertility among the young cohorts. As Abrams points out:

the material that is available suggests that the differences in family
standards within England and Wales are related primarily to age and not
to income. In 1939 young wives on the depressed Tyneside apparently
aimed at much the same size of family as young wives in the prosperous
suburbs of the Home Counties; the outstanding differences in fertility
between Tyneside wives and Home Counties wives were to be found
among those over 35 years of age – i.e., had passed their childhood in a
pre-1918 world; the Tyneside housewives in this age group were producing
relatively 40 per cent more children than their southern sisters.[65]

The general social, economic and ideological trends discussed
earlier may, therefore, have been having more effect on the
younger groups everywhere than the area variations suggest.

If the percentage change in proportions of women married aged
20–24 between 1911 and 1931 for the ten areas are examined, a very
interesting pattern emerges as shown in Table 12. While the
national trend, as discussed earlier, was towards younger marriage,
this was quite definitely *not* the case for many areas. In particular,
areas which manifested the highest percentage decrease in fertility
(the fertility may still have been relatively high) during this period
also manifested a very marked decrease in the proportion of
women married in the younger age groups. In other words, while
the national data on marriage show little correlation with changes
in fertility, at a more local level of analysis, there is clearly a
correlation. This is important, in that it suggests that delayed age

**Table 12**   *Percentage change between 1911 and 1931 in proportion
of women married aged 20–24 for ten 'key' areas*

|  | (%) |
| --- | --- |
| Rhondda UD | − 28 |
| Bethnal Green | − 28 |
| Stoke-on-Trent | − 15 |
| Gateshead | − 5 |
| Burnley | − 1 |
| Edmonton | + 1 |
| Montgomeryshire | + 20 |
| Lincolnshire | + 21 |
| Middlesex | + 24 |
| Hampstead | + 43 |
| Mean (England and Wales) | + 9 |

*Source*: Census (1911 and 1931)

at marriage was for many, but mainly for the working classes, still a very important means of controlling fertility. That is not to say that in these areas an increasing use of birth control may not also have been an important factor, but rather that *both* delayed age of marriage and voluntary control within marriage were affecting the rapid decline in fertility.

Thus, there were many changes occurring at the time, all of which may, to a greater or lesser extent, have affected the decline of family size among the working classes. The problem is obviously highly complex and it is impossible to consider every aspect in depth. Nevertheless, the foregoing discussion suggests that two of the most important areas to consider are those of work (in the broadest of senses) and home, and it is to these realms that we now turn.

# 3 Work before marriage

'Work' is not such an unambiguous term as it is often supposed to be. The vast majority of the population works, and has worked, yet all 'work' is not paid nor is it given the status of paid work – the prime example being housework. People may perform unpaid work part of the year, or part of their lives, and engage in paid work at other times or seasons. Work can be regular or irregular, paid or unpaid, and varies enormously in terms of location, structure and patterns of interaction within the workplace. Type of work, conditions and location seldom remain identical throughout an individual's life-cycle. As a dependant in the parental home it takes one form; when and if full-time paid work starts it takes another. After marriage it takes another, and, for women, after childbirth yet another. It has therefore been considered necessary to divide the discussion into two separate parts: the first, concerned with the effects of the individual's relation to the socio-economic system prior to marriage (and in this chapter, it concerns almost entirely women); the second, dealing with their relation after marriage and childbirth. Unfortunately it has not been possible to examine the individual's initial period of dependence within the parental home, though it is obviously important.

During the period before marriage the majority of single women were engaged in paid work. The majority of married women, as well as those widowed and divorced, were not, as Table 13 shows. By the twentieth century it had become increasingly normative for single women to work before marriage. (For brevity's sake, work here refers to paid work in the labour market.) Among the women interviewed, only three had not worked prior to marriage. Interestingly, it would seem that while many middle-class parents were increasingly accepting the need for their single daughters to go out to work, among some upper working-class parents it was regarded as something of a status symbol if their daughters remained within the parental home. The following extract is from a woman whose

father worked for the railway in Pontypridd, and whose mother
had worked as a farm servant doing some agricultural work as well
as childminding and domestic chores:

My father never smoked nor drunk, he was a deacon in the Chapel, my
brothers never smoked nor drunk – not one of us! ... My mother was
more strict than my father was, my mother, yes, she was very strict ....

*What did you do when you finished school?*

Oh I never done nothing, love, I was a lady, I was. Mind you, I had to do
my work, mind, I had to help, and I had a certain job to do with my
mother – dust and do the bedrooms upstairs and my elder sister could do
downstairs, but I wasn't – I never went out to work, never.

It would seem that her non-participation in the labour force was
intimately linked to her parents' definition of, and concern for,
respectability. For most working-class – and also middle-class –
parents, however, concern for respectability seemed to be attained
through the *type* of employment they put their daughters into (in
*all* of the interviews it was entirely the parents' decision as to
whether their daughters should work, and what sort of work they
should do). Shop assisting and clerical work were regarded by
most as more desirable and respectable than domestic service or
factory work (and factory work tended to be regarded as more
respectable/desirable than service). Different occupations will be
discussed in greater detail later.

**Table 13**  *Female participation rates in Great Britain, by age and marital
status, 1911–31*

| Marital status | Year | 14–24 (%) | 25–34 (%) | 35–44 (%) | 45–54 (%) | 55 and over (%) | All ages (%) |
|---|---|---|---|---|---|---|---|
| single | 1911 | 73.02 | 73.61 | 65.7 | 55.49 | 34.58 | 69.32 |
|  | 1921 | 70.63 | 76.21 | 67.67 | 59.72 | 36.53 | 68.14 |
|  | 1931 | 75.74 | 80.42 | 72.35 | 63.77 | 36.33 | 71.62 |
| married | 1911 | 12.10 | 9.91 | 9.92 | 9.92 | 7.19 | 9.63 |
|  | 1921 | 12.68 | 9.38 | 8.86 | 8.43 | 6.29 | 8.69 |
|  | 1931 | 18.53 | 13.20 | 10.15 | 8.52 | 5.29 | 10.04 |
| widowed and | 1911 | 58.46 | 65.05 | 60.81 | 45.96 | 19.43 | 29.43 |
| divorced | 1921 | 50.06 | 46.41 | 45.14 | 40.28 | 16.82 | 25.62 |
|  | 1931 | 58.17 | 54.76 | 45.25 | 35.58 | 13.78 | 21.24 |

*Source*: Halsey (1972)

**Table 14** *Percentage of women employed, aged 15–64, 1911 and 1931*

| Year | Mean (%) | Standard deviation (%) | Minimum (%) | Maximum (%) |
|------|----------|------------------------|-------------|-------------|
| 1911 | 39.5 | 10.3 | 17.0 | 70.3 |
| 1931 | 38.1 | 12.1 | 12.7 | 69.9 |

*Source*: Census (1911 and 1931)

Whether or not women worked outside the home was, of course, ultimately dependent on job opportunities in the area and these varied widely as Table 14 shows. In areas where employment for women was scarce – primarily rural areas and those characterized by heavy industry such as shipbuilding and mining – many girls left home to work elsewhere, usually as domestic servants. The effects of this on the demographic structure were to create an imbalance in the sex ratio and a consequent lowering of the age at marriage and increase in the marriage rate.

Of course an unbalanced sex ratio *by itself* did not necessarily affect marriage patterns directly, and it is worthwhile considering the link between employment opportunities and marriage. Single women who did not leave the area to work elsewhere almost invariably stayed in the parental home. If they were not employed, although they could be of use to their parents in terms of unpaid domestic labour, they would tend to be a drain on their parents' income. Young women working elsewhere could be an invaluable help financially, in that they contributed to the family income without taking from it in any way in terms of board and lodgings.

It seems that if a daughter's contribution to the family income was not considerable, or not regarded as essential, there was parental pressure to marry early or, at the least, there would not be any pressure *not* to marry early. If, however, her contribution was felt to be essential, then there *would* be some pressure against early marriage, or even against marriage at any age, witness the following account from a woman in Burnley who worked as a weaver, and whose father, after an accident in the weaving shed, set up a herbalist shop:

I used to have to come home, and when I were 19, had six loom and all, and me father were like a rake, me father used to come in – they call him tackler, looked after looms . . . he used to – we could be one night a week out, penny shilling spending money, that's all we got . . . me father he had to give up he had a nervous breakdown when he fell at flywheel . . . so he got a shop in town, herbalist shop, and did we know about it! Me and me sister we used to have to go down there at Sunday after working all week, 9 o'clock till 4 o'clock in the afternoon . . . and I used to have to come home from work and there were no electric irons, they were all gas irons – no gas irons, we used to have heaters, and we used to have 'em in fire, and I used to start ironin' as soon as we'd had the tea and I used to be ironin' till about 11 o'clock at night . . . .

*Did your parents tell you anything about –*

Oh no! We didn't know nothing, oh, and if anyone of us – our Eileen had to be married and our Jack had to be married, but they got married – and if anyone of us had a' come with a child, not bein' married, we'd 'a been – oh, 'struth, we'd 'a been murdered . . . . Oh me father thought none of us should get married, you know, he did!

*Why was that?*

I don't know.

The answer might have been that her father was getting nearly a full week's wages from each child, two unpaid shop assistants, and her mother was getting unpaid domestic help. If she had not married, they would have continued to receive such valuable assistance. It is tempting to wonder the extent to which fear of premarital pregnancy on the parents' behalf was a fear of social disgrace or a fear of losing valuable income and unpaid domestic help. Similarly, it could have been that on a daughter's part, premarital pregnancy was as much a deliberate attempt to gain independence from her parents as a manifestation of ignorance or carelessness. (Most parents under these circumstances, felt the daughter *had* to get married, whereas if she had wanted to, but was not pregnant, they could have refused permission for her to marry.) Whatever the case, there can be little doubt that in areas where girls could find relatively well-paid work easily, they made an important contribution to their parents' income.

It seems, therefore, that an unbalanced sex ratio alone was not necessarily directly linked to age at marriage; the vital intervening variable (which, to a great extent, determined the sex ratio in the first place) was employment opportunities for women. These opportunities must have influenced the prevailing norms and beliefs concerning marriage and age at marriage, particularly with regard to parents' attitudes. Table 15 shows how age at marriage varied among respondents according to their occupational experience. It is interesting to note the low age at marriage among

**Table 15** *Average age at marriage of respondents according to occupation prior to marriage*

| Type of occupation | Average age at marriage | Number |
|---|---|---|
| service/at home | 20.8 | (10) |
| office/shop | 22.4 | (8) |
| factory | 24.7 | (10) |

*Source*: Interviews[1]

those in service; studies of domestic servants in the nineteenth century indicated that this group at that time tended to marry later than other occupational groups.[2] In the twentieth century it would seem that service was regarded as less desirable and respectable than it had been earlier. Whether or not this was a result of a different type of woman entering service is impossible to tell, given the lack of adequate data.

Whatever the case, all of the interviews indicated clearly that once girls left school, they expected, and were expected by their parents, to contribute to the family income and/or to unpaid domestic work within the parental home. Two-thirds of the respondents started work between 1907 and 1916, one-third between 1918 and 1929 (the mean year for starting work was 1915, the mode and median, 1913). Yet by the time these women had their own children, this expectation, although it had not disappeared, had altered considerably. More emphasis was put on the desirability of further education or training, if at all possible, and their children were allowed greater choice of employment than they themselves had had. Although most of their children contributed some of their earnings to their parents, the proportion was greatly reduced.

For the majority of women in the early twentieth century, marriage was a major dividing line between participation and non-participation in the labour market. If jobs were scarce and poorly paid for single women, marriage did not 'matter' so much to them or to their parents, and in these areas a high rate of marriage and a low age at marriage were common. Where employment was plentiful and relatively well paid, but available to single women only (such as residential servants or teachers), there was probably considerable parental pressure to defer marriage. If the woman herself enjoyed her work and wished to continue, then she too would probably have wanted to defer marriage. If, on the other hand, employment was plentiful and well paid *regardless* of marital status, there would probably have been conflict between parents wishing their daughters to remain single for their own benefit, and daughters seeking to break away from parental domination/ exploitation in order to gain greater independence (as they saw it) through marriage. The case of the latter, however, was unusual and, as Glass says: 'whereas employment and marriage were not competing fields in 1851, employment at the present time [1931] tends to cause women not to marry, or at least to postpone marriage'.[3]

The census data showed how the sex ratio, age at marriage, fertility and the proportion of women occupied all correlated closely. When the sex ratio was controlled around the mean, however, the correlation between fertility and the proportion of women occupied in an area disappeared. Was the only relation between women working and fertility simply a result of the area's demographic structure? Leaving aside for the moment the issue of married women working, the fact that the majority of single women did work and yet marked differentials in family size and fertility existed according to geographical area and social class suggests that this must have indeed been the case. But, of course, not all women who performed paid work before marriage had identical occupations, quite the opposite. What evidence is there that variations in women's occupations prior to marriage (and after marriage) influenced their reproductive behaviour?

**Types of occupation**

There was evidence from both the 1911 and 1931 Census of a strong correlation between the proportions employed in certain occupations and fertility which, to a great extent, also correlated with the class structure of different areas. Tables 16 and 17 show how the proportions of men and women in certain occupations correlated with the marital fertility rate. With the exception of areas with a high proportion of men and women in textiles, all the other areas correlating inversely with the marital fertility rate would tend to have a higher than average proportion of the middle classes. To a great extent, the low fertility of these areas, particularly in 1911, may have been a result of their unusual demographic characteristics, namely a high proportion of resident domestic servants which would result in an unbalanced sex ratio, high age at marriage, and so on.

**Table 16** *Strength of correlations (inverse) between fertility and proportions of men and women in certain occupations, 1911 and 1931*

| | 1911 | | | 1931 | |
| Sex | Occupation | $R^2$ | Sex | Occupation | $R^2$ |
| --- | --- | --- | --- | --- | --- |
| female | midwifery | 25.6 | male | commerce | 26.6 |
| male | professions | 25.4 | female | midwifery | 21.5 |
| male | government | 17.5 | male | clerical | 14.8 |
| female | teaching | 12.0 | female | domestic service | 14.4 |
| male | textiles | 8.4 | female | clerical | 12.3 |
| female | textiles | 6.6 | male | textiles | 11.2 |
| female | domestic service | 3.4 | | | |

*Source*: Census (1911 and 1931)

It is interesting to note the extremely high correlation between fertility and the proportion of midwives for both time periods. However, as areas with the highest proportion of midwives corresponded with generally middle-class areas (the City of London, St Marylebone, Holborn, Bath, Bournemouth, Hampstead, Hastings), all that can be said is that the proportion of midwives was a good predictor of middle-class areas at the time, and not necessarily a variable affecting fertility directly. Indeed, as we shall see, the proportions in different occupations seem to be a better indication of an area's class structure generally than a reliable means of analysing differential patterns of fertility and family size. This is the most serious problem when using aggregate data of this type. Other sources,[4] of course, have shown that the family size of the middle classes was lower than that of other social sectors, so it is likely that *both* the class structure and the demographic structure (particularly the sex ratio and age structure) were affecting the

**Table 17** *Strength of correlations (positive) between fertility and proportions of men and women in certain occupations, 1911 and 1931*

| | 1911 | | | 1931 | |
| Sex | Occupation | $R^2$ | Sex | Occupation | $R^2$ |
| --- | --- | --- | --- | --- | --- |
| male | mining | 20.4 | male | agriculture | 4.8 |
| female | manufacturing | 6.8 | female | agriculture | 4.5 |
| female | agriculture | 4.5 | female | manufacturing | 4.3 |

*Source*: Census (1911 and 1931)

fertility of these areas, though which was stronger is impossible to say. Since domestic service was still the most important occupation of women in this period, let us examine it in more detail.

## Women in domestic service

While domestic service still employed more women than any other occupation, residential service was less and less common and was being increasingly replaced by the 'daily'. As McBride notes: 'although service continued to be the major occupier of women until 1940 . . . the middle-class employment of live-in domestics had ended by 1920'.[5] There was, moreover, an increasing number of older as well as married servants.

Between 1911 and 1931 the difference in strength of correlation between domestic servants and the marital fertility rate is surprisingly marked. Why was the correlation so weak in 1911? Looking at the actual areas with over 60 per cent of women employed in domestic service (as a percentage of women employed) in 1911 shows that eight of these fourteen areas were, in fact, rural districts. None the less, only three of the areas had a marital fertility rate above the mean, namely: Rutland Rural Districts, Shropshire Rural Districts and Yorkshire (East Riding) Rural Districts, Hertfordshire, Hereford-shire, Soton and East Suffolk Rural Districts, however, were all only just below the mean. The remaining areas were markedly below the mean, and only two of these were rural districts – Berkshire and Surrey, both of which were probably fairly well stocked with middle-class homes. In other words, it would seem that the weak relationship in 1911 is a result of two different kinds of area: (1) middle-class areas manifesting very low rates of fertility, and (2) rural areas manifesting a higher level of fertility.

In contrast, however, there was a very strong inverse correlation between *age at marriage* and the proportion of women working as servants; this gets stronger with each quinquennial age group. A high age at marriage would certainly tend to depress the fertility rate in such areas, but then why the slight relationship discussed above? It could be that in the rural areas with a high proportion of servants, women were marrying later, but once married still had large families, while women marrying in middle-class areas were controlling their fertility within marriage to a greater extent. It could also indicate that servants working in rural areas usually came from those areas in the first place and tended, once married, to remain there, while servants working in middle-class areas, when married, tended to leave the area and live elsewhere, i.e. the low fertility of such areas would probably not reflect the fertility of the servants *themselves*, but of those they had worked for. These data do not necessarily tell us anything about the individual fertility of servants.

There was a very strong positive correlation between areas with a high proportion of domestic servants and an unbalanced sex ratio (i.e. a surplus of women), but it was not as strong as the correlation with age at marriage. Most puzzling is that when the sex ratio and the proportion of married women of childbearing age were controlled around the mean, a very strong inverse correlation between fertility and women in service resulted. This test would eliminate areas like Chelsea and Hampstead where the sex ratio was highly unbalanced. It would seem to be indicative of lower middle- and middle-class areas characterized by one-servant households with a low level of fertility in suburbs such as Acton, Ealing, Wimbledon and so on.

In the 1931 Census, the rural areas with a high proportion of domestic servants in 1911 have disappeared; all the areas with a high proportion are now concentrated in London and middle-class suburbs in the South-East, and now, of course, there is a strong inverse correlation between fertility and the proportion of domestic servants. It seems likely that the servants in the rural districts in 1911 were farm servants or servants living on farms doing partly agricultural and partly domestic work. The absence of these in 1931 is probably evidence of the considerable transfer of property which had occurred in the countryside during that time.

None of these data, however, tell us anything as to how domestic service as an occupation affected the beliefs and behaviour of the many women who worked as servants prior to marriage. The majority of women who worked as residential domestic servants worked in one- or two-servant households; they were kept in great isolation and allowed little freedom. Their contact with the outside world was minimal; generally the nature of the mistress/servant relationship was to discourage any relationship beyond a communication of orders and duties to be fulfilled. The following extract from an interview with a woman in Essex gives a good idea of a domestic servant's life during the 1920s:

When I left school – I left at 14 – I went into what was known in those days as private service, and I went to Southwold, because I am a Suffolk person, and my mother had friends in the village that we lived, and a lady came to stay with them and she said, 'Well when your daughter leaves school I would like to have her to train – to do the housework proper, you know.' And so I went with her and I was – the agreement was that I stayed with her for twelve months before having a holiday, coming home to my parents for a holiday. . . . I had five shillings a week was my wages, out of that she used to keep a shilling a week for savings and stamps and save it up for me to buy clothes. . . . Well I stayed there for the year and then I came home on holiday. And when I got home my mother said to me, are you happy there? I said, 'Yes I'm all right', but it was a horrible big kitchen and I had to sit in there alone when I'd finished my housework, I had to wear what they call print frocks in the morning and big white aprons and what we would call a dustcap, and in the afternoon I had to have a black frock and a little – a little white cap and white cuffs and a dainty little white apron.

*What sort of work did you have to do?*

All the housework, help with the cooking.

*Was there a cook as well?*

No, she used to do the cooking. . . . I had to do all the vegetables and watch how she done things. . . .

*How did you get on with her?*

I got on all right with her, as I say she quite understood (about having periods) and she said to me one day she said, 'You know when anything happens you must tell me', and that was the way they used to put it to you, they didn't sort of term it as your periods or anything like that you see – when 'anything happened' you had to – when 'anything happened'! I was never allowed out alone there.

*Not at all?*

Not on my own, no. There was another lady round the corner had a maid and I could go for a walk one afternoon a week with her, on Sunday morning I could go to the church with Mr and Mrs Smith and I could go to church Sunday evening with them, but that was my lot.

This respondent, however, left service after twelve months and went on to work as a barmaid, much to the horror of her parents. There was generally a rapid rate of turnover in domestic service, and it would seem that few women remained in the same domicile for longer than two years. A survey of 1899 showed that 36 per cent of the domestic servants had held the same job for less than a year.[6]

Those who remained in service up until marriage, whether or

not they changed employer, seem to have experienced a high degree of isolation both from other women and the outside world generally. They entered marriage with very little idea of what it actually involved. They had had little exposure to new ideals through a work-based social group, except for the all-pervasive ideal that their right and proper place was in the home performing housework. Of those interviewed who stayed as domestic servants until they married (and half found work as shop assistants, barmaids or laundry workers), *all* claimed to have had no knowledge whatsoever of reproduction, sex or birth control when they married, witness the following account:

*Did your mother ever say anything to you about –?*

Oh no! Sex was really out of it all, my mother was a truly old-fashioned mother. . . . I think right up to the time that my first daughter was born I had an idea that they cut you right open to get the baby away. I had a very nice old family doctor and I remember I was terrified not because of having the baby but because I got to be chopped open, I thought, and, he said, 'No, the baby will come out where it went in', you know, that kind of thing, and I think that frightened me even more at the time!

*So nobody had told you anything?*

Not a bit.

It would seem that girls who remained in residential service existed in a sort of isolated vacuum, with little exposure to any beliefs, ideals or information other than those they had gleaned during childhood. When they did marry, if any measures for birth control were taken, they were always taken by the husband (four used coitus interruptus, one the sheath, and three used nothing at all). All but one never discussed sex or family size with their husbands; the taboo instilled by parents and continued by their mistresses apparently lasted through marriage. This is no doubt one reason why their average family size was above that of most other occupational groups (4.0; the maximum was 9.0; the minimum, 2.0). The isolation experienced prior to marriage also seemed to continue during marriage; they all had highly segregated role-relationships, and while three of them did form part of a local social network of women, the rest did not.

Nevertheless, with the increase in 'dailies' during the first four decades of the century, fewer women were experiencing this type of isolation. This could also partly explain the apparent lower age at marriage among domestic servants during this period, in contrast with the relatively late age prevalent during the nineteenth century; for those who wanted or needed to work after marriage, there was now more chance of doing so as a 'daily' – an option which had not been open a few decades earlier.

A comparison of the aggregate and individual data on domestic servants leads to very different conclusions. While the aggregate data revealed a strong inverse correlation between the proportions of domestic servants, the age at marriage and the fertility of an *area*, the individual data showed that for the servants themselves just the opposite tended to be the case. It seems that areas typified by a large proportion of domestic servants were invariably middle-class areas, and middle-class fertility was low. The effect of the work experience and situation on the servants themselves, however, was to isolate them from any social group or network, exposure to new ideals, beliefs or information and to perpetuate an attitude of secrecy and taboo on knowledge and discussion of matters relating to sex and reproduction. This attitude persisted through their married lives, resulting in highly segregated role-relationships, little or no communication between marriage partners on matters relating to family size, sex or birth control, total male responsibility for birth control, and a consequently larger family size than that prevailing among other groups of women who had gone through different types of work experience prior to marriage.

**Women in non-manual occupations**

This discussion will concentrate on women who were employed in the clerical sector. Reference will also be made to women who worked as shop assistants, teachers and nurses, but on the whole there is not sufficient data to examine these in detail, particularly at an individual level. Moreover, while the proportion of women employed in teaching contracted slightly between 1911 and 1931 (from 1.5 per cent to 1.2 per cent), and those in midwifery and nursing expanded marginally (from 0.8 per cent to 1.2 per cent), the proportion of women – and men – in the clerical sector expanded noticeably (from 1.0 per cent to 3.6 per cent for women, and from 3.3 per cent to 5.5 per cent for men). In 1911, 21 per cent of all clerks were women; by 1931, 46 per cent were women.[7]

Looking at the census data, in 1911 there was only a very slight inverse correlation between the proportion of women in the clerical sector and the fertility rate. The correlation between men in the clerical sector and fertility was even less. This was equally true when the sex ratio and proportion of married women of child-bearing age were controlled. There was, however, a positive correlation between women in the clerical sector and the sex ratio. As the numbers in the clerical sector at this time were relatively few, this is probably a reflection of other intervening variables rather than an indication of any direct causal link between men and women in the clerical sector and the marital fertility rate.

What is interesting about the clerical sector during this period, however, is that, while it did expand to a certain extent throughout England and Wales, the most dramatic increase was highly localized in and around London (see Table 18). Thus the expansion of clerical job opportunities was most marked in the South-East.

Parallel with the expansion of white-collar jobs between 1911 and 1931 was an increasingly strong inverse correlation between the proportion of women (and men) in the clerical sector and the marital fertility rate: (see Table 19). There was a strong positive correlation between the proportions in the clerical sector and the sex ratio, so that areas with a high proportion of clerks also tended

**Table 18**  *Proportions of men and women in the clerical sector (as a percentage of all employed) in the areas characterized by a large clerical sector, 1911 and 1931*

| Proportion of males in clerical sector | | Proportion of females in clerical sector | |
|---|---|---|---|
| *1911* | | *1911* | |
| *Area* | (%) | *Area* | (%) |
| Hornsey | 16.0 | Wandsworth | 12.7 |
| Stoke Newington | 13.1 | Hornsey | 9.9 |
| Lewisham | 12.9 | Tottenham | 7.7 |
| Wallasey | 12.9 | Stoke Newington | 7.6 |
| Wimbledon | 9.7 | Coventry | 7.4 |
| *1931* | | *1931* | |
| *Area* | (%) | *Area* | (%) |
| Middlesex RDs | 20.8 | Hornsey | 13.1 |
| Hornsey | 20.6 | Wandsworth | 10.2 |
| Lewisham | 16.8 | Lewisham | 9.9 |
| Wimbledon | 15.9 | Stoke Newington | 9.6 |
| Croydon | 15.8 | Acton | 9.4 |

*Source*: Census (1911 and 1931)

**Table 19**   *Correlation (inverse) between women and men in the clerical sector and the marital fertility rate, 1911 and 1931*

| Year | Women $R^2$ | Men $R^2$ |
|------|-------------|-----------|
| 1911 | 5.9 | 4.5 |
| 1931 | 12.3 | 14.8 |

*Source*: Census (1911 and 1931)

to be characterized by an unbalanced sex ratio, a relatively late age at marriage, and a low level of fertility. In spite of these unusual demographic characteristics, other sources reveal that clerks as an occupational group also had an extremely low level of fertility within marriage relative to other occupational groups as shown in Table 20. Part of this low fertility among clerks might be explained by age at marriage, although of course these data refer to *men*, and their age at marriage matters little compared to that of their wives. Male clerks married much later than men in other occupational groups, although among female clerks relative to other women the differential was less marked, as Table 21 illustrates.

It would seem, therefore, that areas with a high proportion of men and women in the clerical sector (and these correlated very closely) manifested a low level of fertility partly as a result of demographic factors, but also as a result of a low level of fertility within marriage. Why were clerks manifesting such low fertility within marriage relative to other occupational groups?

There are two possible reasons for this, and undoubtedly both

**Table 20**   *Total fertility of various occupational groups, 1931*

| Occupational group | Total fertility (%) |
|--------------------|---------------------|
| miners | 2.765 |
| unskilled labourers | 2.733 |
| agricultural labourers | 2.316 |
| skilled labourers | 2.103 |
| textile labourers | 1.596 |
| professionals | 1.522 |
| civil servants and teachers | 1.434 |
| clerks | 1.349 |

*Source*: Hopkin and Hajnal (1948)

**Table 21** *Proportions of men married in different occupational groups, aged 20–24, 1931*

| Occupational group | Married (%) |
| --- | --- |
| miners | 22.9 |
| unskilled labourers | 20.4 |
| skilled labourers | 18.4 |
| textile workers | 17.7 |
| agricultural labourers | 15.5 |
| professional, etc. | 6.0 |
| clerks | 5.5 |

*Source*: Hopkin and Hajnal (1948)

affected marital fertility among the clerical sector. First, the inter-war period tended to be a relatively difficult era for clerks. As Lockwood says: 'although in bare quantitative terms the clerical and administrative worker was not affected by the depression as much as the average manual worker, those who were actually unemployed were sufficiently numerous to destroy the traditional association of security and blackcoat employment',[8] and 'the characteristic feature of the inter-war years was the "stagnation" of promotion possibilities, even within the clerical grade itself'.[9] Clerks, much more than miners or other manual workers, had a certain 'image of respectability' to uphold: living in the 'right' neighbourhood, possibly owning a house, dressing according to 'proper' middle-class standards, etc., and such a standard of living was extremely difficult to maintain given a period of relative insecurity and poor pay. A large family would certainly have made it impossible to maintain such a standard. The following extract from an interview with a woman in Essex who worked as a typist prior to marriage, whose husband was a clerk for the railway and who had one child, gives an idea of these constraints:

*When you first got married, did you buy a house?*

No. The housing problem then was the same as it is now. If anything it was more tense.... My husband's father was in a position to own some property and there was a ruling, a government ruling that you could gain possession of a house for your family, but he said, 'I'm not turning anyone out for you, if you get married that's your responsibility, but I'm not turning you one out.' So we went and lived in one of them with me mother and had rooms with them. We had our own section of the house....

*Before you got married did you ever talk about what sort of a family you wanted?*

It was never discussed. Never thought of.

*What do you think your preference was? Would you have liked a large family?*

No, I don't think so, we couldn't afford it, and everything in those days was, can we afford it? We couldn't afford it therefore we must wait, and that's how everything was in those days . . . .

Certainly there must have been especially marked constraints on clerical workers both to defer marriage and to restrict their family size. Second, however, it could be argued that for women who had been clerical workers prior to marriage, access to information on reproduction and birth control through their work colleagues would have had considerable influence on their ideals of family size and their knowledge of how to achieve them. The following extract is from a woman who worked as a book-keeper in a department store in Essex, and later married a bus conductor and moved to London:

*When you were growing up, did your mother ever talk to you about –*

I never knew a thing.

*Nothing?*

No. I didn't know a thing.

*Where did you eventually find out?*

One of the girls in the office. They were talking one time and I wasn't sure about something and I said to them about it – and they told me. And that was after I was – oh I don't know whether I was engaged or just before I was engaged [i.e. in her early twenties]. No, my mum never discussed *anything* like that with me. When I was 14 I had the shock of my life – I couldn't think – I just screamed!

*Did your mother tell you then?*

She told me that, you know, oh everyone – all girls had it, but she didn't – never *explained* anything to me . . . . That's why I didn't stop at school! It was over that – the only reason I left school . . . . But you never used to talk about sex or anything of that, not years ago. I was brought out more in the office down there! Because of course Jane [a colleague], she got married several years before I left. And then of course the typist – she *had* to get married! and Jane was ragged and talking her so – and of course I was in between the two of them at my desk, you see. Oh we had some good times down at the office. There was something I said to Jane one day – I forget what it was – and she absolutely killed herself laughing. 'Cause I thought – about once every three months or something – I didn't know you had intercourse when you wanted or anything of that, see – I thought it was once in three months! Now Jane, she roared!

The fact that many offices were organized on a less hierarchical and more informal basis than occupations like domestic service or even shop assistants may have led to the formulation of fairly coherent social networks among work colleagues. Given the likelihood that some would be older and married (unlike residential service where they would all – if there were more than one – be single), it is probable that a fairly explicit exchange of information and values occurred, such as that described in the extract above. These women were also likely to have greater exposure to the media, given their greater freedom outside work, more substantial pay, and the fact that they would usually be working in an urban environment. *All* of the women interviewed who had worked in the non-manual sector prior to marriage had quite explicit ideas and information on marriage and sex by the time they married, although those working in office jobs tended to have a more detailed knowledge than those who had worked in shops. The information they had acquired, with only one exception, had all come from work colleagues.

In spite of the small number of interviews, it is interesting to see how the average age at marriage and family size of women who worked as clerks compares with those of women in other occupations (see Table 22). The family size of clerks was thus small relative to other groups, and yet they were not marrying late. While financial constraints must have been an important factor affecting their ideals of family size, it is also probable that their work experience before marriage was an important influence on both ideals of family size and knowledge of reproduction and birth control.

**Table 22** *Average age at marriage and family size of respondents according to occupation prior to marriage*

| Occupation | Age at marriage | Family size | Number |
| --- | --- | --- | --- |
| domestic servants | 20.5 | 4.0 | (7) |
| shop assistants | 22.0 | 2.7 | (4) |
| clerks | 23.2 | 1.0 | (4) |
| factory workers | 24.6 | 1.8 | (10) |

*Source*: Interviews[10]

There is, however, one other factor where there was a marked differential between women who worked as clerks and women in other occupations prior to marriage, and that is the family size of their parents, as Table 23 shows. The family size of clerks' parents was noticeably less than that of all the others. Now, while only two of all the respondents received any explicit information on sex from their parents, and a taboo on discussion of it seemed to prevail between parents and children in *all* social sectors, there can be little doubt that the beliefs and norms of an individual's parental home are of great importance, even if specific communication of information is lacking. In other words, those women going into the clerical sector would most probably have accepted already a small family as normative, while women in other occupations would not. Women going into other occupations must therefore have *changed* their norms and values from those experienced during childhood quite drastically from, say, a norm of seven or eight children to one of two or three. For clerical workers the change was relatively slight, from a norm of two or three to one or two.

It seems from the evidence here that both the economic constraints on clerical workers during the period and the greater opportunities for female clerks (and the expansion of their numbers) to gain information prior to marriage from work colleagues would have affected the very low level of fertility manifested by clerical workers during the inter-war years. Further, their concentration in certain areas in the South-East, areas with demographic characteristics which would contribute to low fertility rates, is important when considering patterns of differential fertility. The expansion of the clerical sector *outside* the South-East was too slight to have had a marked impact, at an aggregate level, on the fertility rates in such areas.

**Table 23** *Average family size of respondents' parents according to occupations prior to marriage*

| Respondents' occupations | Family size of parents | Number |
| --- | --- | --- |
| clerks | 2.8 | (4) |
| domestic servants | 6.6 | (7) |
| factory workers | 7.0 | (10) |
| shop assistants | 8.3 | (4) |

*Source*: Interviews

## Women in factories

The census data showed an *inverse* correlation between the proportion of women employed in textiles, and a *positive*, although weaker, correlation between the proportion of women employed in manufacturing, and fertility. Both would be classified as 'factory work'. In certain ways, areas with a high proportion of women in textiles and those with a high proportion in manufacturing were similar: they did not manifest any markedly unusual demographic characteristics as many areas did; the sex ratios were relatively balanced, and the proportions of women married in each age group neither particularly high nor low. Why, then, the different correlation with fertility? Could the difference be a result of variations in the relations of men to the economic system in such areas? Did women in textile areas have greater knowledge of, and access to, contraception and abortion? Or is it simply a result of other intervening variables leading to an ecological fallacy?

Taking first those areas with a high proportion of women employed in manufacturing, in both 1911 and 1931 there was a slight positive correlation between fertility and the proportion of women employed in manufacturing ($R^2$ – 6.8 in 1911, 4.3 in 1931), but virtually no correlation with the latter and either the sex ratio or age at marriage. When the sex ratio and proportion of married women of childbearing age were controlled around the mean, however, then there was a very strong positive correlation between fertility and the proportion of women in manufacturing.

The most marked positive correlation between the two in 1911 was when areas with over 33 per cent of the total female population occupied were selected. There were, however, only three areas manifesting a very high proportion of women in manufacturing and a high fertility rate: Shoreditch, Bethnal Green and Finsbury. As all of these are in London, it is possible that a variety of intervening variables were affecting the correlation. On the other hand, the high correlation in these areas could reflect the *nature* of their occupations. For instance, many women in these areas were working in very small factories or at home as outworkers.

In Bethnal Green, for example, a great deal of the women's work was carried out in small companies or in outwork. Therefore, there was often an isolated type of work situation, with less opportunity for interaction and exchange of information between work colleagues. The categories of manufacturing and dressmaking

– where the majority of women were employed – encompassed a wide variety of occupational subdivisions, probably with little contact between them. This, of course, is in marked contrast with the work situation of textile workers. Table 24 shows the results of looking at the numbers of women employed in different sectors of manufacturing in 1911.

On the other hand, Bethnal Green was a fairly close-knit community and had been for some time. It is highly likely that strong social networks existed among married women there – and also among men. It is probable that those living there were relatively unaffected by many of the national trends discussed earlier, and that information between women would be of a fairly traditional nature.

The majority of men in Bethnal Green were employed in manufacturing, transport and communication, or building. Most of these jobs were unskilled or semi-skilled, and insecurity and underemployment were common. Moreover, the majority of these jobs were very much male-dominated (unlike the textile industry) and, while wages were poor relative to other areas, they were a good deal higher than those which working women in the area could earn. Marriages were therefore likely to be characterized by segregated and unequal role-relationships, and the traditional values among local social groups were apt to deem large families and female responsibility for birth control normative. Relative

**Table 24**　　*Women employed in different sectors of manufacturing, Bethnal Green, 1911*

| Sectors of manufacturing | Number of women employed |
| --- | --- |
| tailors | 2533 |
| paper box, bag, stationery | 2056 |
| cardboard box makers | 1574 |
| boots, shoes | 1129 |
| shirt makers | 1089 |
| hair and feathers | 815 |
| skins and leather | 487 |
| French polishers | 450 |
| upholsterers | 169 |
| cabinet makers | 39 |

*Source*: Census (1911)

lack of exposure to information and new values meant that such control was likely to be irregular and unreliable.

In Stoke-on-Trent, however, there was a high proportion of women in large-scale manufacturing and a relatively high rate of fertility. Work was concentrated in large-scale pottery factories, although men's work and women's work was generally separate. But Stoke also had a large proportion of men in mining and a large Roman Catholic community. The high fertility rate may well have been a result of other factors.

Turning to those areas characterized by a high proportion of both men and women in textiles, there is then a stronger correlation with fertility, but here it is an *inverse* one. Such areas were beyond any doubt predominantly working-class; in Burnley in 1911 the proportion of men in professional and administrative occupations was 2.8 per cent (the national mean was 5.4 per cent, that of Hampstead, 15.9 per cent), and the proportion of domestic servants was 4.6 per cent (the national mean was 14.0, that of Hampstead, 38.0 per cent). Further, these areas were *not* unusual demographically; the sex ratio was relatively balanced and the proportion of women married in each age group was actually slightly *above* the mean. There was no correlation at all between the proportion of men and women in textiles and either age at marriage or the sex ratio.

In all areas, however, there was an exceptionally strong positive correlation between the proportion of married women working and the proportion of women in textiles ($R^2 - 54$), as well as a strong inverse correlation between married women working and the marital fertility rate. All of this is strong evidence suggesting that when a married woman is directly engaged in economic activity outside the home there are significant effects on fertility.[11] The census data gives no indication as to *why* this might be the case, and this will be considered in greater detail in Chapter 4.

At an individual level, was there anything unique about the work situation of single women in textile mills which could have affected their ideals of family size? The interviews showed that young women in weaving, like young women in other occupations, received little explicit information on sex or reproduction from their parents. The following extract is from a woman in Burnley who worked all her life as a weaver, married a glass blower, and had one child. It is typical of the responses from other women who had worked as weavers:

*Could you talk to your mother about more personal things?*

No, no. no. She never would, she were a real old-fashioned type were me mother, really old-fashioned, no. No she never told us anything .... Y' had to find out things for youself, yeah.

None the less, they certainly did find things out for themselves and, it seems, from a generally earlier age than did women in other occupations.

The interviews did not reveal one common source of information; some claimed to have gleaned a great deal by the time they left school from school friends; one did get some information from her mother; the majority got their information from work colleagues. Where they did differ markedly from other groups, however, is that there would seem to have been a somewhat different relationship between young men and women, involving both sexual 'messing around' and apparently a certain amount of exchanged information. The following extract is from a woman who worked as a weaver both before and after marriage, married a weaver and had one child:

*Did people talk about that sort of thing in the mill?*

Well, I mean they do, among your friends an' that, you know, I mean to say, you get together and when you get older you start courtin' an' y'get to know different things, but − y' get some good friends at mill an' all.... Well, I know our Bessie what's dead, his mother she worked where I did when we were young, and I'd two loom in at door, and Henry's mother − she 'ad 'im before she were married − we worked at door at mill and, of course, we were there, me an' two lads see, and d'you know, she used to come down and put weft, an' she were like *that*! [i.e. very pregnant] An' she used to give us such a mouthful if we looked, you know! Well, I think we knew someat then, someat wrong.. when she 'ad 'im she were only about 16.... Well if y' went out, many lads 'd start messing − well y' sort of found out, you know.... But when I got older if I went wi' any lads, if they started, oh I never went no more − we used to parade up Manchester Road an' on St James Street, y'know, to get off −

*Is that how you met your husband?*

Oh, he used to come to our house you see, 'twere a friend of one of me brothers, you see, an' he used to come an' he never left me alone! Me mother used to − 'course mother had to be married with me − she used to say, eh, put your hand over your mouth you! She did, an' if any of us had had a child, not being married wi' 'em, God help us!

*Did you know people who tried to get rid of pregnancies?*

Oh yes, this here friend o'mine, lived on Stoney Street I think then, an' were passing bottom o' stairs, well they'd a chamber there and 'twere full o' blood, an' Alice says to her, 'What's this? Who's been hurting theirself?' An' she'd had three an' she'd been pushing a knitting needle or something up her to try and get rid –

Her remarks about when she was working with the two lads would suggest that the three of them shared an understanding, if not a joke, about the girl who was pregnant; there is no mention of embarrassment with the lads there. Similarly, the next extract from the woman quoted earlier whose father ran a herbalist shop shows how, although little was apparently *said* between parents and children, there was none the less an implicit understanding after a certain age that the children knew all about it:

I know me youngest sister – I were 19 when she were born, and I'd been working in the mill all day and we never – me mother never had bed downstairs, but bein' a big house she had bed put down front room – lovely room we had then in that new house . . . an' she were only one that she had to have it brought by instrument, 'twas only one, and I were up all night, and doctor come and he were boiling water for t'instruments and there were I – I weren't at room – me dad were up, 'twere only men, I'd been working all day at that, an' I were off me work an' I had all that family [seven brothers and sisters] to look after, an' me father had to go back an' I'd all that gang to look after . . . I mean I haven't had a big family of me own, I know, but I knew about it at home . . . me mother used to say, 'Don't be as daft as me, don't be as daft as me, true.'

First of all, it is interesting that *both* the unmarried daughter and the father were present when the mother was in labour. In other interviews, it was either the father who was present, with the children (even older ones) well out of the way, *or* occasionally the elder daughter would help while the husband was out of the way. There seem to have been far less rigid divisions according to marital status, age group and sex among these families. While matters were seldom discussed openly, there was a tacit under-standing and what would appear to be a shared belief-system between parents and children, men and women, which was definitely lacking among other respondents with different patterns of work experience.

Further, the fact that the mother told her daughter not to be 'as daft as me' with regard to family size seems to reinforce this argument. While there were obviously certain taboos on discussion of topics relating directly to sex, there was none the less evidence of certain shared assumptions and beliefs between parents and children and boys and girls which were definitely *not* present among respondents from other occupational groups. After a certain age, when children had acquired information from various sources outside the home, there was an attitude of suppressed defiance, almost ridicule, of parents' unwillingness to discuss such matters openly, witness the following account from a woman who worked as a weaver; her mother worked as a charwoman and married a hauler in the textile mill:

Do y'know, if anyone used to come in our house an' say, 'Oh so-and-so's got a baby', I've seen her [mother] go [furious expression] because I've been in there, yes ... I were once washing up an' this woman came in to tell us about this girl that had had this baby, an' she weren't married, y'see, oh an' she came in an' she just said, 'oh Lucy's got her baby like', an' I looked up an' saw me mother!!! No, me mother never told me a thing – we'd to find out at school. We used to go out an' y'know when we used to play out – so-and-so'd had a baby like, an' they started. When I see me mother get that big, I thought, *well*, you've no need to be like *that*!

There was no evidence among these women of beliefs that babies were born from your navel or that they chopped your stomach open to get the baby out, as were common among women who had worked as domestic servants or stayed at home. Nor was there evidence of the acute embarrassment felt between men and women if matters relating to birth or sex arose that was evident among other occupational groups. Sexual divisions there were, age divisions there were, divisions between parents and children there were; divisions, however, were noticeably less rigid and less marked than among other occupational groups. To a great extent, this must have been a result of the occupational structure of textile towns like Burnley, where it was common for all ages, marital statuses and both sexes to be engaged in the same, or similar, work situations. Frequently the whole family or most of the family, would be employed in the same mill, much as had been the case in Lancashire in the nineteenth century. This situation, it is argued, resulted in a more generally shared belief-system and information networks between age groups and sexes. It is therefore not surprising that all of the women interviewed in Burnley had gone into marriage with a very clear idea of what it actually involved, that more of these women discussed ideals of family size with their husbands than among the other occupational groups, that nearly two-thirds of them had extremely joint marital role-relationships once married, and that their average family size was very small. It is quite possible, however, that these distinctive features were not so much a result of women's work experience prior to marriage *per se*, but were more a result of the unusually high proportion of married women working there and the consequence thereof. This will be discussed in greater detail in Chapter 4.

To conclude, the participation of single women in the labour market had two principal effects: first of all, availability or non-availability of employment in a geographical area affected the demographic structure there, which in turn affected patterns of, and attitudes to, age at marriage and in turn fertility. Second, at an individual level, the type of occupation in which a single woman was employed had important effects on the formation of her ideals, attitudes to and information about, marriage, sex and birth control. These in turn affected her behaviour pattern within marriage. The more isolated the work situation, the less information and exposure to new ideals and values there was, and, once married, the more segregated such women's marital role-relationships tended to be. Conversely, the larger the work situation and the greater the chances of interaction with other individuals of different marital status, age and sex, the greater were the chances of exchange of information and exposure to new beliefs and attitudes and the greater the likelihood of a joint marital role-relationship once married.

Of course the situation was more complex in reality. Women working in predominantly single-sex occupations (domestic service, dressmaking, decorators in the pottery industry) would undoubtedly have experienced different patterns of social group formation and participation and exposure to different types of social networks than women working in occupations where there was a relatively balanced proportion of men and women doing the same jobs (for example, textiles). The work experience, family organization and family size of girls' parents certainly had important effects on the formation of their values, norms and ideals relating both to work and to marriage and the family. Further, the actual *nature* of their work affected their beliefs and values, their perceptions of themselves and of their roles as women in society; girls staying at home or working as servants must have had very different views of work, domesticity and so on than girls who had for several years performed the same, or similar tasks as men in a workplace completely divorced from the home, where the work itself bore no relation to domestic chores.

Unfortunately it has not been possible to explore all of these dimensions to the problem, nor to look at more than a minimum of occupational types. It is hoped, however, that it is now evident that employment opportunities for women before marriage were not simply affecting demographic variables in a given geographical area, but that the structure and nature of the occupations into which girls entered and their work experience therein were of importance in affecting attitudes to marriage and ideals of work, children, family organization and family size.

It now remains to examine patterns of work after marriage, and then to try and assess the extent to which women's attitudes may, or may not, have changed after marriage.

# 4 Work after marriage

The full scale and nature of married women's work is not wholly clear from the census data; seasonal work is totally absent, as is most part-time work. The fault does not, however, lie entirely with the census enumerators. Many married women apparently did not consider seasonal or part-time work as 'real' work. This was evident in the interviews, where many women stated quite clearly that they never worked after marriage, yet later in the interview it emerged that some had kept lodgers, some had done seasonal farm work, and others had done part-time charring and/or washing. Their interpretation of 'work' tended to be of paid work on a full-time basis which took place outside the home. All census data on married women's work will tend, therefore, to under-represent the true scale and rate of participation of married women in the labour market.

## Married women in the labour market

The census data for 1911 revealed a very strong inverse correlation between the proportion of married women working and the marital fertility rate ($R^2 - 47.0$). This is in line with the findings of other research.[1] The minimum percentage of married women working in any area was 2.0 per cent, the maximum was 23.2 per cent. The important question is whether the employment of married women in such areas only affected the fertility *rates* by distorting the demographic variables in some way, or whether employment affected the fertility of the women themselves at an individual level.

The employment of married women on a large scale was a highly localized, and completely urban, phenomenon. Geographically, married women's employment was concentrated mainly in three areas: in and around Lancashire (including Stockport in Cheshire and Bradford in Yorkshire); in the Midlands; and in

*Work after marriage*

certain districts of London, two in the West End and three in the East End. It was shown earlier how the sex ratio, the proportion of women married (particularly those aged 20–24), the proportion of women occupied and the marital fertility rate for the different areas all correlated very closely. The data suggested that employment opportunities for women had a strong influence on the sex ratio of an area, and in turn on trends in age at marriage and also fertility. The fewer women there were occupied, the lower the age at marriage and the higher the marital fertility rate tended to be. But our concern here is with the effects of women working, when they were married, on these variables. Let us look at the eighteen areas with a high proportion of married women working in greater detail. Table 25 shows the demographic characteristics of these

**Table 25** *Percentage of married women working (as a percentage of all women aged 14–64) in areas where over 10 per cent worked, and principal demographic characteristics, 1911*

| Area | Married women occupied (%) | Sex ratio (females to males) | Marital fertility rate | Married women aged 20–4 (%) |
|---|---|---|---|---|
| (mean) | (5.3) | (107.6) | (167.0) | (23.7) |
| Blackburn | 23.2 | 115.3 | 136.1 | 21.7 |
| Burnley | 22.9 | 111.6 | 138.7 | 26.6 |
| Preston | 17.9 | 117.2 | 155.9 | 22.4 |
| Bury | 16.3 | 111.6 | 128.7 | 20.8 |
| Rochdale | 14.7 | 114.4 | 126.7 | 23.5 |
| Leicester | 14.5 | 114.5 | 147.8 | 22.3 |
| Shoreditch | 14.4 | 103.1 | 222.7 | 29.0 |
| Oldham | 12.9 | 108.7 | 145.8 | 25.6 |
| City of London | 12.7 | 95.0 | 98.9 | 6.9 |
| Stoke-on-Trent | 12.5 | 104.4 | 203.2 | 31.8 |
| Stockport | 12.3 | 113.5 | 147.2 | 26.1 |
| Bethnal Green | 12.2 | 104.6 | 221.3 | 28.8 |
| Nottingham | 12.0 | 115.9 | 115.3 | 25.1 |
| Finsbury | 11.8 | 106.1 | 209.6 | 28.0 |
| Blackpool | 10.2 | 129.6 | 105.3 | 16.2 |
| Birmingham | 10.2 | 107.3 | 186.5 | 27.1 |
| Bradford | 10.2 | 116.1 | 193.2 | 20.8 |
| Holborn | 10.1 | 104.9 | 136.3 | 18.6 |

*Source*: Census (1911)

**Table 26**   *Different areas by type*

| Area type 1 | Area type 2 | Area type 3 |
|---|---|---|
| Blackburn | Shoreditch | City of London |
| Burnley | Stoke-on-Trent | Blackpool |
| Preston | Finsbury | Holborn |
| Bury | Birmingham | |
| Rochdale | Bethnal Green | |
| Leicester | | |
| Oldham* | | |
| Stockport | | |
| Nottingham | | |
| Bradford† | | |

\* sex ratio below the mean
† not exact 'fit', but closest to this type

areas in 1911[2] and the proportion of married women occupied.

It is clear from the data contained in Table 25 that, among the areas with a high proportion of married women working, there is a considerable variation in the level of fertility and in other demographic characteristics. Moreover, it is evident that a high proportion of married women in employment is *not* always associated with low fertility. We can identify three quite distinct 'types' which correspond only to some extent with the geographical divisions mentioned earlier. First of all, there are those areas with a sex ratio somewhat above the mean, the percentage of married women aged 20–24 clustered fairly close to the mean, and a marital fertility rate in the range 126–56 (i.e., below the mean). Second, there are those areas with a sex ratio slightly below the mean, a relatively high proportion of women married aged 20–24, and a high marital fertility rate. Third, there are those areas with a low proportion of women married aged 20–24, a low marital fertility rate, but without a common sex ratio characteristic. Table 26 shows the different areas by type. Although the areas have been grouped according to their demographic characteristics, it is apparent that they also tend to fall into three distinct occupational types, which may provide some clue as to their different patterns of fertility.

The principal occupation of women in area type 1 was work in the textile industry, although Leicester also had a high proportion of women employed in dressmaking (17 per cent in dressmaking,

19 per cent in textile manufacture). The principal occupations for women in type 2 were manufacturing and dressmaking. Among the three areas in type 3 the main occupation was domestic service. Let us consider each type in more detail.

First, in area type 3 with low fertility, the areas were all distinctive because they had a *low* proportion of domestic servants who were residential, in relation to other types of service, while they were all characterized by a high proportion of domestic servants. The mean percentage of residential servants for all areas was 73 per cent; the figure for Blackpool was 59 per cent; Holborn, 42 per cent; City of London, 41 per cent. The rest of the women employed as domestic servants in these areas worked on a daily basis in institutions. This would explain why a high proportion of married women were able to work; married women could work as servants in institutions, but not as residential servants in private households. Hence in these areas marriage and work were not necessarily *alternatives*;[3] the step of marriage did not commit a woman to a domestic/childbearing role to the same extent as it did in other areas and/or occupations. Other factors, however, probably contributed to the low fertility of these areas.

They were all very much middle-class areas. Blackpool, too, had a highly unbalanced sex ratio as well as a high proportion of older people, and presumably a large number of lodging houses and hotels. The City of London, on the other hand, was demographically and occupationally 'peculiar' for different reasons, which also resulted in a low level of fertility. The low proportion of women to men here did *not* result in a high rate of, or low age at, marriage; quite the contrary. This must have been mostly a result of the high proportion of women in domestic service (37 per cent of all women aged 14–64 were domestic servants; although the proportion who were residential was relatively low, it still represented a substantial proportion of the female population of childbearing age who were single), and also partly a result of the main male occupations in the area. 18 per cent of all males were employed in the professions, government or as clerks – the national mean was 8 per cent. Further, of course, the City was not primarily a residential area for married couples; it was first and foremost a work area with large numbers of people commuting into it during the working week and living elsewhere. It would seem reasonable to conclude, therefore, that the low level of fertility of this area type was primarily a result of its unusual demographic and class structures. The presence of a large number of married women working would not seem to be directly linked to the fertility pattern at an individual level.

Second are the areas in type 2, where some of the high fertility rate may be explained by the somewhat unbalanced sex ratio and the relatively high proportion of women married in the age group 20–24. These variables alone, however, cannot offer a complete explanation, as in other areas with similar characteristics the level of fertility was much lower. Nor is there any immediately obvious relationship between fertility and the class structure of these areas as measured by the male's relation to the economic system: Shoreditch, Finsbury and Bethnal Green were predominantly unskilled areas, while Birmingham and Stoke-on-Trent were mainly skilled. Did the fact that a large proportion of married women were working here and/or the type of occupation they were in have a direct effect on fertility, or was it simply that there were a number of intervening variables – not obvious here – that affected the fertility rate? Certainly this type is the most puzzling and atypical, as we find a high proportion of married women working associated with above average fertility.

The main occupation of women in these areas was manufacturing and dressmaking. I suggested in Chapter 3, with reference to Bethnal Green, that the often isolated nature of employment in manufacturing for women in the London areas, the existence of 'traditional' social groups, the prevalence of outwork,[4] in conjunction with the predominance of unskilled labour among the men,[5] could have led to highly segregated marital role-relationships. All of these factors may have resulted in less knowledge of efficient means of birth control, less sharing of decision-making on both family size and use of birth control, and hence higher fertility. While there is little data available on outwork, what there is suggests that many children worked with and helped their parents before leaving school, and that truancy was still common. B. Westover, for example, noted that 'often children were expected to help with the work [outwork tailoring] particularly the fetching and carrying of articles, which meant that they were frequently absent from school',[6] and also that young girls were expected to perform tasks for their mothers such as sewing on buttons after they returned from school. Thus in areas characterized by unemployment and underemployment for men and outwork for women, it is probable that children were not regarded as an economic liability to the extent they were among other groups. Further, where outwork was common among married women, it is likely that employment after marriage and childbearing were less incompatible than in areas where home and work were distinctly separate. This would fit in with other studies[7] which show that where women work at home employment and fertility are not negatively correlated in the manner typical of advanced industrial societies.

In Stoke-on-Trent and Birmingham, however, these factors would not have been relevant, for most work, it seems, was carried out in workshops or factories. It is possible that the high level of fertility in these areas was more a result of other intervening variables, such as a large proportion of Roman Catholics,[8] than a result of high fertility among married women who worked in manufacturing there.

In areas of type 1 the association between fertility and employment is in the predicted direction, and analysis of these areas is therefore more straightforward. We need, however, to consider the possibility that the low fertility is a function of demographic variables. Taking Burnley as an example, in 1911 the overall sex ratio of the population was 111.5 females to males, and the surplus of females was most marked in the age groups 15–19 and 25–34. In 1931, the overall sex ratio was 113.7, and the surplus was concentrated in the age groups 20–49, but especially 30–49. One would expect such an imbalance (although, of course, by no means equivalent to the dimensions of areas like Hampstead) to have some noticeable effect on both marriage patterns and fertility.

The marriage pattern and age at marriage in Burnley, however, were not in any way unusual. Given the unbalanced sex ratio, one would expect a relatively low proportion of women married, but this was not the case. In 1911 the proportion married aged 15–19 was above the mean and so was the proportion married aged 20–24. The same pattern applied for the older age groups. Given that in 1911 the marital fertility rate was below the national mean (although not as low as some of the areas in this group), the sex ratio and the proportions married do not seem to have had any direct effect on fertility; indeed, when all textile towns were analysed, there was then no correlation at all between the three variables. In other words, although the demographic variables must have had *some* effect on fertility in these areas, it is apparent that there must have been other factors generating the unusually low level of fertility.

In 1931 the proportions married in Burnley *decreased* slightly for all age groups except the 15–19 year-olds. For virtually all the age groups the proportion married was equivalent to the mean for England and Wales, and was actually higher than Bethnal Green and Stoke-on-Trent. The marital fertility rate, however, was well below the national mean. Again, the demographic variables would seem to have had only a marginal effect on fertility here. The decline in the proportion of women married aged 20–34 must have contributed to the decline in fertility, but by itself can neither explain the phenomenon of low fertility at both periods of time, nor the decline between 1911 and 1931.

Let us consider the employment pattern of the area in more detail. The occupational structure of Burnley was quite distinctive. First of all, in both 1911 and 1931 over two-thirds of all women aged 15–64 were employed, more even than in Hampstead. Second, in 1911 23 per cent of all women aged 15–64 were *both* employed *and* married (there are no figures on marital status for 1931), which was considerably greater than in any other area mentioned with a high proportion of married women working (for example, Stoke, 13 per cent, Bethnal Green, 12 per cent). Third, all but 15 per cent of these women were employed in *one* industry – textiles – while there was also a very high proportion of men employed in the same industry (40.4 per cent in 1911, 28.2 per cent in 1931). The proportions employed in other occupations were small enough so as not to have distorted the pattern to any great extent. Do these three distinctive occupational features of Burnley (which are virtually identical to those of other textile towns in Lancashire) throw any light on the unusually low fertility of the area, and on the way in which employment may affect fertility?

The exceptionally high proportion of women working in Burnley would mean that the majority of women there would have had work experience involving exposure to a cohesive social group and social networks prior to marriage, while many would have continued to be part of these after marriage as well. The fact that nearly all of them worked in the textile industry, which was organized on a large-scale basis, employing a large number of people of both sexes, all ages and all marital statuses in the same premises, would mean that social groups and networks were probably common to men and women of all ages and marital statuses. Weaving, which was the principal occupation in textiles here, was by no means an exclusively female occupation (although male weavers were usually in charge of a greater number of looms and were assigned a young female assistant – a 'tenter' – which meant that they usually had a greater income, as wages were based on piece-work).

During this period wages were relatively low for both male and female weavers,[9] and although in other areas men would be the sole breadwinners on a similar wage, it was apparently normative here for married women to work, and their income was regarded as essential. Excessive childbearing would, of course, put a considerable strain on the family income; at least several weeks' wages would be lost during childbirth, and another child meant more money to be spent on a childminder if the wife chose to return to work – which was often the case. Children would therefore conflict with the wife's role as breadwinner, and a small family would usually be regarded as desirable by both husband and wife. But why should this be peculiar to textile towns, and not apply to other areas where women worked after marriage and where male wages tended to be low?

One answer may lie in the fact that towns like Burnley had a long and distinctive tradition behind them; they had not, for instance, been greatly affected by in-migration since the early nineteenth century. During the early course of their development in the late eighteenth and early nineteenth centuries both married women's and children's work were regarded as normative and essential, particulary as spinning had been women's work in the first place, long before the industrial revolution.

The exclusion of young children from the production process during the course of the nineteenth century must have had a dual effect on textile families: first, it would have acted as a deterrent to large families by making children more of a liability economically and by reducing their 'value' as contributors to the family income. Second, it must have put an added premium on the wife's role as wage earner. Previously perhaps three or four children working might have been equivalent in wage terms to the wife working; now three or four children meant both greater financial strain and a hindrance to the wife's wage-earning capacity. If, of course, there had been a substantial rise in the *male's* earning potential, women might have gradually withdrawn from the labour market, stayed at home, and not had to face conflict between childbearing and rearing and wage labour.

But this was not the case. Although during the nineteenth century, wages in textiles were relatively high (declining rapidly during the twentieth century), both men and women in textiles tended to regard women's work after both marriage and childbirth as normative and necessary. In other words, unlike many other areas and occupational groups, marriage and work for women were not regarded as mutually exclusive. It would be interesting to see to what extent a decline in family size among textile workers in the nineteenth century coincided with the exclusion of children from the labour market, but this is a problem outside our time period.

Why did such a pattern not apply in areas such as Bethnal Green, where men's wages were low, employment available for married women, and yet where there was a high level of fertility? One important difference was that, whereas in Burnley men and women tended to be employed in the same occupation often doing identical work, this was *not* the case in Bethnal Green. Here couples would almost inevitably be employed in different occupations, where there were quite definitely 'men's jobs' and 'women's jobs'. Further, while textile workers would be earning similar wages (although the male's would be slightly higher), in Bethnal Green the men's work, even if low-paid relative to other jobs for men, was usually considerably higher than the women's work in that area. This would tend to result in a more unequal and segregated type of marital role-relationship, with couples belonging to distinctly separate social groups and social networks. Decision-making and communication among such couples was probably far less of a joint process – and thus usually less efficient – than among couples in textiles. Textile towns like Burnley also had a strong political tradition of both socialism and feminism, and this was not the case in Bethnal Green.

The comparison of the three different area types, with their varied fertility and demographic structures suggests, therefore, that it is not simply a question of *whether* women work after marriage, but the *type* of occupation and occupational community in which they live that is the crucial factor affecting ideals of, and patterns of, family size and the ability to achieve these ideals. Nevertheless, the question remains as to why some women work after marriage and others do not.

Why did so many women in textile towns continue work both after marriage and after childbirth, in marked contrast to the rest of England and Wales at the time? Obviously job opportunities existed in greater quantity than in many other areas, but this is not a wholly satisfactory answer. It is often assumed that women are 'better' at intricate manual work like weaving – yet many men were also weavers and apparently equally competent. The responses of the women interviewed revealed three essentially interrelated answers as to why they worked after marriage: first of all, it would seem that they all *enjoyed* working; second, it was generally considered normative to work after marriage; and third, there were economic reasons for doing so. The following extracts illustrate these points; they are all from women who worked as weavers after both marriage and childbirth. A woman with two children had this to say:

Oh I started work when I went half-time for school for 12, you see ... one week I went for morning and t'other week I went for afternoon, see, that was when I was leaving, you see. I always wanted to be a weaver, that was my one aim – to be a weaver, an' I had a auntie, she'd a' liked me to be in teaching, something like that, but I says no, no, I says, I want to go to make cotton, I want to be a weaver, because I thought it was – well, I thought it was fascinating making cotton ... oh yes, I did *enjoy* weaving, so of course if you do enjoy a job you do it well.

Another, who had had one child, said:

I worked till I were 59, I think it were, 58 or 59, then I had to give over with legs ... it were standard thing going out to work ... I mean, I don't know as I ever wanted to stop home – but when I could work I did so.

This enthusiasm about work was *never* present among women who had worked as domestic servants or shop assistants, although it was evident to a somewhat lesser extent among those who had worked as clerks. All of the women seemed to accept working after marriage as normative, and so did their husbands, except for one woman's husband who worked as a bus driver. When asked how her husband felt about her working after she married, she replied:

Well – I worked seven month before our Edith were born, I were – well, an' he used to stand at bus office, an' he used to have park at other side when I were going home at tea time, an' he used to say, don't speak to me!

The embarrassment (or perhaps shame) felt by her husband would seem to indicate that married women working was only normative among certain occupational groups in the area. His attitude was much like that of those from the south-east of England, where working after marriage was considered a shame, an admission of failure on the husband's part, and where it was certainly not normative among the majority of the population.

The following extract from an interview with a woman who was married to a weaver and who had one child shows a similar acceptance of work:

I couldn't afford to stop at home really, you had to go to work you know, because I'd a extra mouth to feed, really, and he wanted – being a bab – he wanted all sorts o' stuff, you know.

*Is that what most women did?*

Oh yes, yes. Their mothers looked after their babies .... And then at weekend you'd be doing all your catching up on what you couldn't do during the week, you know, ironing and washing and baking – as a matter of fact I think I've worked harder at weekend than I did when I went out to work! .... Oh it were hard life, but I think I'd rather – I liked weaving, I used to like weaving, I wouldn't let loom stop like – mind you, before I were married I never used to bother much, but when I got married I thought, well, more money, you know.

One or two of the women were virtually forced to work for financial reasons alone, as a result of their husband's inability to work. The majority, however, worked because they felt *both* wages to be essential. Nevertheless, although the textile industry certainly was in a depressed state during the inter-war period, unemployment was not as high as in some other areas (such as the mining districts),[10] nor were wages as low as in many other industries where, however, it was not normative for the wife to work. Why, then, was it acceptable for married women to work here and not in other areas or occupations?

The employment structure was, and had been, one with an unusually large number of jobs available for women; this had essentially changed very little since the nineteenth century. Up until the First World War, too, textile workers were among the better paid of the working class. After the war, however, their wage rates relative to other occupations declined, and this must have reinforced, to some extent, their perceived need for married women to work. Married women were, of course, an essential part of the local labour force, and one of the key factors to their continued participation in it may have been that the textile industry was still by and large labour-intensive, compared with other sectors which had become more capital-intensive and where there was less need for a large labour force. Moreover, no measures had been enforced restricting jobs to unmarried women. Undoubtedly one of the most important reasons for married women working must simply have been that the job opportunities were available.

None the less, it was by no means impossible for married women in other areas to find employment, although it would not have been on the same *scale* as in Lancashire, and yet in such areas there was strong evidence of a prevalent norm *against* married women working among many sectors of the working class. The extract which follows is from a woman who worked as a tailoress in a factory in Essex before marrying; her husband was at the time an unskilled labourer earning very low wages; she married when she was 26 and they had one child. When asked for how long she had worked as a tailoress, she replied:

Right up till I married, and I *wanted* to go out to work, 'cause me home was new and everything – I didn't have much to do. But my husband said, 'No', he said, 'I married you to keep you and you're not going out to work', so I didn't go no more – 'till my husband was out o' work.

Note how it was the *husband* who forbade her going out to work, while she herself would have preferred otherwise; this was very common, particularly among couples from the South-East. The next extract is from the woman quoted earlier who had worked as a book-keeper, married a bus conductor at the age of 25 and had two children:

'Course when I – they wanted me to keep on at work, and I told them I was going to leave. The manager said, 'Why must you leave? Can't you stay on?' I said, 'No', I said, 'My husband said I either get married and stop at home or don't get married at all.' I said, 'Another thing, if I'm living in London,' I said, 'what's it going to be?' I said, 'We got to be out here at half-past seven in the morning and my husband's shift work,' I said, 'I shall never see anything of him! We shall have no married life or anything else.' 'Oh, but', he said, 'look what you can do for the children later on if you save that money.' I said, 'Yes, I can start them at the top,' I said, 'what about if I go down to the bottom and can't keep it up?' I said, 'I'd rather start them at the bottom and take them to the top' – which luckily we did.

For these two women and their husbands, marriage and work were seen as most definitely mutually exclusive roles for women, regardless of employment opportunities or pay. In the textile areas, on the other hand, they were not regarded that way. It must be remembered that most textile workers' parents had also been in textiles, and that often both their father and mother had worked full-time after marriage and childbirth; there was a strong tradition of married women working which did not exist to the same extent in other areas and occupations. Thus both geographical and social mobility may have been important factors affecting attitudes to, and norms of, married women working.

The sharing in textile towns like Burnley of work experience and workplace between men and women, husbands and wives, parents and children led to a generally shared set of norms and values among textile workers. This in turn had important effects on their patterns of family organization and decision-making concerning family size, which will be discussed at greater length in Chapter 5. In areas with a high proportion of married women working, but where a sharing of occupational experience and workplace was *not* the case between men and women (such as those in area type 2), then different patterns of social group formation, social networks, family organization and decision-making processes resulted. Even in Stoke-on-Trent, for example, while there was a high proportion of both men and women, married and single, employed in the pottery industry, individual jobs within that industry *were* differentiated according to sex; almost all of the women worked as decorators, while none of the men did.

## Men in the labour market and married women at home

As discussed earlier, the majority of married women at this time did stay at home and did not participate on a full-time basis in the labour market. Not being economically active meant, of course, that these women were 'invisible' in the census data dealing with employment. It is therefore necessary to examine the relationships of *men* to the economic system and to deduce, if possible, any common characteristics or variations in women's role of non-participation from these data.

Areas characterized by a low percentage of married women working were mainly of three occupational types: those with a high proportion of men in agriculture; those with a high proportion of men in mining; and those with a high proportion of men in manufacturing. As we would expect, most of these areas in 1911 also manifested moderate to high fertility. There were, however, several areas which were atypical, characterized by a low proportion of married women working and low fertility. These areas also manifested an unbalanced sex ratio (a high ratio of women to men) and a low proportion of women married aged 20–24, which would both contribute to a low fertility rate. They were also, however, predominantly middle-class areas, and we can assume that the middle-class pattern of small family size also affected the low fertility there. Let us examine the three types of area mentioned above in greater detail to see if any conclusions can be drawn as to why married women in these areas tended not to work, and if this directly affected fertility in any way.

First, the areas with a high proportion of men in mining. In 1911 there was an inverse correlation between the sex ratio and the proportion of men in mining ($R^2$ – 11.0); mining areas were typified by an unbalanced sex ratio (a high ratio of men to women). Further, there were strong correlations with age at marriage, in particular with the quinquennial age group 20–24 ($R^2$ – 21.0) and with the proportion of women occupied (inverse, $R^2$ – 39.0). Mining areas were thus also characterized by a very low age at marriage and a very low proportion of women working.

These factors suggest that the pattern governing the fertility of mining areas at this time may have been something like this: with few job opportunities for women, many (particularly young women) left the area and found work elsewhere, primarily as domestic servants in urban areas. This created an unbalanced sex ratio in the mining areas which was further exacerbated by the in-migration of young men from rural areas seeking employment in the mines. A high ratio of young men to women, and lack of employment opportunities for women, meant that an exceedingly high proportion of women married, and married early. This in turn meant greater exposure to risk of pregnancy which would tend to result in both a relatively large family size and a high rate of fertility in mining areas. This was the converse of the pattern in textile areas.

There is certainly evidence that miners had a high level of fertility during this period. The average number of live births for women born 1861–5 was 4.66;[11] the average family size of the parents of the women interviewed who were married to miners (corresponding roughly to the cohort above) was 7.1.

What is interesting, however, is the very rapid decline in fertility and family size which occurred in mining areas and among miners' families between 1911 and 1931. Taking areas which in 1911 had over 30 per cent of males employed in mining, Table 27 shows the decline in fertility there. The average family size of the eleven women interviewed who were married to miners was only 2.5. The national equivalent, that is, for women married between 1914 and 1929, was 2.4.[12] The census data for 1931 shows little change in the demographic structure of mining areas; there is still an unbalanced sex ratio, a high proportion of women married in the 20–24 age group, and an even lower proportion of women occupied. The big change is in the marital fertility rate; there is now a strong *inverse* correlation between the proportion of men in mining and the marital fertility rate ($R^2 - 19.0$). The difference between the fertility of mining areas in 1931 and England and Wales as a whole was very slight, why? Let us look at one area in greater detail, the Rhondda UD, chosen because it had the highest proportion of men in mining of all the mining areas.

The decline in fertility which occurred in the Rhondda between 1911 and 1931 was over 50 per cent. Some of this can be explained in terms of a less marked imbalance in the sex ratio between the ages of 20 and 40; nevertheless, there was still a marked surplus of males in these groups in 1931. Despite a decline in the proportion of women married in all age groups up to 34, the proportions were

**Table 27**  *Marital fertility rates and percentage decrease in mining areas, 1911 and 1931*

|  | Males in mining, 1911 (%) | Marital fertility rate, 1911 | Marital fertility rate, 1931 | Decrease (%) |
|---|---|---|---|---|
| Rhondda UD | 74.2 | 234.6 | 108.6 | 53.7 |
| Aberdare UD | 64.1 | 215.1 | 89.5 | 58.4 |
| Durham RDs | 60.7 | 218.1 | 122.4 | 43.9 |
| Merthyr Tydfil UD | 55.0 | 207.1 | 99.9 | 51.8 |
| Wigan | 41.9 | 190.0 | 121.4 | 36.1 |
| Derby RDs | 37.7 | 195.1 | 108.4 | 44.4 |
| Glamorgan RDs | 36.7 | 205.3 | 103.9 | 49.4 |
| Carnarvon RDs | 36.1 | 148.1 | 105.8 | 28.6 |
| Barnsley | 36.1 | 193.2 | 115.6 | 40.2 |
| Denbigh RDs | 34.2 | 197.3 | 112.0 | 43.2 |
| Northumberland RDs | 34.1 | 176.5 | 101.7 | 42.4 |
| Yorks., West Riding RDs | 31.6 | 194.7 | 117.9 | 39.4 |
| Brecknockshire RDs | 30.3 | 198.3 | 116.6 | 41.2 |
| mean (mining areas) |  | 198.0 | 109.5 | 44.7 |
| mean (England and Wales) |  | 167.1 | 102.7 | 38.5 |

*Source*: Census (1911 and 1931)

still well above the mean. It is interesting to note, however, that while the *national* trend during this time was for a decline in age at marriage, just the reverse was the case in the Rhondda.

This decline in the proportions marrying in the younger age groups was probably one of the main factors affecting the rapid decline in fertility; the decline was not necessarily only a result of increasing use of birth control within marriage. It seems likely that both delayed age at marriage *and* an increasing use of birth control and also resort to abortion were important factors affecting the decline of family size and of fertility in these areas.[13]

It is possible that the Rhondda may be a good example of differential fertility between age groups. While the proportion of women aged 20–29 remained fairly stable (7.8 per cent in 1911, 7.3 per cent in 1931), the proportion of women in the older childbearing age groups of 30–49 increased from 10.8 per cent in 1911 to 13.3 per cent in 1931. The evidence is by no means conclusive, but it does seem possible that the rapid decline may have been more a result of changes in fertility occurring among the younger cohorts, and the fact that family size among miners was still large, relative to other occupational groups in 1931, might be a result of the older cohorts continuing to reproduce at a high level, while the younger cohorts were not.

There was a great reduction in the proportion of young dependants and an ageing of the population generally, which was also, of course, a national trend. In 1911 nearly 40 per cent of the population of the Rhondda was comprised of dependants, 37 per cent of whom were 14 or less, and 3 per cent of whom were 65 or over. By 1931 only 34.5 per cent of the population was made up of dependants, while only 29.5 per cent were 14 or under and 5 per cent were 65 or over. This was a result both of greater longevity *and* the decline in fertility.

The occupational structure of the Rhondda is striking; the proportion of women occupied at both dates was minuscule compared with England and Wales as a whole, while the over-whelming majority of the men was employed as miners. What is particularly interesting about this area, and others in South Wales, is that it was very much a 'boom' town, with young male migrants pouring in from rural Wales, Somerset, Devon and Cornwall from about 1851 to 1901. From 1901 the influx decreased, and from 1911 to 1931 there was a fairly heavy flow of out-migration (the population decreased by 14 per cent between 1911 and 1931).

Parallel to this was a steady trickling of young women leaving the area to work primarily as domestic servants in the south-east of England until the early twentieth century. In other words, the Rhondda was by no means a stable and homogeneous community with a long tradition behind it, but was more a *mélange* of people, mostly first or second generation migrants, from a number of different areas. How were these characteristics associated with fertility?

First of all, most of the migrants into the area were young men from rural areas. Of those who came from rural Wales, many would have come from a socio-economic system where smallholding still prevailed, where the relations of all family members to the economic system were often similar, and were thus likely to share a set of common values and norms. Further, the economic situation in these areas was likely to have been one deterring early marriage because of land scarcity, but where, it would seem, once married, marital fertility tended to be relatively uncontrolled. Children in such areas could still be a valuable asset in the production process, even if less so than they had been a few decades earlier. Abortion was apparently quite common in rural areas of Wales,[14] which would suggest that control of fertility, when it was exercised, would tend to be primarily the woman's responsibility. If this was the case, then the fact that it was young unmarried men who were leaving to go into the mining towns suggests a severance with traditional channels of information on these matters, i.e., that male migrants would be relatively, if not wholly, ignorant of the possibility of controlling fertility, much less the means of doing so, on arrival in a mining town.

The position of the young male migrant into the Rhondda was one where, up until 1911, he could find employment readily with high wages; there was thus little deterrent to early marriage. In fact, early marriage was probably desirable for him, given his distance from his nuclear family (although there would probably be kin in the area). Once married, however, his situation would be very different to that of his counterparts who had remained in the rural areas. First of all, his workplace was distinctly separate from his home. Second, his wife had nothing whatsoever to do with wage-earning or the production process in which he was engaged and, as she may well have come from a different background to his, they were less likely to have shared a common set of norms and values. These factors would have led in many instances to the formation of a distinctly segregated marital role-relationship.

Given the likelihood of a segregated role-relationship, the greater power of the male within marriage (by virtue of his being the sole breadwinner), and the probability that he knew little about controlling fertility (although he may well have known of *coitus interruptus*), it is highly likely that first generation male migrants thought little about limiting family size, except possibly after the wife had borne a large number of children and/or was suffering from poor health. Further, up until 1900 infant mortality was still very high, and it was more than likely that some of the children born would die in infancy. Up until 1911 a large number of children still meant both a boost to the family income once they could work and a reasonably viable 'insurance scheme' for old age, a factor which must have been of no little importance considering the very real dangers of mining.

The wife in such a community was likely to be part of a social group, with its own social networks, quite distinct from those of her husband. If she wanted to limit the size of her family, but her husband was unaware of her desire, or uninterested or unwilling, then her means were essentially limited to abortions and abortifacients, and probably also a variety of other 'folk' remedies passed on by word of mouth (for example, urinating, or sitting up, directly after intercourse). Maternal mortality was very high in both the rural areas of Wales and in towns like the Rhondda, and, indeed, increased during the first three decades of this century. While there are no reliable figures on the incidence of abortion, the high rate of maternal mortality would suggest that there was also a high rate of abortion. Given the high level of fertility, it could be surmised that abortion was probably used more as a 'desperate remedy' after repeated childbirth than as any effective means of limiting family size during the early years of family formation.

After 1911 the situation began to change in a number of ways. The First World War helped to break down the generally isolated and parochial nature of mining towns. Many young miners who fought in the war were introduced to the availability and advantages of the sheath. Employment became far less secure; there was no longer any reason to suppose that children would or could be any real asset to the family income, while the institution of old age pensions, and better conditions for miners generally, meant children would be seen as less necessary as 'insurance policies'. In-migration ceased abruptly. Most young people getting married would be second, or even third or fourth, generation migrants with an established social network. Infant mortality had declined rapidly, and people were increasingly aware of the importance of health and hygiene; young miners and their wives may well have been less willing to see the effects of the stresses and strains of repeated childbirth on the wife's health and the comforts of the home. Unemployment meant more miners were often spending more time in the home, which may have led to a greater awareness of what housework and childcare involved.

The economic depression and the cessation of in-migration undoubtedly affected the community in a number of ways, its patterns of social interaction, belief-systems, etc., and it is likely that during the first few decades of the century communities such as the Rhondda 'settled down' and became generally more homogeneous than had previously been the case. While there may have been a tendency towards more joint role-relationships in marriage, these trends probably also resulted in a consolidation of social groups and networks. This, combined with the dramatic economic changes after the war, the changing position of children in society and in the family, would help explain, to a great extent, changing ideals of marriage and family size and the resultant decline in fertility which occurred after 1911.

It is interesting to note the average family size of respondents' parents according to place of origin: of those whose fathers were born locally, the average family size was 5.0, while of those who had migrated to the area, it was 9.8, or nearly *double*. Further, of those who had worked as miners prior to migration, their average family size was 6.2, while those of farmworkers was 11.0. Migration, place of origin and type of occupation prior to migration would seem to be very important factors to consider in any analysis of fertility and family size, factors which so far have not been given much attention at local and regional levels.[15]

The fact that the family size of miners continued to be greater on average than that of most other occupational groups may simply be a reflection of changes occurring very rapidly and a certain 'lag' in adjusting to them. For example, the possibility that the average family size and fertility rate were 'inflated' by the reproductive behaviour of older marriage cohorts who started their families when the Rhondda was still a 'boom' town may have distorted the pattern. None the less, certain distinctive characteristics

of the area still persisted, in particular, the almost total exclusion
of women from the labour market, their relative lack of exposure
to new ideals and information through work experience prior to
marriage, and the fact that mining remained a totally male
occupation. These factors probably continued to have important
effects on patterns of social group formation, marital role-relationships and ideals of family size regardless of other changes.

The fact that so few women worked in mining areas was largely
a result of the economic structure – there simply were very few
jobs women could do. Not surprisingly, the interviews with women
in the Rhondda revealed that it was also not considered normative
for married women to work, although if work had been available
the norms might well have been otherwise, witness the following
extract from a woman who worked delivering milk before marrying
a miner at the age of 20; they had three children:

*Did you ever work after you were married?*

No, no. Well they didn't years ago, the women didn't work years ago, only
through the war I think that the women have had to do it more, aren't
they? There was nothing years ago – only service, unless you could get in
a shop, and years ago there was hardly any money in the shop.

There was, however, less evidence here of a strong ideology
against married women working than was the case with women
interviewed who lived in the south-east of England. Two of the
miners' wives did work after marriage, one full-time and one part-
time, and none of the other respondents expressed the idea that
working after marriage was in any way shameful. Perhaps this was
a result of the high level of unemployment in mining areas during
the period, when any supplement to the family income was
welcome, whether it came from husband or wife. The next extract
is from a woman who worked as a barmaid before marriage; her
father was a miner, and she had married a miner at the age of 18
and had two children; her husband had had to give up full-time
work six or seven years after their marriage because of ill health,
and they lived on unemployment benefit and her earnings (which
she did not declare) from then on (he spent most of the dole
money on drink and betting):

Oh I went out to work, when the children got old enough I was working
very hard, every day – on the QT, on the quiet, on the QT, oh yes . . .
went out working doing a day's washing for two shillings perhaps, comin'
home and there's a basketful waiting for me. Oh I had to turn round and
do that lot.

*For the family?*

No! For outsiders. For Jones the fruiterers down there, the butcher's shop, oh I was doing a lot of washing – that's beside my own. ... I brought it into the house after I came home doin' a day's work. Well the end of the week then, I was going off to scrub the school with my mother. She cleaned the school, the girl's school . . . . I don't say that I'm sorry I did it because – I kept the family going.

The next extract is from a woman who worked as a shop assistant before marriage; her father was a miner and her husband had been a miner, but was almost totally blind by the time they married and they lived on unemployment benefit; she married at the age of 20 and they had two children; when asked whether she had ever worked after marriage, she replied:

No, never worked no more. Oh – I went out working in *houses* to earn a few shillings, yes, I worked with a family, my mother's and my sister's, and took in washing – to friends – the lady across the road 'ad a little shop, so I used to do her washing. Then another person I used to wash for, down the road, I went on a Sunday night to fetch the basket of washing and wash 'em on Monday and iron – if they were dry – iron Monday night . . . and then I used to go out – to anything! And then when a shop would go idle and they were letting it to somebody else, I done it in several places, we'd have perhaps fifteen shillings – and I scrubbed 'em all . . . . Then I did a house over up the other road, 'cause the painters had been in papering and painting and they were letting it to sell it, it was terrible . . . and I had fifteen shillings for cleaning that house. And I'd do *anything* to earn money!

It is interesting to note that she first stated that she never worked, and then qualified that statement by saying she worked 'in houses', as though work in houses really did not count as work, even if it was paid. This attitude reveals a great deal about women's work and the definition of it by others as well as by the women themselves. Work within the home or in a domestic situation, paid or unpaid, was perceived as the rightful place for women, and thus did not really 'count' as work. As virtually the only work available to married women in areas like the Rhondda at this time was of this type, it was apparently not seen as conflicting with the accepted definition of a woman's role, and was regarded simply as an extension, albeit a paid one, of her domestic situation. In the South-East, however, even paid domestic work after marriage was regarded as undesirable among upper working-class families. One reason for this was that values and ideals concerning the private nature of the family were generally more developed in this area, and for a married woman to do paid domestic work for others was essentially an infringement of her family's privacy and also, presumably, respectability. It would seem, therefore, that the attitude to married women working in mining areas was intermediate between the prevalent attitude in the South-East and that in areas such as the textile towns of Lancashire, where it was generally accepted as normative for married women to work full-time outside the home doing non-domestic work.

Now let us consider the areas with a high proportion of men employed in agriculture. When all 178 areas in 1911 were analysed, there was a surprising lack of correlation between fertility and the proportion of men in agriculture, while there was a marginal positive correlation between fertility and the proportion of women employed in agriculture ($R^2 - 4.5$). There was only a slight inverse correlation between the proportion of women in agriculture, the sex ratio, and age at marriage. Only when areas with over 45 per cent of men employed in agriculture were selected was there a strong positive correlation with fertility ($R^2 - 13.0$); there was then also a strong correlation with age at marriage. Thus it would seem likely that in predominantly rural areas a similar pattern to that of mining areas prevailed (low age at marriage, few employment opportunities for women), which could partly explain the relatively high rate of fertility there.

In 1931 the correlation between men and women employed in agriculture for all areas included in the study was still very slight. Taking areas with a high proportion of men employed in agriculture, however, a similar pattern to that of 1911 emerged, that is, a strong positive correlation with the proportion of women married in the younger age groups (15–19, $R^2 - 18.0$; 20–24, $R^2 - 16.0$), a strong inverse correlation with the proportion of women employed ($R^2 - 11.0$) and the sex ratio ($R^2 - 13.0$), and a strong positive correlation with the marital fertility rate ($R^2 - 28.0$). It seems likely, therefore, that in these areas both employment opportunities and the demographic structure were affecting fertility.

Table 28 shows the rate of decline of fertility between 1911 and 1931 in areas with a high proportion of men employed in agriculture. Whereas in 1911 all of these rural areas were clustered quite near the mean, and six of them were actually below it, by 1931 all but two of them were above the mean, some of them quite markedly so. The data show quite clearly that the decline in rural areas was neither as rapid nor marked as in other areas (compare, for instance, the figures in Table 28 with those for the mining areas) – why was this the case?

It could have been partly a result of changes in the demographic structure. Or it might have been a manifestation of the relative isolation of rural inhabitants from social groups, networks and the expanding media. Certainly agricultural labourers were one of the worst hit groups economically during the inter-war period; they were not even covered by unemployment benefit until late in the 1930s.

If certain crucial demographic variables are considered for the rural areas discussed above, then several important factors emerge (see Table 29). *All* the areas with the exception of Cardiganshire had a ratio of females to males which was below the mean. For eight of the areas, as would be expected, the proportion of women married aged 20–24 was also above the mean. To a certain extent this could explain the relatively high fertility of these areas, although the correlation is not that clear-cut (the area with the

**Table 28**  *Marital fertility rates and rate of decline between 1911 and 1931 in areas with over 50 per cent of males employed in agriculture in 1911*

| Area | Males employed in agriculture (%) | Marital fertility rate, 1911 | Marital fertility rate, 1931 | Decline (%) |
|---|---|---|---|---|
| Isle of Ely | 72.5 | 175.5 | 106.9 | 39.0 |
| Lincs. (Holland) | 70.0 | 187.8 | 122.3 | 34.9 |
| Montgomeryshire | 65.5 | 175.0 | 130.8 | 25.3 |
| Radnor | 63.9 | 200.7 | 124.3 | 38.1 |
| Huntingdonshire | 60.8 | 153.3 | 103.7 | 32.4 |
| Herefordshire | 60.3 | 165.9 | 117.1 | 29.4 |
| West Suffolk | 58.7 | 169.2 | 95.8 | 43.4 |
| Cardiganshire | 57.9 | 170.3 | 124.4 | 27.0 |
| Lincs. (Lindsey) | 57.6 | 175.0 | 112.3 | 35.8 |
| Anglesey | 57.1 | 162.9 | 115.7 | 29.0 |
| Norfolk | 55.8 | 165.5 | 108.8 | 34.3 |
| Cambridgeshire | 55.6 | 156.8 | 97.7 | 37.7 |
| East Suffolk | 54.3 | 165.1 | 109.2 | 33.9 |
| mean (England and Wales) | | 167.1 | 102.1 | 38.9 |

*Source*: Census (1911 and 1931)

**Table 29** *Selected demographic characteristics of predominantly rural areas in England and Wales, 1911 and 1931*

| Rural district | Sex ratio | | Females married aged 20–24 (%) | | Females married aged 30–34 (%) | |
|---|---|---|---|---|---|---|
| | 1911 | 1931 | 1911 | 1931 | 1911 | 1931 |
| Isle of Ely | 92.3 | 95.0 | 36.2 | 42.6 | 79.0 | 84.4 |
| Cambridgeshire | 100.8 | 100.5 | 23.8 | 29.7 | 72.5 | 75.6 |
| Lincs. (Holland) | 96.9 | 97.7 | 31.2 | 39.3 | 78.2 | 81.9 |
| Lincs. (Lindsey) | 96.9 | 98.0 | 28.7 | 34.0 | 74.3 | 77.9 |
| Herefordshire | 103.4 | 103.7 | 16.1 | 26.1 | 65.1 | 68.0 |
| Huntingdonshire | 98.1 | 100.3 | 27.9 | 32.1 | 69.0 | 74.9 |
| Norfolk | 99.5 | 99.7 | 25.4 | 31.9 | 72.1 | 75.8 |
| East Suffolk | 95.3 | 96.2 | 26.2 | 30.4 | 71.8 | 74.4 |
| West Suffolk | 97.8 | 97.8 | 24.3 | 29.1 | 70.9 | 73.5 |
| Anglesey | 104.7 | 104.7 | 18.5 | 22.9 | 62.4 | 64.5 |
| Cardiganshire | 117.6 | 110.6 | 10.7 | 17.8 | 52.1 | 57.6 |
| Montgomeryshire | 97.8 | 96.3 | 17.4 | 21.7 | 64.5 | 66.2 |
| Radnor | 94.2 | 93.4 | 14.8 | 26.3 | 67.7 | 69.7 |

*Source*: Census (1911 and 1931)

highest proportion of females married in both age groups, the Isle of Ely, had one of the lowest marital fertility rates in 1931). More significant perhaps is the marked increase in the proportions of women married in both age groups in all areas between 1911 and 1931. This could explain a great deal of the relatively slow decline of fertility in these areas, and contrasts noticeably with the mining areas, where fertility declined much more rapidly, but where the proportions married also declined. Note, also, that the four Welsh areas displayed distinctly different characteristics to those of the areas in England. While their sex ratio was below the mean (except Cardiganshire) and the proportions of women married were extremely low for both 1911 and 1931, yet their fertility rates were above the mean.

One reason for the difference between the Welsh and English areas might be sought in different patterns of landholding. In most of England at this time the prevalent socio-economic system in agricultural areas was one of landowners, tenant farmers and wage-earning labourers, although after 1911 there was an increasing number of medium sized landholdings as a result of many tenant farmers buying land from impoverished landholders. In much of

Wales, on the other hand, a pattern of smallholdings still prevailed, and it would seem from the relatively high proportion of women employed in agriculture there that it was still quite common for members of the family to work a holding together, more or less as an economic unit.[16] In other words, the relations of family members to the socio-economic system were still very different in Wales, and this must have affected patterns of family organization as well as ideals of family size. In spite of compulsory education, for many Welsh smallholders, women and children could still be of vital importance to production, and this was certainly not the case in most of England.

Another possibility is that ideas of family size were affected by patterns of migration.[17] While most rural areas experienced a certain amount of out-migration from the mid nineteenth century, the four Welsh areas discussed experienced them to a far greater extent than any other English areas. Up until 1911, it could be said that the Welsh rural areas were 'feeding' the labour force for the nearby mining areas, as well as the domestic servant population in South-East England. Thus children who were not needed on the smallholding still had outlets available to them if and when they became a burden to their parents. From 1911, however, and especially after the First World War, these outlets became increasingly closed.

The low proportion of women married in the Welsh rural areas suggests a pattern of fertility control not unlike that prevailing in pre-industrial society, where under a system of smallholdings, delayed marriage was a more common form of restricting fertility than control exercised within marriage.[18] It seems likely, too, that the availability of employment for young men in surrounding mining areas may have, in some ways, been equivalent to the situation in certain areas of England during industrialization. That is, lack of land (which restricted early marriage) sent many young men to mining areas where ready employment meant there were no longer any restrictions on early marriage. The influx of young rural male migrants undoubtedly contributed to both the low age at marriage and high fertility of the mining areas, while the problem of land availability in rural areas continued to deter early marriage and resulted in a lower level of fertility than that prevailing in the mining areas. Further, the out-migration of young females from both the rural and mining areas to work elsewhere further exacerbated the unbalanced sex ratio and would have also affected patterns of early, and low age at, marriage, which in turn contributed to the high rate of fertility in the mining areas.

After 1911 the pattern changed. Rural migration into mining areas virtually ceased. Agriculture was in a state of depression. Lack of employment opportunities for children in either agriculture or mining must have affected ideals of family size, not to mention the effects of a lengthier period of dependence for children (school leaving age rose from 10 to 14). Indeed, the marital fertility rate in the rural areas did decline between 1911 and 1931. On the other hand, the proportion of women married increased, which suggests that control of fertility was being increasingly exercised more efficiently within marriage.

Little has been said so far about the relation of married women to the economic system in these areas. While few married women were employed on a wage basis in agriculture, it is evident that in the Welsh areas characterized by smallholdings, the wife was frequently directly involved in the production process. Marriage and childbearing were not mutually exclusive.[19] In most of the English areas, on the other hand, few married women worked, except on an occasional or seasonal basis. Home and work in such areas were usually quite separate, whereas in the Welsh areas they were not. The work of married women in England would tend to be more as an occasional boost to the family income, while that of married women in Wales was essential throughout the year. Such differences would have had important effects on beliefs, norms and values. While there is no adequate data available, it is suggested that the nature of the relationship of married women in agricultural areas in England would result in a more highly developed domestic ideology and a greater privatization of the family. These factors would tend to result in a reduction in ideals of family size and different ideals of family organization.

Married women in the agricultural areas of Wales, on the other hand, would have been less prone to these influences, although they were certainly affected by the economic depression during the inter-war period. Their ideals of family size were most likely to have been affected by the lack of 'outlets' available for children elsewhere. Perhaps one or two children were needed to help run the smallholding; more than this would present such couples with a serious problem. In other words, their motives for restricting family size during this period were probably different in many ways to those of their English counterparts, even if the net result was very similar.

Third, and finally, let us consider the areas with a high proportion of men in manufacturing. When all 178 areas were considered, there were no obvious correlations between the proportions of men and women in manufacturing, the demographic variables, and the marital fertility rate. This was undoubtedly a result of the diversity within the category of 'manufacturing', which included a wide variety of industries: some small, some large, some male-dominated, others female-dominated or mixed. If we consider those areas with a high proportion of men employed in manufacturing and a low proportion of married women working, there are

**Table 30**   *Areas with a high percentage of men employed in manufacturing and a low percentage of married women working, 1911 and 1931*

| Area | Year | Sex ratio | Women married 20–24 (%) | Women occupied (%) | Marital fertility rate |
|------|------|-----------|---------------------|--------------------|----------------------|
| Gateshead | 1911 | 102.2 | 31.3 | 28.6 | 204.2 |
|  | 1931 | 104.0 | 29.9 | 32.9 | 135.6 |
| South Shields | 1911 | 103.9 | 35.5 | 24.0 | 197.3 |
|  | 1931 | 106.3 | 32.2 | 25.4 | 127.9 |
| West Hartlepool | 1911 | 102.8 | 29.8 | 26.2 | 191.7 |
|  | 1931 | 104.1 | 30.7 | 28.6 | 133.7 |
| Barrow-in-Furness | 1911 | 91.1 | 28.6 | 25.8 | 178.4 |
|  | 1931 | 94.5 | 27.3 | 26.8 | 95.9 |
| St Helens | 1911 | 91.9 | 35.9 | 25.0 | 237.1 |
|  | 1931 | 95.7 | 31.1 | 27.9 | 135.4 |
| Lincoln | 1911 | 101.0 | 28.6 | 29.6 | 156.3 |
|  | 1931 | 106.1 | 26.4 | 31.2 | 84.7 |
| Newcastle | 1911 | 103.2 | 25.2 | 33.1 | 182.4 |
|  | 1931 | 106.1 | 25.3 | 37.2 | 119.6 |
| Burton-upon-Trent | 1911 | 99.3 | 23.9 | 29.1 | 146.5 |
|  | 1931 | 103.6 | 27.2 | 31.7 | 104.0 |
| Middlesbrough | 1911 | 95.6 | 34.4 | 24.5 | 200.1 |
|  | 1931 | 98.1 | 35.4 | 28.1 | 135.0 |
| Swansea | 1911 | 98.2 | 30.1 | 29.5 | 200.4 |
|  | 1931 | 103.5 | 27.8 | 26.1 | 107.4 |
| mean (England and Wales) | 1911 | 107.6 | 23.7 | 39.5 | 167.1 |
|  | 1931 | 108.8 | 25.9 | 38.0 | 102.7 |

*Source*: Census (1911 and 1931)

a number of similarities, as shown in Table 30. All these areas, with
the exception of Lincoln, were areas of heavy industry: shipbuilding,
steel manufacture, etc. These industries were almost entirely male-
dominated, and all had a low proportion of women working
(although this increased between 1911 and 1931, contrary to the
national trend). The sex ratio was below the mean in both 1911
and 1931, and the proportion of women married aged 20–24 (with
the exception of Newcastle in 1931) was above the mean. Not
surprisingly, most of the areas also had a marital fertility rate
above the mean. Unemployment was high in these areas in 1931,
but analysing all 178 areas there was only a slight positive correlation
between unemployment and fertility ($R^2$ – 8.0). The decline in
fertility between 1911 and 1931 in these areas, however, was
relatively slight (except in Barrow and Lincoln); this cannot by any
means be wholly explained by demographic variables. Is there any
way in which the occupational structure could explain such
trends?

Let us look at the occupational structure of one of the areas in
somewhat greater detail, that of Gateshead. There was a low
proportion of women occupied both in 1911 and 1931, although it
did increase somewhat between those years. The largest proportion
of women working was in domestic service. Only just over 3 per
cent were employed in manufacturing. There was also a very low
percentage of married women working. These factors suggest that
few women in Gateshead were gaining access to new belief-
systems or networks through work experience either prior to, or
after, marriage. Of course it is likely that once married many
would become part of a local, community-based, social network
which would almost certainly be separate to that of their husbands.
This was likely to result in highly segregated role-relationships
within marriage, little sharing in communication of ideas or decision-
making, and could thus have resulted in relatively inefficient
control of fertility within marriage.

The principal occupations of men in Gateshead were manufacturing (primarily shipbuilding and allied industries), employing
33.5 per cent of all men in 1911, 27.1 per cent in 1931; transport
and communication, employing 15.4 per cent in 1911, 13.3 per
cent in 1931; and mining, which employed 13.1 per cent in 1911
and 10.2 per cent in 1931. Most of these occupations would be
classified as skilled or semi-skilled, and were entirely male-
dominated. The fertility of the skilled and semi-skilled sectors on a

national level was lower than that of the unskilled or miners.[20] Why, then, was the marital fertility rate here notably higher than in areas like the Rhondda or Bethnal Green? The categories of 'skilled', 'unskilled' etc., give us no idea of occupational variations, and only provide information about the position of *men* in the labour market. What we need to know is the relations of all family members – men, women and children – to the socio-economic system. Perhaps women who had worked as domestic servants in these areas and married shipbuilders had different ideals of family size and different family-building behaviour from women who had worked as servants and married miners or agricultural labourers.

Again, there is virtually no individual data available on these questions. It is only possible to conclude from what data is available that in areas of heavy industry such as Gateshead, employment opportunities for women were very few, whether single or married; some left the areas to seek work elsewhere, thereby creating a somewhat unbalanced sex ratio. For those who remained, many of whom would have been unable to find employment, marriage must have been perceived – and they may have been pressurized into seeing it by their parents – as the only available option to them. Early marriage thus tended to be prevalent, and would explain part of the high fertility rate. Scarce job opportunities, mostly in service, must also have resulted in little exposure to new values, beliefs or ideals through work experience prior to marriage. It is likely that many women retained the norms and values acquired during childhood up until marriage, and probably after marriage as well. The decline in early marriage between 1911 and 1931 was probably a reaction to the high unemployment in these areas, and one result of this was a moderate decline in fertility by 1931, although other factors would also have affected the decline.

Thus, whether or not married women worked was primarily dependent on whether job opportunities were available. None the less, it was also dependent on the prevailing norms among various groups in certain areas; relatively plentiful job opportunities for women in an area did not necessarily result in a large proportion of married women working. Where married women did work in large numbers it was a result of a combination of factors: available work, perceived economic necessity to work, and an acceptance of work as normative. The relation of the husband to the economic system was also a crucial determinant of married women working or not: if his occupation was different to his wife's, if it was male-dominated, if he perceived his wages as sufficient to support his family without his wife working, or if his own social/occupational group perceived them as such, then he was likely to regard his wife's role as a purely domestic one and be opposed to her taking employment outside the home. The more insecure he perceived his own situation as being (and this, particularly during the inter-war period, could easily change during his life-cycle), the more likely he was to accept the need for his wife to work.

What can we conclude from these data about the relationships between married women working and fertility? Like other studies, there was strong evidence of an inverse correlation between married women working and fertility. Further analysis, however, revealed a rather more complex picture, where the association by no means always applied to all areas. It would seem that the crucial factor was not *whether* married women worked or not, but the type of work they did. Where work was carried out outside the home then there was a fairly consistent inverse correlation with fertility. Where work and home were not mutually exclusive, then married women working was often associated with a higher level of fertility. This, too, is consistent with other studies. Nevertheless, correlations are not equivalent to explanations. We cannot assume that separation of home from work *causes* a reduction in fertility – consider, for example, the pattern of high fertility under such conditions during the early period of industrialization or the incidence of high fertility and a high proportion of married women working in the 1950s. We want to know how and why women perceived the problem, and how their perceptions affected their behaviour. This is the topic of Chapter 5.

# 5 Family life: organization and domestic ideology

Comparing the different groups of women interviewed, the most striking general difference between those women who worked and those who stayed at home was a marked contrast in their attitudes to, and ideologies of, the home, the family and work. Those who stayed at home tended to give detailed and elaborate accounts of family life, leisure pursuits and incidents concerning their children. This was more marked, however, among those women from the south-east of England than amongst those from South Wales. The responses of women from the South-East to questions related to their work prior to marriage were usually brief and often mono-syllabic. For those who worked full-time the opposite tended to be the case. Accounts of their work were detailed and elaborate, while responses to questions concerning family life were far less so. This difference suggests that meanings attached to certain phenomena tend to vary in their degree of importance to an actor in proportion to that actor's time spent, and degree of involvement, in a particular activity.

To illustrate this difference more fully, the following extracts are quoted at length from two women. The first worked prior to marriage as a tailoress in Colchester and later took in lodgers when her husband was unemployed; she had one child.

*What did you do before you were married?*

Oh I was a tailoress, bespoke tailoress, yes.

*What did that involve – did you work in a factory?*

In a factory, yes, there was – downstairs 'twas all bungled, but we had separate coats for the – they were measured – say, if you went to a tailor and, say, 'I want a suit made', they'd take all your measurements and when they cut 'em out – we worked for all the tailors round the town – and we had to baste 'em up and they went back to that person to fit on, any old traces they used to alter it, and then that used to come back for us – unpick, and then make it up. . . .

*Did you and your husband go out together much?*

Oh we went to – yes, and David went out with us Sunday nights and if we had a walk out, he went out with us till he was about 13, well then he got this little boy that were goin' to get him this paper round, so of course we let him go with the boys. . . . We used to like walkin' on the Hythe Quay and over the Wivenhoe Park, and we used to go to the Wivenhoe 'Flag'. My husband used to have a glass of beer, I used to have a glass of beer if I fancied, or a shandy, and we used to buy David a ginger beer or somethin' like that, you know, and biscuit, and then we used to walk home by the road, but if we felt tired and we thought the boy was a bit tired – after he left his pushchair – we used to catch the bus home to Hythe Station Road, and then we had to walk Station Road just up Spurgeon Street, over the bridge and up Spurgeon Street and we were home. Oh yes, we had some lovely times over there, yeah, we did, we used to go when my husband was on different shifts . . . well, when the blackberries were on and he was on six till two, he used to come home at two for his dinner. I used to keep his dinner hot, my husband's, and he'd wash and we'd have a cup o' tea and then David used to come out o' school about four, quarter past, well he either had my dad to go home to or Tom's mother lived just be me up the hill and a little bit further . . . and they'd look after him and we used to fill the flask up – 'at's when the flask first come out – fill the flask, take some tea with us, and we used to pick blackberries over Wivenhoe Park – and they were great big 'uns! Oh dear, they were beautiful! And we'd set down in the grass and we'd have our tea and we'd have a little cuddle! And then we'd pick blackberries till we were tired and come home. And then the next day I'd make blackberry jelly with 'em, I made a lot of jelly, and we'd have blackberry and apple pudding the next day. Well I was doin' this one day, my husband was on six till two, and I was makin' this jelly I wanted to do it in the mornin' 'cause I knew in the afternoon my husband didn't come home till two, by the time he'd had his dinner that there wouldn't be a lot o' time, but the next door neighbour had gone over to Walton for their school treat, and Mr Rose, he come home in the dinner, well of course all the bedroom windows was open – and the WASPS! Oh goodness! Oh I didn't know what to do with meself! So I kept putting the pan over and turned them out. Well, when Mr Rose came home dinner time, I said – we used to call him Peter – 'Oh Peter,' I said, 'I'm smothered in wasps!' 'Whatever are you doin'? he said. 'Makin' jelly,' 'Oh,' he said, 'you shouldn't do that till the sun's set! After they've gone to bed,' he said, 'so,' he said, 'never mind, I'll light a little fire in the garden.' So he got some old newspapers and rubbish and he lit a fire – and they don't like fire, they all went. So when I knew I hadn't got any more I run upstairs and shut the windows. Makin' jelly! Oh when my husband come home he did laugh! 'Well,' I said, 'nobody told me!' That was funny – but that jelly turned out lovely.

The detail with which she remembered and described such apparently trivial incidents betrayed the great pleasure and meaning these occasions held for her, in contrast with the relatively curt and concise account of her work experience. Compare that with the next extract from a woman who worked as a weaver both before and after marriage, as well as after her child was born:

*Did you and your husband spend your spare time together?*

Oh yes! I'll tell you what we used to do – we used to go out walks, we used to walk miles and miles, take us tea wi' us, m' sister an' her husband as well, an' me husband's sister an' her husband. Oh yeah, we used to walk miles – set off at Sunday morning about 10 o'clock and get back about 10 o'clock at night, yeah . . . .

*What did your work as a weaver involve?*

Well, you know warps? Well they put warps in t' loom and take beams out and then they've got to gate warps up – that were heaviest part o' tackling is putting warps in t' loom, but they used to have something called a gantry and if they were away from where warps are they used to run 'em in on this gantry and then lower 'em down with chains into looms. But when I worked up that fancy place, we had double beams as well, we'd a beam at top an' all, we had a beam come up this way to loom and top would come down that way t' loom. They had them for things we used to call sponge cloths, but they were like towellings, and you know like your loops in on your towel? Well, what they used to do, your top beam used to be weighted a different way than what your bottom was weighted, and it used to come in slacker, you see, they'd come in slacker and it'd cause that loop to stand up. Well, when your tackler were getting a warp up or when he'd got it ready he used to measure a piece 6 inches and he'd snip thread 6 inches away, and then when it were pulled out he'd stretch it and it had got to measure 10 inch, and then he got the thickness of the towel you see, instead of – you get me towels now, some of them are flatter and harder, and you get some towels are thicker, only you got more o' what you call pimp on you better towels, 'cause they take more yarn, won't they, but we used to weave them sort an' all . . . . Men'd have six looms, and they'd have what they call a tenter – it's a young school leaver and he used to take ends off and sort of help out, help to keep looms going, and then, you see, when you'd been tenting a long while, when they thought you were capable enough, you'd go on t' looms then, you get two looms and then you'd go up to three and then you'd get up to four. Well, you see, six loom weavers would have to have a new tenter then . . . you used to get what you earned off looms, see. Well these here what we used to call papoons, what were for Indian turbans and things like that, they used to be in 3 yard lengths and you used to have to weave 20 lengths to make what we call a piece. Well, you get paid so much for those pieces and then after you wove that you'd go on weaving till you wove another 20 lengths and that were another piece. Well, when it used to be piece-work like that, same as you might have one time, we used to make wage at dinner time, only you'd have to be trying t' hurry up and keep that one on to try and get another two. Well sometimes you'd have only about eighteen in, well you see that'd go on for t' week after, so the week after you'd have like two full pieces and one week you see – you wouldn't have same wage each week. Well in weaving they used to call it corving. They used to say, I'm corving for two off this, and you'd try to get those two pieces off in the time when your wages were made up.

While the family outings were obviously a source of pleasure to this woman, she was not able to recall them with anything like the detail shown by the first woman, or with the same detail she described her own work.

Interestingly, both these women were extremely similar in background; both of their fathers had been labourers, both of their mothers had worked after marriage (the mother of the Colchester woman as a tailoress doing outwork, the mother of the Burnley woman as a charwoman). The Colchester woman married at 26, the Burnley woman at 24; both had one child. Their husbands would have both been classified as 'skilled': the husband of the first woman was a baker (although later unemployed), the husband of the second woman, a glass blower. Further, they had both worked in a factory prior to marriage. The principal difference between them lay in their relation to the economic system after marriage; the Colchester woman did not work at all after marriage until much later, when she took in lodgers; the Burnley woman worked full-time in a textile mill all her life, except for brief interruptions during childbirth and illness.

These extracts have been quoted at length to show how the women's different relations to the economic system were associated with two very different ideologies of the home, the family and married life. The Colchester woman spent the vast majority of her married life in the home with her family performing domestic tasks, and the home, family life and household jobs were extremely significant and important to her. She glorified and elaborated fairly minor incidents like country walks and making jam and they were incidents of great meaning and pleasure to her. Indeed, her home, family, household chores and leisure pursuits were, essentially, her entire world as a married woman.

For the Burnley woman, on the other hand, these events did not carry the same meaning. She also remembered going on country walks with her family, and enjoyed them. She made jam and baked her own bread, too, as well as going for the occasional drink with her husband. Yet they were not the centre of her married life. Her most detailed and elaborate memories related instead to her working life, which apparently had far greater significance for her than her memories of family life. Such differences in beliefs must also have had important effects on family organization and attitudes to children and family size.

Each respondent's marital role-relationship was analysed in terms of joint or segregated participation by husband and wife in the following areas: leisure pursuits, household chores, childcare and decision-making concerning family size and use of birth control.[1] Dividing them according to whether the respondents worked full-time, part-time or stayed at home after marriage and childbirth, the pattern illustrated in Table 31 emerged. The highest proportion of joint role-relationships occurred among those who worked full-time, the lowest among those who worked part-time, while the proportion was equal among those who stayed at home. Of those who worked full-time outside the home, all but two of the women from this group worked as weavers; of the remaining two, one worked as a charwoman, the other as a clerk. Their husbands were overwhelmingly skilled working class: four were in textiles, one was a glass blower, one a miner, one a joiner, one an engineer, and one a bus conductor. Of the four couples who were *both* weavers, *all* had joint role-relationships. Of the couples who had segregated role-relationships, one was a miner, one a joiner, and one a bus conductor; all of these men were also regular drinkers, which the others were not.

**Table 31** *Respondents' relations to economic system and type of role-relationship*

| Relation to economic system | Segregated role-relationship (%) | number | Joint role-relationship (%) | number |
|---|---|---|---|---|
| worked full-time | 33 | (3) | 67 | (6) |
| worked part-time | 75 | (3) | 25 | (1) |
| stayed at home | 50 | (8) | 50 | (8) |

*Source*: Interviews

The marital role-relationships and family organization of those couples where both partners worked as weavers were quite distinctive, especially with regard to housework. Among other couples whose role-relationships have been classified as 'joint', the husband's main role in the house and with the children was that of helping out, while the woman still performed the bulk of the chores (and also usually the dirtiest ones). Among these weaving couples, however, household duties were shared quite evenly and equally between husband and wife, witness the following extracts. The first woman was married at 26, her mother was in textiles, her father a labourer at the foundry; she and her husband worked in textiles all their lives, and also in the same mill for a long time; they had one child:

*Did your husband help out much in the house?*

Oh he were a good one for it – doing potatoes and cutting meat up, he'd do all that, he'd clean windows and that.... We'd all so much work to do when we'd come home from work, one'd iron and one'd mop out bathroom floor – we all had his work picked out.

The next extract is from a woman who married at 18, whose mother was a weaver and whose father was a miner; she, too, worked in the same mill as her husband for many years; they had two children:

*Did your husband help out much in the house?*

Oh, he did everything... an' on a Friday night Jennie – when she were about 12 – used to go through the house with her dad while I went shopping with me mother... an' when we used to get back everything were all spick 'n' span.

*Would your husband do any cooking?*

Oh, he could wash and bake with anybody! Nothing he couldn't do, anybody that knew him, yes.

*Did he help out when the girls were babies?*

Yes, oh yes – well, he did, an' he has another brother lives at Hebdon Bridge and he's just the same, oh yes.

These couples also spent most of their leisure time together, going to the cinema, playing cards with friends or relations, going for walks or the occasional drink together. The impression given by all of them was of a definite sharing between husband and wife in all aspects of their married life: work, home and leisure. This seems to have been primarily a result of their identical relations to the occupational system – not just that they worked after marriage, but that they all did the *same* work, leaving home and returning at the same time, often working with the same group of people. There were few divisions between them in terms of workplace, occupation, social group, home or leisure, and they seem to have shared a common set of ideals, norms and values.

Among those couples where the woman worked full-time, but in a different occupation to that of her husband, these characteristics were by no means so pronounced. Half of them had segregated role-relationships, half joint. If their husbands helped, which many did, the jobs they would and would not do were clearly defined, and their work was usually more helping out than real sharing. Some would do a great deal in the house, but did not share leisure pursuits with their wives or children; others would share leisure pursuits but do little in the house; one did neither.

The next extract is from a woman in South Wales who married at 18, had two children, and worked full-time soon after marriage when her husband became unemployed:

*Did you ever go out much with your husband?*

No I didn't, no, he wasn't that sort. No – *he* used to go out – plenty! But not me, he didn't take me out. No – there was, I used to tell him after I got married, 'People think that I'm not married to you because you never see me with my husband.' He wasn't that – he wasn't sociable that way. He wouldn't say, like, 'Let's go out and have a drink tonight, or let's go out and visit somebody.' He wouldn't've, really now! . . . He wouldn't come to have a cup o' tea nor what. If anybody wanted to invite us out, he'd say, 'Oh you go, I won't come.' Now *he'd* go out every night of the week drinking – *every night of the week*! Yeah, but he wouldn't ask me to go . . .

*Would he help out much in the house?*

Yes he was good in the house – when I was out working he'd, yes, he'd heat the children's food, perhaps he'd go and make the beds – he wouldn't do a lot of scrubbing and rubbing – wash dishes, clean the fire irons, and he'd put them under the table till I came back to show that they were nice and clean and all, make the beds, make the food for the children – he was really *good* with food . . . . Oh he'd cook a good dinner and he'd see that the children would have it on the – he'd look at the clock, the children would come home from school and they didn't have to play around waiting for their food, 'twas always ready. He was good like that, yeah. He had his good points, oh yes, there's good in a bad one and bad in a good one, in't there?

His help in the house, however, as she stated later, was essentially a result of economic necessity, rather than a result of any ideals that it was something he *ought* to do. The wife had to work for financial reasons, he was unemployed, and someone had to feed and look after the children, so he did it. In the next extract, the woman worked as a weaver and the man as a bus conductor; she was 30 when she married, and they had one child; both of their parents had worked in textiles:

*Did he help out in the house much?*

No, no, but I tell you what he did do. That motor place, there were him an' another man that had this pub an' they worked together, they were always like pals, and this other fellow . . . an' him used to do a lot o' work, see, in their spare time, and they used to earn money and used to buy all sorts for t'home and he used to buy our Elsie meals. . . .

*Did he help out with Elsie?*

No. He'd work and then he'd buy us something . . . . I come home one dinner time an' I said to him, 'Oh, there's a sale up on Nicola's Shop, and there's a lovely' – 'twere like a three piece, navy blue – oh an' it were nice. He says, 'Well have it'. I says, 'I haven't time, I've only an hour.' An' you know, when I come home, 'twere on settee!

This was the same woman whose husband asked her not to talk to him when she was coming home from work through the bus station; while he reluctantly agreed to her working, he was none the less embarrassed about it with his own, distinctly separate, social group, and apparently made his feelings about the set-up obvious to her by taking no part whatsoever in domestic chores or routine. His only contribution was financial. The next extract is from the woman quoted earlier who worked as a weaver and whose husband was a glass blower:

*Did he help out in the house much?*

Oh yes, he used to help, yes. He'd do washing and things like that, but he couldn't cook, no . . . he'd clean up and help to wash up. He didn't like going out – when me legs were bad, he'd go when he were forced, but when I could go he wouldn't go then, you know, he didn't used to like shopping.

They did share most of their leisure time together, particularly walking and going to the cinema, and he used to go out to the pub on his own on Friday nights. Their relationship was, in the main, a joint one, but not to the extent of those couples where both husband and wife were weavers.

Among this group there was only one couple where the husband apparently did nothing in the home or with the children, and did not share any of his leisure time with his wife or children. He worked as a joiner and she was a weaver; she married at 23 and they had three children:

*Would your husband help out with the housework?*

No he wouldn't – he wasn't that way gifted, no, he always wanted to be out. It does make life a bit hard work like.

*Would he help with the children?*

No, he wasn't gifted that way was Fred, no.

*Did you go out with him much after you were married?*

No, no, no – well, I – no – I went to whist. He used to like to go for a drink . . . through t'week I didn't go out like on me own, no, well, you can always find sommat to do, can't you?

Thus even among couples where both partners worked full-time, the nature of their relations to the economic/occupational system as individuals had a marked effect on their organization of, and attitudes towards, married life. Where both were engaged in the same occupation then there was a marked sharing, equality, between them concerning both housework and leisure; when they were in different occupations, however, their degree of sharing was noticeably less. This was primarily a result of belonging to different social groups with different belief-systems. It may also have been the case that as those men who worked in different occupations also tended to be in male-dominated occupations, where there was a very different meaning attached to work, women and their work were probably regarded as inherently inferior to theirs. Where both husband and wife were in the same occupation, doing essentially the same job, such differentiation and beliefs of superiority/subordination did not exist.

Let us consider next the group of women who stayed at home after marriage. I have already noted that half of them had joint role-relationships and the other half, segregated. This is not really surprising, as those women were quite diverse in terms of their own occupational experience prior to marriage, their husband's relation to the economic system, and the communities in which they lived. Just over half of them had been in isolated occupations or had stayed at home before marrying (three were at home, four were domestic servants, one delivered milk), the others were in much less isolated occupations (two worked as shop assistants, two as clerks, two in factories, and one as a barmaid). Of the husbands' occupations, two were in commerce, one was a clerk, two were in semi-skilled occupations, ten in skilled.

The role-relationships among this group were very different to those observed among the weaving couples. There was far less sharing of household work and childcare between partners. Of those with a joint role-relationship in this group, the husband's role wthin the home was quite definitely one of helping, 'giving mum a break', and there were certain jobs he simply would not do, in particular, ironing, changing nappies and scrubbing. Washing up, some cooking, and playing with the children or taking them out were the principal tasks; witness the following two extracts. The first is from a woman in Essex who had worked as a domestic servant, whose husband was a policeman, who had married when she was 18, and had two children. When she was asked whether her husband helped out in the house or with the children, she replied:

Well, he was quite good with the children and he'd take it in turns getting up at night, you know, for bottles or anything like that, he was always good like that. But no, he didn't like doing anything in the house whatsoever. I remember that I went on a holiday once... and when I came back a fortnight later, there wasn't a thing in the house to use to drink out of – basins, cups, pie dishes – he'd used the lot! I've never seen so much washing-up in my life! I had a copper – it was an old-fashioned house – and I had a copper and even *that* was full of crockery. It took myself and a neighbour – what, quite three to four hours to clear this washing out.... I never attempted to have a holiday on my own from that day to this!

The second woman, who had worked as a clerk, married a bus driver when she was 25, and had two children, had this to say when asked the same question:

Oh yes. Oh he'd always help me – wash up and doing me shopping or anything like that.

*Did he help when the boys were young?*

Oh yes. Oh yes, and he used to look after them, and if he had to go on duty and I was getting his meals and that, he'd look after them, take them out and that.

*What about changing nappies and things like that?*

No – I don't think he did that. I can't remember whether he did. Of course the men didn't help so much, not then, looking after children like *that*. As

I say, he would see to them and amuse them in the garden....

What was distinctive about these couples, where the woman stayed at home and they had a relatively joint role-relationship, however, was that their 'jointness' was centred far more around the *children* and the family as a whole than it was among those couples where both worked. Children and married/family life seemed to have had very different meanings to them. For example, among the couples where the wife worked, leisure pursuits were usually shared between husband and wife rather than between them and the children, whereas just the opposite was the case with this group: leisure pursuits almost invariably involved parents *and* children. Witness this account from a woman in Essex who had worked as a shop assistant, married a male nurse when she was 23, and had four children:

*Did you ever work after you were married?*

No, no.

*Not at all? Why was that?*

Well, you just didn't think of it in those days. You never thought of it. Well, they would have thought it was a shameful thing if a woman had to go to work in those days.... When you were married, well, you had your family and your home to look after.... But our time was fully occupied, but we were very happy. We had no television... no radio or anything like that... but when the children were small we used to – my husband used to have two days a week off... before the children went to school we used to take them out on picnics and all that sort of thing, long walks and all that... and then when they got a bit older they could have bicycles, buy a five shilling bicycle, you know, and rig it up and make a good job of it. My husband used to do that, so eventually we all had bicycles and we used to go out for cycle rides cycle to Mersea and Clacton and Walton and all that sort of thing and we thoroughly enjoyed ourselves. That was our pleasure and we used to have a real good time.

*What would you do in the evenings?*

Play games, play cards, anything the children wanted.

*Did you ever go out to the cinema?*

We couldn't afford it.... We just didn't think about it... you know, we were quite happy in our home-life and looking after the children and taking them out and all that sort of thing. As I say, amusing them in the house and all that.

*Would your husband help with any of the housework?*

Oh definitely. Oh yes, and he'd help looking after the children if I was busy.

**Table 32**    *Percentage of respondents' children continuing school*

| Respondents' relation to economic system | (%) | Number |
|---|---|---|
| at home | 50 | (15) |
| full-time work | 33 | (11) |
| part-time work | 13 | (4) |

*Source*: Interviews

It is interesting to note the proportion of respondents' children who continued school after 14, according to the woman's relation to the economic system (see Table 32). Why was education apparently more important to the couples in this group, considering that the class backgrounds of *all* the respondents were quite similar?

The reasons were essentially twofold. First, just as these women seemed to glorify their roles as housewives and their domestic duties by virtue of spending all their married life within the home, so they also elaborated and glorified their roles as mothers and the importance of children. Children were an essential part of their ideology of the home and family. Second, a distinctive feature of these couples was the woman's lack of integration and participation in a social group or network. Whether because of actual physical isolation, or a deliberate 'policy' on the part of herself and/or her husband, isolation from a social group tended to result in great emphasis on, and importance attached to, family life, domesticity and particularly children.

Let me illustrate this by quoting two extracts, one from a woman who had a joint role-relationship but stayed at home, and one from a woman who had a joint role-relationship but worked. The first woman, who had worked as a shop assistant, married a miner when she was 23 and had two children. Here she shows her involvement with her children:

Oh my husband was a wonderful man. Never took a ha'penny pocket money when he was on the dole, not a ha'penny. And they were giving shoes out in the school now to the children, and my son came home crying, and I said, 'What's the matter with you?' 'They're all having shoes in school,' he said, 'but I can't have any,' he said. 'Well, why is it?' 'I dunno,' he said, 'go down and see.' So I thought all right, I'll go down to see now, well, to satisfy him. 'Well, no,' they said, 'he's tidy!' 'Yes,' I said, 'I do keep him tidy – *I'm* going short,' I said, 'not him.' Well, no, they wouldn't give him shoes because he was too tidy. I said, 'It's *I* gotta go short, not the children!' And he came home crying' another day – well his first long trousers it was – and he was a big boy to go to school, but he wasn't the age to leave, you see. Well he come home cryin' this day. 'Well, what the devil's the matter?' I said to him. How is it he hadn't got a patch on his trousers, 'cause so-and-so got one! And when he'd come home from school I'd make him change, put old clothes on so he'd have his good trousers to go to school, see, well he wanted a patch on it. I said, 'Now don't be so soft,' I said, 'that little boy's got a hole and that's how he got a patch.' 'Well – I'll make a hole!' 'You do! You do and you'll go back to school in the afternoon, mind,' I said – cryin' 'cause he didn't have a patch on his trousers – now then!

The second worked as a weaver both before and after marriage, as well as after her children were born:

*Would you rather not have worked?*

Well, you can always do wi' plenty when you've children – I'd three children – when you've children in house, can't you really, but you see you must say, it was a thing you did in them days . . . .

*Did you want to have three children?*

Well, don't know . . . . I'd a' liked another little girl! I'd just one girl.

*You wouldn't have liked to have six or seven children?*

Well, no, I don't think I would! Well, I mean they're hard work and all when you're young, and then when you've to go out to work and all, you've things to consider, haven't you.

*Who looked after the children when they were little and you were working?*

I couldn't tell you really, just neighbours, that's all I could say, neighbour looked after one – Doris, when I'd only Doris.

To the first woman her children were a great source of interest and pride to her, and the slightest incident took on a great deal of meaning and significance. She spent a lot of her time looking after them, of course, far more than the second woman. Certainly the children were important to the second woman, but definitely not to the same extent. Several of the weaving women boarded the children out during the week with mothers and mothers-in-law, and only saw them at weekends; this did not, however, seem to be a great source of pain or regret to these women; witness the following account from a woman who married a textile worker when she was 25 and had one child:

*Who looked after him when you went to work?*

Well me mother looked after 'im, me mother practically brought 'im up really, you know what I mean – it was always grandma, nobody else except his grandma, see. And when he were old enough he went in the army, 'cause he had to go in, it were national service then... and when we got to know he were coming home me mother says, 'He'll come here first!' I said, 'He won't, he'll come here first!' And d'you know... I went to the hairdressers an' I said, 'Oh will you be sharp, me son's coming home like'. 12 o'clock an' he hadn't come! Oh I said, 'Let's go to bed, he'll not be here tonight', when all at once a knock at door, shouts 'Hello!' and it were him and he'd knocked me mother up an' me dad was still in bed and he went upstairs and woke him up, then he come downstairs an' me mother made him his – an' I were one 'at 'ad made 'im a steak pie, like, you know! An' he had his supper like... when she opened door an' she said he just come in an' he grabbed her! ''Ey grandma!' You know – well he didn't grab me when he come home. He got hold o' me like, but he didn't make as much fuss like he did with me mum, see.

*Did you wish you could have stayed at home with him?*

No – well I knew he were being looked after, an' he used to stay with her all week, an' I only used to bring him home at weekends, see, then I'd take him back again at Sunday, an' practically, well, I think 'e'd more feeling really for me mother than what he had for me.

*That didn't worry you?*

Well, no. No, it didn't.

If we examine the role of social groups for the respondents, the criterion used to analyse whether or not they belonged to such a group was the extent to which they had any social contact either with neighbours or work colleagues, other than in times of emergency, and if such contact was fairly regular. To some extent, this is similar to Bott's measurement of 'network-connectedness', but considers specifically social interaction between *women* and not simply between couples. Table 33 gives the result of dividing

**Table 33**  *Participation in a social group according to marital role-relationship*

| Social group | Joint role-relationship | | Segregated role-relationship | |
|---|---|---|---|---|
| | (%) | number | (%) | number |
| strong | 40 | (6) | 65 | (9) |
| weak | 60 | (9) | 35 | (5) |

*Source*: Interviews

respondents according to role-relationships. Of course the 'joint' category in this table comprises many women who worked full-time, yet this category is still noticeably weaker in social group participation than the segregated category. Dividing respondents according to their relations to the economic system, the differences became even more marked, as Table 34 shows. The weakness of social group participation among women who stayed at home is striking; the strength among full-time workers is hardly surprising, given that the majority of such respondents were working in large factories. Why was social group participation so weak among those staying at home?

On the whole, it was *not* a result of actual physical isolation from other women. Of the six women who lived in rural areas, two were part of a social group and four were not. The two who were part of a social group lived in small villages; of the four who were not, one was married to a policeman and felt 'a policeman's wife never has friends, nobody wanted to know you'; of the other three, it seemed primarily a result of a deliberate 'policy', and to a lesser extent, a result of physical isolation. Witness the following comment from a woman in Essex who had worked as a barmaid before marrying a decorator at the age of 20; they lived in a hamlet where there were only three cottages; they had four children; asked whether she had many friends, she replied:

I had friends, but we weren't living near them anywhere you know, I was never one to make a lot of friends, I was always one to keep myself to myself.... Even now I'll be quite friendly with anybody, but I would never think of going to someone else's house.

Among many of the women, but in particular those staying at home and/or having joint marital role-relationships, there existed a definite taboo on entering other people's houses, except in times

**Table 34**  *Participation in a social group according to women's relation to the economic system*

| Economic relation | Strong participation (%) | number | Weak participation (%) | number |
|---|---|---|---|---|
| at home | 14 | (2) | 86 | (14) |
| part-time | 60 | (3) | 40 | (2) |
| full-time | 89 | (8) | 11 | (1) |

*Source*: Interviews

of emergency. Interestingly several respondents stated that not visiting neighbours was a result of their husband's wishes – wishes which were often more akin to orders as this extract shows:

*Did you see much of your neighbours?*

Yes.

*Did you pop in for cups of tea and that sort of thing?*

No. I don't think we did that so much, you know, my husband didn't like this popping in business!

*What if you were ill or something?*

Oh, they were good then, yes.

Another interview illustrates the same point:

*How did you get on with your neighbours?*

I hardly knew them. I've never gone in people's houses, you know, having cups of tea and things like that. I've always been friendly with my neighbours.

*Why do you think that was?*

Well, in the first instance, when I got there, my husband said to me, 'Now listen, I don't like neighbours in the house having cups of tea and gossip and I don't like coats hanging on the door.' So I suppose really that it was a habit that I never went into other people's houses.... But with the neighbours we were always friendly, if she needed help I'd help her and when my father died she came in and helped me and it's always been like that. But I've never been in the habit of going in and sitting and listening to a lot of gossip.

These attitudes were far more pronounced among the women from the South-East and, in particular, among those women who said it was considered shameful, and whose husbands felt it to be shameful, for a woman to work after marriage.

The norms and values were, it would seem, an integral part of the domestic ideology of couples where it was firmly believed that the male should be the sole breadwinner (and where, in terms of employment, he was capable of being so), where the woman's place was quite definitely in the home, and where the home was above all a private area reserved for the family and for family activities. The ideals also tended to go hand in hand with joint marital role-relationships. The effects of ideals of family size, decision-making, and use or non-use of birth control will be discussed after I have examined those women who stayed at home, but had segregated marital role-relationships.

The husband's relation to the socio-economic system for women who stayed at home and had segregated role-relationships was varied. Five were married to skilled workers, two to semi-skilled workers, one to an unskilled worker, and two to men who were in commerce. The occupational experience of the women prior to marriage, however, was far more uniform: seven had worked in isolated occupations (i.e. domestic service or stayed at home), while of the remaining three, one had worked in a factory, one as a shop assistant and one as a clerk. Given, too, that those occupations classified as isolated were also wholly domestic in nature, then the consequence was that the women saw themselves, and their roles, once they were married, as entirely domestic and also isolated. Such beliefs and perceptions were conducive to the formation of a more segregated marital role-relationship. Further, the nature of their occupations, in contrast with, say, factory work or clerical work, was such that they were unlikely to have experienced much interaction with, communication with, or collaboration (in a work sense) with *men* on a basis of sharing and/or relative equality. Once married, the experience of this was likely to continue between husband and wife within the context of the family.

Segregation and isolation within marriage frequently led to bitterness and an atmosphere of undeclared warfare, as is evident in the following extract from the Essex woman quoted earlier, who had worked as a barmaid and married a decorator. Her hatred for her husband is evident in her intermittent use of the word 'it' when she refers to her husband (as well as to the girlfriend).

*Did he ever help out with the housework and things like that?*
No.
*The children?*
No. Hopeless.
*What about when you were ill?*
Just had to get on with it.
*Did you go out together much?*
No. Never.
*Did he go out?*
Oh yes, drink, drink, drink.
*Did you ever go out on your own?*
No. I was at home . . . . Oh one occasion he brought a girl home. He did. Yeah.

*What were you supposed to do?*

Entertain it. Yes. The funny part was he brought a fellow with them – tried to palm me off on him. So whether it was daft or not, that's what it done. Another time it came home and I said to him, you got any money? It said, 'No' – now this was really horrible – he said, 'No' (my mother was here), so I said, 'Well, it's time you had some' – I hadn't had any for weeks and weeks, my mother had kept me. And you know those old-fashioned purses? They sort of lap over – well, he threw one into my lap, and of course I thought it was full of money. But it weren't – it was full of whatsits [sheaths]. My mother sat there on the couch – I was *never* so embarrassed in all my life. I just took it and threw it in the fire – we had an open fire – and mum looked at me and said, well that's something to do with a purseful of money, isn't it? When he threw it at me he said, 'That's all the money I've got.' So you can imagine what life has been.

*Why have you stuck it out?*

Left him twice. Well I came back the first time because Linda got married. And I was worried about Jack, you see, being an asthmatic.

*You left the kids here?*

Yes – there'd be no fun in taking the kids with me, that'd be what he wanted.

Among all the couples in this group there was virtually no sharing of leisure activities by husband and wife, and while some of them were obviously fairly content with the situation, it was only among these couples that there were examples of real cruelty and bitterness. Nor did the husbands help out in any way with the housework. Most of them, however, took an interest in the children, and would spend some time with them. Not surprisingly, there was little evidence of any glorification of domesticity and family life among these women. While they were all devoted to their children – 'my kids were everything to me' – it was a devotion unlike that evident among the 'joint' couples. The women often used the children against the husbands in a number of ways; many became over-involved with, and over-indulgent with the children in an apparent attempt to compensate for their lack of shared time and affection with the husband.

Some of these women obviously found refuge, as it were, with friends and neighbours. A high proportion of them formed part of quite tight-knit social groups although, whether they became involved as a result of the segregated nature of their marriage, or vice versa, is difficult to tell. The general impression was that it was the fact that the husband himself belonged to his own social group, usually centred around pubs or clubs, that drove the wife to seek friendship and company among other women in her community. The following interview is quoted at length, as it shows very clearly a number of the characteristics of these couples: the isolation of the wife, the domination by, and often cruelty of the husband, the lack of family life and an ideology of family life or domesticity, the lack of communication between partners, and the potential influence of a social group on such women in terms of beliefs, ideals and information – and often very misleading information. This woman had worked in a factory, married a miner when she was 21, and lived with her husband's brother and his wife for several years after their marriage; they had two children:

My husband was a very dominant man, very strong – headstrong – gambler, used to spending money, all his money on himself. Now he had it to share with me, but he was too – he was so that he wouldn't let me go to work, all my friends would drop like that, you see, getting married like that, I was dropped from everybody. There was no invitations to the wedding, it was a registry office wedding, and we had a day at New Brighton and that was it. And the next day him and his brother were out, and his wife and me sat with our noses to the window watching traffic go by, and we did that *every* night. He never stayed in one night at home for years, her and I were together on our own . . . . Now for two years, short of two years, every month there was a row – terrific row! Because I was – had a period. I was called everything under the sun because I didn't conceive. Well, I used to talk to his mother and I was on the verge of a nervous breakdown one time and I went home to my mother and she said, 'You married the wrong man, you're not properly mated.' And his mother said, 'You should never a' married him, he isn't for you, he isn't your kind.' But after this holiday with me mother and that, when I came back . . . we did! Well, nine months after the boy was born. Well, you see, a *boy* – I was everything the world wanted – *he*, the child, was everything he wanted, it was marvellous what a difference *that* made!

*He treated you better after that?*

Oh yes. Yes, there was – he still had me where he wanted me, he still went out and left me.

*Did he drink?*

Yes, Oh yes, yes, shocking. That's where he went every night, drinking. Every night from the day we were married . . . and Emma and I sat there with our noses to the window, and she was slightly deaf – she was very quiet, you couldn't – she wouldn't give me any information about – any kind, she wasn't that kind of person . . . . She'd go out and leave me in the house and chat to another woman, and this woman would ask her questions, like, how much do they pay you for living with you?... So she'd tell her, well, we bought in for ourselves, me husband gave me a wage, you see, and I did all the buying in, I did all the cooking, she did hers.... But she was always first, first in the morning to get her husband off, and then I'd do it afterwards, and this woman used to put her up to things, and she'd come back in sometimes and she wouldn't speak to me, she'd sulk for weeks on end, and I never knew what was wrong. So sometimes I couldn't bear it, and I'd say to me husband, 'What's the matter with her? She hasn't spoken to me for nearly a fortnight, ever since she went to Win's she's never spoken to me.' He says, 'Have you done aught you shouldn't do?' I says, 'Not that I know of.' 'Have you not cleaned your room up or have you not done this?' I said, 'No.' He says, 'Have you been out anywhere and not told her where you were going?' I said, 'No', because living with them I felt obligated to.... So he says – he called her Liz, her name was Emma! – 'Oh,' he says, 'what's matter between you and wife, Liz?' She said, 'Nothing.' 'Nothing? There must be,' he says, 'come on, get it off your chest.' 'Well,' Win says, 'you should pay me a bit more for use of t'cruet!' I'll never forget it as long as I live! He said, 'BLOODY HELL, is that all you want?' He says, 'I'll buy a pound of salt and a packet of pepper', he says, 'why haven't you said sommat before now?'

She then describes how after some years of marriage, they slept in separate bedrooms; for three years she haemorrhaged and never told her husband. Finally she went to a doctor, who diagnosed it as a fibroid on the womb, and told her that she would have to be operated on immediately.

The doctor asked all sorts of questions, like, he says, 'You have two children, haven't you?' He says, 'Boy and a girl? You don't want any more, do you?' You know, penny never dropped with either of us, so we said, 'No.' Well we didn't, I didn't want any more, and he was happy, he'd got his lad and I'd got the girl, and nothing penetrated at all. All we were frightened of was, was I going to die? So he said, 'You're all right? You're satisfied?' 'Yes', and still didn't tell us anything, so I went in January 3rd – scared to death, terrified.... Anyway I woke up, the nurse came round and she was smackin' me face with something wet about 6 o'clock and she said, 'Come on, come on, it's time you woke up, you been asleep long enough,' she says, 'come on, your husband'll be in in a minute or two and all your worries are over now,' she says, 'you'll never have any more periods'. OH MY GOD! I couldn't have been more shocked! I says, 'WHAT?' And she knew she'd gone too far – 'cause I'd had a hysterectomy and he never told me I were ever having one.... Well, from that minute on I deteriorated. I was terrified because as a wife, we women when you get together as neighbours, anybody who'd ever had that, well, was the talk of the neighbourhood sort of thing. Oh, after I'd had one that was it. Well, you were always told by neighbours your husband would never touch you again after *that*, no feelings, it was like doing nothing and nobody, to be rude, husbands never wanted wives that had had that operation. So that was the first thing that come into me head. I thought, he's just started to be nice to me and now he'll never want me again . . . . Well on Sunday night I could feel myself, oh it were beautiful, floating out through the window, lovely, and they were all round the bed in the night . . . and you'd drainage pipes and all sorts of things and neighbour from across the road said, 'Don't you want to live?' I said, 'Well, I didn't know they were going to do that to me. My husband won't want me.' Well, when he come at Monday night they had him over there, shouted at him – a woman, motherly woman, she says, 'Do you know you nearly lost your wife last night? Everybody was awake, they were all round her bed fighting for her life.' He says, 'What for?' She says, 'Well she learned that she's had this hysterectomy and she thought you wouldn't want her any more. We know it's an old woman's fallacy, but we all believed it.' 'And oh,' he says, 'we'll alter that.' He comes across, he says, 'You've only one thing to do lass', he says, 'that's get better and come on home,' he said, 'I'll show you whether I want you or not.' He could see the other side of it! He could see he could have aught he wanted without any bother! Selfish, selfish . . . he were a singer, you know, used to go in clubs singing. I gave up, gave up going, yes . . . every club he went to he filled, and he could sing, and he used to sing old loving mother songs – and he used to make 'em cry, and they used to love him. When he used to come off the stage there'd be first one woman and then another, arms round his neck, and come and sit here and have a drink with me – he'd pay for the table's round of drinks while they sat there on their own. Well, too much of it, that got me down, I'm not going any more, I said, I'm sitting there like cheese at fourpence – and I didn't drink, well, he'd buy me a drink to make it look as though he was looking after me – that drink would last me all night, he could top it up with lemonade . . . . Oh yes, he'd umpteen women, different women. One half of the world doesn't know how the other half's living, and what's upsetting me now is I've got me freedom, I can do what I like, I can manage on me pension – but me health's gone!

Throughout this interview it was evident that she did not accept her husband's behaviour, her position and their role-relationship, and that her ideal would have been a more joint marital role-relationship. A few of the women in this group did seem to accept the situation, but the majority felt, like this woman, that their marriage did not work out as they would have liked it to, which suggests that the ideal of a joint role-relationship was fairly normative among many sectors of the working class at this time.

Let us now consider how the relations of couples to the economic system and their type of family organization affected ideals of family size, decision-making about use of birth control as well as their success or failure in achieving their ideal. Looking first at the relation of women to the economic system after marriage, Table 35 gives the ideals of family size which they expressed, and which they believed were those of their husbands.

Of the women who stayed at home, it is interesting to note that *all* had a clear ideal of family size, and that they, much more than the women in the other two groups, had a high proportion who would have liked to have had four children. This would probably have been a result of their economic situation as full-time housewives and mothers; the home and the family were the centre of their lives; children did not conflict with their roles, but rather enhanced them. Why, then, did many of them not manage to achieve their ideals of family size? Table 36 attempts to answer this question. Of the women who did achieve their ideal, all but one had a joint marital role-relationship; of those who had more than their ideal, all but one had a segregated role-relationship. This certainly suggests, in spite of the small numbers involved, that Rainwater's hypothesis that marital role-relationships are a crucial determinant in the achievement of a couple's ideal of family size was valid in the past as well as the present.

It is interesting, too, that among this group (i.e., women at home), only 20 per cent of them used reliable methods of birth control:[2]

**Table 35**   *Ideals of family size and achieved family size according to women's relations to the economic system*

| Ideal number of children | At home | | Part-time | | Full-time | |
|---|---|---|---|---|---|---|
| | wife (%) | husband (%) | wife (%) | husband (%) | wife (%) | husband (%) |
| 1 | 25 (4) | 6 (1) | 20 (1) | 20 (1) | 22 (2) | 11 (1) |
| 2 | 44 (7) | 56 (9) | 20 (1) | 20 (1) | 56 (5) | 44 (4) |
| 3 | – | – | – | – | – | – |
| 4 | 31 (5) | 6 (1) | – | – | 11 (1) | – |
| didn't care | – | – | 60 (3) | – | 11 (1) | – |
| didn't know | – | 32 (5) | – | 60 (3) | – | 45 (4) |
| achieved family size | 2.5 | | 4.4 | | 1.9 | |

*Source*: Interviews

**Table 36** *Percentage of women at home who achieved, or did not achieve ideal of family size, and reasons*

| Achieved ideal | Those who had more | | Those who had fewer | |
| | accident | husband's decision | health reasons | didn't happen |
| (%) | (%) | (%) | (%) | (%) |
| 38 (6) | 12 (2) | 12 (2) | 25 (4) | 12 (2) |

*Source*: Interviews

two used the sheath, one a diaphragm, one was sterilized (for health reasons), while nine used withdrawal and two used nothing at all. Of the couples who had more than they wanted as a result of 'accidents', *all* were using withdrawal. Of those who did achieve their ideal, one used withdrawal, two a sheath, one a diaphragm, one nothing at all (one, or both, were apparently subfecund) and one had a hysterectomy. Achievement of family size was, it would seem, at least partly a result of using more reliable means of birth control.

The question arises, however, as to why couples with a joint role-relationship came much nearer to achieving their ideal of family size than those with a segregated role-relationship. First, those with a joint role-relationship tended to have discussed such matters *before* marriage, while those with a segregated role-relationship did not. The following extract is from a woman who worked in textiles before marrying a miner at the age of 26; they had two children:

*Did you ever talk about the size of family you wanted before you were married?*

Oh yes, oh yes, definitely. With my husband, Oh yes, definitely. We had an understanding *there*.

*Before you got married?*

When we was – after we was engaged. But yes, oh definitely. No, he was very, very good, very respectable in – he respected my feelings in every way and I *so* appreciated it, and I think that's why it was that I – I settled so well down here [she had come from Yorkshire and moved to the Rhondda when she married]. Oh it was lovely. 'No,' he said, 'Mary, we won't have any children until you say yes.' And so I thought, well, he's respecting my feelings and – so that was nice.

Bearing in mind that women who had joint role-relationships when married, also tended to have worked in non-isolated occupations before marriage, it would seem that this experience had important effects on their ability to discuss topics relating to sex and birth control with their husbands both before and after marriage. Women who had worked in isolated occupations, and who often had segregated role-relationships once married, had seldom discussed such matters before marriage, and many not even after marriage. The next extract is from a woman in Essex who had worked as a domestic servant, married a crane driver at the age of 21, and had six children:

*Did you ever discuss, before you got married, about having children?*

No, dear, no... I was innocent for a long time I think, really, you know.

*When you got married did you talk about such things?*

No, no − it's just that I went a long, long time [before they could have any children], and I did suffer, so I went to the doctor's and he gave me some medicine and that must have put me right. We wanted children, definitely, oh definitely, yes.

*But you never sat down and thought when, or how many?*

No, no.

*Did you want to have lots of children?*

Oh we never even really thought about it, it just happened, I guess, and we loved them and that was it.

*You never took any precautions?*

Did! That's − eight years, or nine years rather!

*How did you find out what was available?*

Oh, I think my husband, I think.

*So then you decided you wanted to have the other ones?*

No, no, it was one of those accidents, I guess.

What distinguished the couples with joint role-relationships in this group from those with segregated role-relationships was not only that they tended to discuss their ideals of family size and birth control between themselves before and after marriage, which the segregated couples did not, but that, although all used mostly male methods of birth control the joint couples made their decisions about family size *together*, while among the segregated couples if and when such a decision was made, it was invariably the husband's decision. The following two extracts illustrate this: the first is from the woman in Essex married to a male nurse; they had a joint role-relationship. Asked whether she and her husband had planned their family, she had this to say:

Well, we didn't really, because I had womb trouble when I was 18 and the doctor told me then that I should never have any children – he was the doctor of both of us, you see, and he said, 'I suppose you're getting married one day, so you must tell that young man of yours that you'll never be able to have any children.' And we talked it over for a while, he said I could adopt some perhaps. But I'd only been married for about three months when I – and I told the doctor, you see, and he said, 'It can't be. It's impossible!' And he said, 'It's no good for you thinking about it. You can't carry it!' Then after the first one he said I mustn't have any more – but of course, there you are, after only a year and nine months I had the second one. I was very bad that time and he said, now definitely, you mustn't have any more children. And I said, 'Well what have we got to do about it?' So he told my husband he must wear sheaths. Well, we both wanted boys. I wanted a boy and so did my husband, we were very fond of boys. And after six years I said, 'Oh let's risk it.' And we did, and the first boy again that was a very thing . . . but anyway, I got over that and I fell again in two years, and the other one was no bother.

The second extract is from the woman quoted at length earlier in the chapter, who had worked in a factory and married a miner:

*Did you want more children after that [the first]?*

No, no. But he decided that after nine years I'd had it easy long enough – so I started again!

*You didn't have any choice in the matter?*

No, no. It was deliberate. It was deliberate – but I wasn't bothered – no, oh no. He was careful, say what you call careful – there was no precautions those days, nothing that we knew anything about – there was just careful.

Hence the ability of women who stayed at home after marriage to achieve their desired family size, and use of birth control, depended to a great extent on the nature of their marital role-relationship. This, in turn, was by and large determined by their work experience prior to marriage. Among couples with a joint role-relationship decision-making on family size tended to be a shared process, although the actual methods used were usually male methods. For the couples with a segregated role-relationship, however, decision-making was rarely a shared process, but was usually the man's responsibility, regardless of his wife's ideals or feelings – which, of course, were often not known to him.

Of the women who worked full-time outside the home, this group had the largest proportion wanting only one or two children (78 per cent). Most notable is that *none* of these women had more children than they wanted (see Table 37). Why should this have been the case? Unfortunately, many of the women in this group would not give precise information about use of birth control. It became apparent, however, that many had very detailed information on abortions and abortionists: five gave detailed, personal information, two gave abstract information acknowledging the fact that they knew it went on, but did not know anyone personally, while two claimed to have known nothing about it at all. The comparable figures for women staying at home were three, ten and three. One woman admitted to having tried to induce an abortion on herself:

I remember when I had my little boy I was going in a hot bath and they said, 'Oh take a hot bath and this, that and the other.' I tried everything but – nothing came of it. Jump off the table – yes! done that, too, put clothes up and jump down! Oh, thinking it would shake it about – but then I wasn't lucky enough.

The detail of some of the accounts, the fact that many knew of abortionists, their names and addresses – as well as the knowledge of certain home-made abortifacients did make me suspect that some of them may well have had abortions themselves, but were unwilling to admit it. There is, of course, no way of proving it, but their detailed knowledge coupled with their high achievement of their ideal of family size (as well as their unwillingness to discuss what they themselves had used) made such a suspicion at least plausible. Moreover, there had been a long tradition of widespread use of abortion among women in the textile towns of Lancashire since the early nineteenth century.

Even among those couples where both were weavers, the woman did not, or would not, give information on how the decision was reached to have a specific number of children. Certain remarks, however, did seem to imply that such decisions

**Table 37**   *Proportion of women at work who achieved, or did not achieve, their ideal family size, and reasons*

| Achieving ideal (%) | Having more (%) | Having fewer than ideal reasons | |
| --- | --- | --- | --- |
| | | *health* (%) | *'didn't happen'* (%) |
| 67 (6) | – | 22 (2) | 11 (1) |

*Source*: Interviews

were *not* usually shared, but were left to the woman. This would make sense, too, in view of the previous discussion on abortion.

Within this group there was little relation between couples' marital role-relationships and their achievement or non-achievement of their ideals of family size. Of those who had fewer children than they wanted, all had joint role-relationships; among those who did achieve their ideal, six had segregated, and three joint, role-relationships. This could be taken, again, as indicative of greater female responsibility for childbearing and birth control among this group; there is, at least, no evidence to suggest that this was not the case. On the other hand, it is possible that the apparent reluctance of these women to discuss such matters was a manifestation of the fact that they were far less important to them than to those who stayed at home. Consequently, they had trouble remembering much about them. While their cursory, often evasive, replies to questions relating to birth control could have been a result of embarrassment, their general willingness to discuss abortion suggested that this was not the case. Decision-making on family size and type of birth control would therefore seem to have been far less important to them; they were important in so far as they affected their ability to work, and it seems likely that they sought abortions if necessary, but as matters concerning husband and wife within the context of the family, they did not seem to play much part. There was little evidence of any ideal to have a small family so that the children could receive a better education or 'have a better chance in life', as was prominent among those women who stayed at home.

Analysing the reasons women offered from both groups for having smaller families, there were quite marked differences between them (see Table 38). The high proportion of women at home who gave economic reasons, in marked contrast with those at work is significant. Some of these women, of course, were married to miners who were unemployed, but there were also several whose husbands were in relatively well-paid and secure jobs who still gave this as a reason. Further, the financial situation of women who were working was, on the whole, very poor at this time; the majority of them were underemployed, and wages were very low among weavers. Why, then, were economic motives more important to those at home?

This seems to have been essentially a result of their family organization and marital role-relationships. As decision-making

**Table 38**    *Reasons for not having more children, all respondents*

| Reasons | Women at home (%) | Women at work (full and part-time) (%) |
|---|---|---|
| Economic – 'couldn't afford it' | 38 (6) | 15 (2) |
| Education — 'to bring them up well' | 19 (3) | – |
| Health – 'doctor's advice, painful birth' | 45 (7) | 15 (2) |
| Work – 'difficulties, conflict etc.' | – | 54 (7) |
| Childhood experience – 'too much of kids at home' | – | 15 (2) |

*Source*: Interviews

among those at home tended either to be a shared process or the husband's responsibility, then there was also a greater tendency for his ideals and values to dominate. Given his role as sole bread-winner, then it is also likely that economic reasons would predominate, as reasons relating to pain or the drudgery of looking after children would not be his primary concerns.[3] Few women, however, expressed economic reasons in purely financial terms, but tended rather to emphasize the standard of living aspects:

Two was enough to – to bring them up as we'd like to. You know, in the ordinary way, so that they didn't go short of anything – and we'd do what we could for them.... I said, 'Two,' I said, 'and give 'em a good education if we can.'

Economic reasons often went hand in hand with education reasons and the desire to give their children a 'good start' in life. Such reasons were invariably given by couples with a joint role-relation-ship where there was a highly developed ideology glorifying the family, the home and the importance of children generally.

There was no evidence of these ideals among the couples where both worked full-time. When they did give economic reasons they tended to be specific financial reasons, for example, that the husband was often ill and irregularly employed and that having more children would have meant financial disaster to the family. The lack of reasons expressing concern with a certain standard of living, and in particular expressing concern with their children's upbringing and education can be seen as indicative of the general lack of a domestic ideology among this group. The home, the family and children were not in any way glorified by these women as they were by those who had stayed at home all their married lives. In other words, while the achieved family size of these two groups was very similar, their *reasons* for having small families – and also it would seem their means of achieving such – were quite different.

It is worthwhile considering the high proportion of women in the 'at home' group who gave health reasons for not having more children. There were essentially three types of health reasons: first, women who had had a difficult and/or painful experience of childbirth and who themselves decided they did not want to experience it again (two women); second, those who had had a difficult and dangerous pregnancy and/or birth and were advised by their doctors not to have more children (three women); third, women who, as a result of a difficult pregnancy or birth, were either unable to have any more children or who had had a hysterectomy (two women).

These reasons were hardly mentioned by the women who worked after marriage. Of the few who did give health reasons, *all* were as a result of a hysterectomy. While this evidence is, of course, neither representative nor in any way conclusive, it does suggest that among women who stayed at home, ideals of health and the notion that pain could be avoided, were part of their general ideology. There was evidence that among the working women, doctors' advice was, to some extent, not always taken too seriously and was often disregarded, while among those at home (with one exception, quoted earlier), a doctor's advice was usually taken very seriously indeed.[4] Of the next extracts, the first two are from women who stayed at home (the first, married to an agricultural labourer, had worked as an unqualified teacher before marriage; the second, quoted previously, worked in a factory before marrying a baker).The first woman shows how she took her doctor's advice to heart:

When I married I was all set to have four boys. I was quite determined to have four boys and I wouldn't have minded, I don't think, if I'd have had ten boys – I love boys and I grew up with boys [she had nine brothers]. ... Anyhow, when she came and she was the little girl that she was ... she was definitely her father's girl. ... I thought, 'Never mind, I'll have my day when I have my son.' Well she was five when my husband had a very serious illness. We couldn't have another child before then because plainly we couldn't afford it ... . He had this very serious illness and it went to his lungs, and in those days there wasn't any cure for tuberculosis.... Well he finally made his recovery, you see, and we go to doctor and say, you know, that we didn't want her to be the only child. So she said, 'Well I can't advise you one way or the other but', she said, 'you do realize don't you that you might bequeath to a child what your husband has suffered, and you wouldn't like that?' And so we had to make a decision. Now if ever I've regretted anything in my life, I regretted listening to that doctor's opinion. I wish we'd gone ahead whatever the consequences, because if I had have had the little boy I wanted – or the boys – even if they hadn't been very well, I would have fulfilled a maternal desire that I had.

Another woman shows a similar willingness to listen to medical opinion, asked if she only wanted one child, she replied:

Well I had a very bad time with him – I was 30 when I had him, and I was in labour five days – 's truth, it's the honest truth.... We never went towards any more, because when the nurse told my husband and me that I hadn't got to have more children – there was no french letters in them days or nothing and nothing could do, but we were very careful – if we'd have had another one 'at would've been a great mistake, you see.

The third was asked whether the doctor had tried to persuade her not to go back to work; she said:

I weren't working just then when I were feeding him – he said, 'You keep him on that because he's gaining.' But anyway – somebody told me to take some beetroot wine and I talked t' doctor, an' no, he said, 'Just keep on with my pills.' But I didn't, I made this here – and it made blood you see, an' it were cheap then, beetroot. And you'd to peel it and cut it in slices and put that demerara sugar on and let it stand all night – twenty-four hours, and then you'd to get a bottle o' Guinness and mix it together. Well it did me good.

Her failure to take the doctor's advice is echoed by another woman:

In them days, you see, they couldn't have any free doctor, you used to have to cure yourselves.... An' when me dad had that herb shop the people 'at had it before they'd bought a recipe off some old lady, they give a lot of money for this recipe, an' it were called Pounds Ointment. An' we had me brother what died – his wife's cousins they'd a boy 'ad ringworms, oh, an' they were bad, and they took 'im t'hospital, they couldn't do anything at hospital wi' him, and doctor couldn't do anything. So he said, 'Have you tried that Pounds Ointment what Joe's father sells?' .... Anyway, it cured 'em. So she went to doctor's and doctor says to her, 'Well what've you been putting on?' 'Well, who would think, we've been to that herbalist's shop, we got some ointment.' WELL! You've never saw such a hullaballoo about that in all your life! If my father had sold that ointment in a shop he'd 'a been fined a thousand pound.... Were doing doctor out of a job! Well, we could sell it from home, but we were stopped from selling it at shop – 'cause it did more than they could do at hospital – than doctors could do!

The fact that women at home took more heed of professional medical advice – and none ever mentioned getting medical advice or herbal remedies and so on from friends – suggests that these couples were more influenced by the growing emphasis put on ideals of health and hygiene through national institutions such as welfare clinics, schools and the media. These probably had more impact on this group, particularly those with a joint role-relationship, as a result of their general isolation from social networks either through work or community. Their isolation would also have been reinforced by suburbanization and mobility, particularly in the South-East, which not only isolated couples but also severed their relations with traditional communities and networks.

Arguments for having fewer children on the grounds of health, education and the desire to maintain a certain standard of living were far more pronounced and elaborate among women at home in the South-East than among those in South Wales. This must have been a result partly of the severe economic situation among those in Wales; when they did give economic reasons they were usually related to unemployment and particular financial problems rather than to the maintenance of a certain standard of living. None the less, education and health were also important reasons given by the women in Wales. The fact that their reasons and their ideology of the family was generally less elaborate than those of their counterparts in the South-East was probably a result of living in a more traditional community with greater participation in community-based social groups. Among those who did not work after marriage, the more isolated the women were from social groups, the more joint their marital role-relationships tended to be, and the more liable they were to be influenced by national trends and ideologies.

In conclusion, the basic difference between women who worked and women who stayed at home after marriage was in their ideologies of the home, the family and children.[5] This ideological difference was primarily a result of their different relations to the economic system, but was also affected by their work experience before marriage as well as by their husband's relation to the economic system. Couples engaged in the same occupation (and, of course, by this time these formed a tiny minority in England and Wales as a whole) were unique in the way in which their working lives and family lives were identical, and in the way they shared responsibility for housework and childcare.

Among couples where both worked in different occupations or where the woman stayed at home, the crucial influence on marital role-relationships seemed to have been the woman's work experience prior to marriage. The precise nature of her work was also very important, in particular, whether or not it was isolated and domestic. Participation in community social groups and networks was strongly related to the nature of a woman's marital role-relationship; those with a joint role-relationship seldom belonged to a local social group and their ideology concerning the home and children was much more elaborate. Decision-making on family size tended to be shared, although the ultimate decision was the husband's (the majority used male methods of birth control) – a reflection, no doubt, of his superior power.

Women, who had a segregated role-relationship and stayed at home, usually participated more in local social groups, had a less developed ideology of the home and children, seldom discussed topics relating to family size or birth control with their husbands, and left decisions on such matters to the husband. Their ideals of family size were not clearly defined or formulated, and their average achieved family size was distinctly greater than that of those with joint role-relationships. In other words, ideals of family size and the ability to achieve those ideals, were associated with the family organization of a couple, which was in turn related to both the husband's and the wife's participation in the labour market, and occupational experience, before and after marriage. These factors seem to have been more important to the achievement of desired family size than was the type, or efficiency, of birth control used. To examine why this should have been so, and to consider the patterns of birth control of these men and women, and their beliefs and ideas about contraception, we must now examine birth control in the early decades of the twentieth century in more detail.

# 6 Birth control: clinics and communication

The history of contraception and of the birth control controversy is now quite well documented,[1] and it is not intended to reiterate it here, except in as much as it relates directly to the problems under consideration. Birth control, in one form or another, was no invention of the nineteenth century. With the exception of the development of the sheath with the vulcanization of rubber in the nineteenth century, there were no dramatic innovations in contraceptive technology until after the Second World War. Methods which were available to the population of England and Wales between 1900 and 1939 had also been available earlier; as Peel notes: 'with the exception of the oral contraceptive, there is not a single birth control method in existence today which was not already available, and available in greater variety, in 1890'.[2] Abortion and *coitus interruptus* had been known for centuries.

The questions relating to birth control that concern us here relate to the extent to which different methods were used by different sectors at different times, and the light this might shed on the debate so far. To what extent, for instance, were most working-class men and women already well aware of the possibility of controlling fertility by 1900? Where did they get such information? Why was it that birth control apparently became more prevalent among the working class during the early part of this century? To what extent was the middle class attempting to encourage preventive means of birth control and discouraging abortion, and what were their reasons? Was the decline of family size among the working class, as has often been assumed, simply a result of increased knowledge of more reliable means of birth control? Was it a case of diffusion? All of these problems will be considered, as will questions of communication patterns and information networks. It is also hoped that they may illuminate some of the points discussed earlier concerning women's work, social group formation, trends of centralization and privatization, role-relationships and the decision-making process regarding family size.

## General trends

Birth control, in one form or another, has been used since time immemorial. Abortion, *coitus interruptus* and infanticide were all means of fertility control well-known among ancient civilizations. Primitive mechanical and chemical means have also been known and used for centuries (goats' bladders as sheaths, crocodile dung as a spermicidal pessary, half a lemon used as a diaphragm, and so on), as well as a variety of folk and herbal preventives and abortifacients, some more reliable than others. The extent to which these methods were used, and by whom, is almost impossible to gauge; evidence like Wrigley's on Colyton suggests that some form of birth control was known and practised in pre-industrial society.[3] Birth control and population as issues of *public* interest and debate, however, were primarily products of the nineteenth and twentieth centuries.[4] Why was this the case?

The early 'birth controllers' of the first few decades of the nineteenth century, for example, Place, Carlile, Owen and Knowlton, were directing their information at working-class women in industrial areas, and the emphasis was not so much on 'teaching the ignorant' as on trying to persuade them to use *preventive* means instead of having frequent recourse to abortion. All evidence available indicates that abortion was known prior to industrialization, and certainly during industrialization; why the campaign at this point in time to condemn it? As Maclaren notes:

As early as the 1830s repeated reports were made of factory women seeking to induce miscarriages . . . . The recourse to abortion or infanticide (the two often confused in the public's mind) was presented by middle-class observers as the most damning evidence of the immoral influence of factory life on women.[5]

The condemnation of women working, of the immorality of factory life, and of abortion at this time coincided very closely with a consolidation of middle-class domestic ideology and the sanctification of the family. Fear of working-class political power, of the 'threat' which working women posed to middle-class values of domesticity and the family were all inextricably linked, and resulted in a general condemnation of factory life, women working and abortion. The three continued to be condemned by the middle class and resulted in state legislation on all of them during the course of the nineteenth, and early twentieth, century. Thus considering the evidence up until 1939, it seems that the birth control movement by the middle classes for the working classes was not so much a mission to instruct the ignorant, but rather a mission to convert those practising methods regarded as diametrically opposed to middle-class ideology to the use of methods more acceptable to their own ideals and values.

Up until the end of the nineteenth century, and for some sectors well into the twentieth century, the most common forms of birth control were *coitus interruptus* and abortion/abortifacients. *Coitus interruptus* is essentially a *male* method of contraception, while abortion is a *female* method. Further, *coitus interruptus* (and other mechanical means) is basically a *private* means of controlling fertility known only by those practising it; induced abortion, on the other hand, is a more *social* act involving interaction with individuals outside the nuclear family (although of course abortion can be induced privately and individually, but this is generally less effective and far less safe). The regular and relatively successful practice of *coitus interruptus* within a marriage presupposes male responsibility for control; it is also a form of power. Whatever the wife's wishes and ideals concerning childbearing and family size, the ultimate decision is a matter concerning the male alone. Abortion, on the other hand, is essentially the woman's responsibility and the ultimate decision lies in her hands.

Now, it is argued here that middle-class reaction against the prevalence of abortion in industrial areas during the nineteenth and twentieth centuries was basically a protest about, first of all, the family structure of working-class families, i.e. that female responsibility for fertility control was wrong in that it gave the woman power within the marriage. This power was reinforced by her role as wage-earner in the labour market; married women working and the practice of abortion were both seen as direct threats to middle-class values of male supremacy economically and within the family itself. Second, the fact that abortion was a social act involving initial transfer of information between women, and frequently also the performance of the act by one woman outside the nuclear family on another, was contrary to the increasingly dominant middle-class idea of the private nature of the family and married life.

The fact that middle-class agitation against abortion, especially during the nineteenth century, was expressed primarily in terms of morality indicates the threat the middle class felt to its own

ideology of women, children and the family. Parliamentary
legislation on abortion during the nineteenth century can be seen
as an attempt to impose the middle class's own morality and
ideology on the working class:

the distinction traditionally made as to whether or not the child had
quickened, retained in the laws of 1803 and 1828, was removed by the act
of 1837. In a similar fashion the 1861 Offences Against the Person Act
made it a crime for a woman to abort herself, whereas the acts of 1803,
1828 and 1837 had only penalized the abortionist.[6]

The evidence seems conclusive that, first, knowledge of the
possibility of controlling fertility was prevalent among the working
classes from the start and, second, that what the middle classes
objected to most was the way in which they achieved such
control, not the fact that they exercised it.

The reason for differential fertility between the middle classes
and the working classes cannot necessarily be reduced either to
differential knowledge at this time, or to differential efficiency.
*Coitus interruptus*, the principal middle-class method during the
nineteenth century, was no more reliable (albeit safer) than abortion.
One can only conclude that when the working classes manifested
relatively larger family size than the middle classes, it was because,
for various reasons, they wanted larger families.[7]

The differences, however, cannot simply be ascribed to social
class. The essence of the debate of *coitus interruptus* versus
abortion was one of female versus male *vis-à-vis* power and
responsibility within marriage. The prevalence of abortion among
the industrial working classes from the nineteenth century suggests
a radically different family structure, and the fact that it was
apparently most common in areas of high female employment
(particularly *married* females) suggests that the relation of both
men and women to the socio-economic system had profound
effects on family organization and the distribution of power within
marriage. Further, the social nature of abortion, in contrast with
the private nature of other types of birth control, is indicative of
the importance of social group formation and social networks
among many working-class women at this time. The type of birth
control used, therefore, might in a very general sense be seen as a
gauge of marital role-relationships and power relationships and the
relative prevalence and importance of social group formation.

Thus it is suggested that where *coitus interruptus* was used regularly and reasonably effectively (as far as this can be established), such marriages would tend to be characterized by a greater degree of power on the part of the husband. This was undoubtedly the case among middle-class sectors when family limitation became increasingly normative from the 1860s onwards. Of course, it is quite likely that the woman also wished to control childbearing, nevertheless, the ultimate power to do so, or not to do so, lay with the male  Perhaps this helps to explain why economic motives have generally been assumed to be of prime importance when the middle classes began to limit family size. Financial and money matters were very much part of the male preserve, and it is therefore likely that given the fact that the ultimate decision was his, economic motives were apt to be uppermost in the decision-making process.

In most working-class sectors, however, the female tended to remain the person who took prime responsibility for the family and the home, and it would seem that this responsibility continued, at least among certain sectors, until well into the twentieth century. As Hoggart points out:

[financially] the wife is by tradition responsible; the husband is out, wage-earning. He wants food and his own sort of relaxation when he comes home. I suppose this explains why, as it seems to me, the wife is often expected to be responsible for contraceptive practices  . . . The husband's shyness and an assumption that this is really her affair often ensure that he expects her to take care of it . . . .[8]

In working-class families where the wife did not work, the husband would of course have greater power, yet the wife still retained a fairly high degree of responsibility and power in many sectors with regard to the family and home, probably more than in most middle-class families. In these situations, too, with the wife not working, marital role-relationships would tend to be segregated; an integral part of this segregation was the wife's responsibility for the family, and thus often for family limitation as well. The information and means available to her came either from her social network and/or through advertisements. Hence the prevalence of abortions, abortifacients and methods such as Rendell's pessaries among many of the working class, a situation readily exploited by commercial firms from the late nineteenth century onwards:

it is obvious that by the 1890s a major shift was occurring. In the previous decade new vulcanization processes permitted the production of thinner, more comfortable sheaths, diaphragms, and pessaries. Cheap postal rates and advertising in the penny press gave entrepreneurs access to a mass market. Surgical shops blatantly advertised their wares in window displays and distributed leaflets. By the turn of the century the channels of birth control information ranged from the local barbershop to the advertising columns of the national press.[9]

The situation changed and varied, of course, between areas and sectors as well as over time. It seems that by the turn of the century more working-class couples were using the sheath, as well as *coitus interruptus*, abortion and abortifacients, and pessaries. The following data gives a very general idea of the pattern of change in the twentieth century; social class 1 represents the middle classes, social class 2 the skilled working class, and social class 3 the unskilled sector. Note, however, that *coitus interruptus* is often assumed by working-class couples as not constituting a means of birth control and therefore may well be under-represented in the working-class groups: 'There seems much confusion on this matter of *coitus interruptus*. Most patients do not consider it as a contraceptive method at all, and, as mentioned already, we always make special reference to it when asking them about their previous experiences with birth control.'[10] Further, the use of appliance methods is qualified by 'at some time' and does not necessarily imply regular and careful use by any of the three groups (see Table 39). Of course there is no data in this table on abortion. It seems most unlikely that only 4 per cent of the unskilled sector was using any sort of birth control prior to 1910; even given a relatively high level of fertility among this sector, clearly it was *not* the case that 96 per cent of the unskilled sector was reproducing the biologically maximum number of children during the nineteenth century. There is no way of knowing precisely what proportions sought and obtained abortions, but there is no doubt that abortion and use of abortifacients were common. Data such as these must therefore be treated cautiously.

Abortion was still very much a topic for discussion and also investigation during the inter-war period. Marie Stopes wrote in a letter to *The Times* that:

experience at our Clinic has brought staggering facts to light. Two illustrations will suffice:

(1)   That in 3 months I have had as many as 20,000 requests for criminal

**Table 39** *Percentage distribution for each marriage cohort, distinguishing three social classes, according to proportions (a) whose use of birth control has always been restricted to non-appliance methods, and (b) who had at some time used appliance methods*

| Date of marriage | Social class 1 | | Social class 2 | | Social class 3 | |
|---|---|---|---|---|---|---|
| | non-appliance (%) | appliance (%) | non-appliance (%) | appliance (%) | non-appliance (%) | appliance (%) |
| before 1910 | 17 | 9 | 17 | 1 | 2 | 2 |
| 1910–19 | 45 | 15 | 28 | 11 | 28 | 5 |
| 1920–4 | 30 | 26 | 43 | 17 | 39 | 15 |
| 1925–9 | 21 | 37 | 39 | 21 | 48 | 15 |
| 1930–4 | 24 | 40 | 34 | 28 | 38 | 25 |

*Source:* Lewis-Faning (1949)

abortion from women who did not apparently even *know* that it was criminal.

(2)    That in a given number of days, one of our travelling clinics received only 13 applications for scientific instruction in the control of conception, but *80* demands for criminal abortion.

Thus the fall in the birth-rate at present is clearly not to be attributed solely to the use of 'birth control' but to a much larger extent is due to criminal abortion.[11]

During the 1920s an Inter-Departmental Committee on Abortion was set up, and the final report was published in 1939. The conclusion was that, as far as could be known, criminal abortion had probably been increasing; the committee estimated that between 300 and 400 abortions had probably occurred daily on average over the past five years, and that approximately 40 per cent of those were criminal abortions. Various studies of hospital gynae-cological departments from 1900 to 1936,[12] estimated that from 16 to 20 per cent of all pregnancies ended in abortion, and the Inter-Departmental Committee confirmed that this was likely. Further, they found that abortion was most likely to be induced as a result of economic problems[13] and that:

if account is taken of marital status, both the mortality statistics and the figures of cases treated in hospital show that the overwhelming majority of abortions occur among married women . . . . There was some suggestion, too, that abortion is relatively more common in the case of mothers in the higher age groups than in the case of younger mothers.[14]

It seems probable from this evidence and from the data on marriage patterns in Chapters 4 and 5 that the decline of family size among the working class during the first four decades of this century was not so much a result of increased knowledge and availability of reliable birth control methods, but was a response to their changing relations to the socio-economic system, a view that fits with the arguments of others that developments in birth control alone cannot account for declines in fertility. The means by which couples achieved smaller families were varied: delayed age at marriage, increasing resort to induced abortions, and increasing use of birth control – including *coitus interruptus*, mechanical and chemical means. While it is quite possible that one couple may have resorted to all three means at various stages, it is likely that certain means were more prevalent among some sectors than others. We will therefore examine differentials in use of birth control, type of birth control, and, where possible, recourse to abortion, looking primarily at the data provided by the records of the mothers' clinic.

## Class and birth control: the clinic data

The data for the Manchester and Salford Mothers' Clinic affords a useful breakdown of contraceptive use prior to coming to the clinic. Users of the clinic cannot, however, be deemed wholly typical, even of their class, despite many statistical correspondences with national data.[15] It is probable that those women who did use the clinic were either more highly motivated (whether by economic pressure, awareness, or health reasons), or more desperate (they had on average more pregnancies than other women of their age and social class) than others from the same class. None the less, if such qualifications are borne in mind, the data are still of interest (see Table 40). Comparing these with Lewis-Faning's findings (see Appendix 1) reveals quite marked discrepancies. Much of this can be accounted for in the clinic data by differences in numbers of years married (see Table 41) and age of marriage (see Table 42). The lower the social position, the earlier the age of marriage (a national trend, of course), and the later the first visit to the clinic. The point becomes even more obvious if the data are presented as in Table 43. The high proportion of unskilled workers' wives coming to the clinic after eleven or more years of marriage suggests that recourse to contraception was, for many of these women, a desperate last attempt to control childbearing, while for the others, there would seem to have been a greater element of

**Table 40**   *Use of birth control, and type, prior to coming to the Manchester and Salford Mothers' Clinic, by husband's social class, 500 cases, 1928–33*

| Social class | None used (%) | Non-appliance (%) | Appliance (%) |
| --- | --- | --- | --- |
| routine non-manual | 35 | 29 | 35 |
| (clerks) | 20 | 27 | 43 |
| skilled manual | 29 | 27 | 43 |
| semi-skilled manual | 22 | 40 | 37 |
| unskilled manual | 50 | 20 | 30 |

*Source*: Clinic data

**Table 41**   *Mean number of years married at first visit, by social class, mothers' clinic*

| Social class | Mean years married |
| --- | --- |
| routine non-manual | 6.7 |
| skilled manual | 7.3 |
| semi-skilled manual | 7.1 |
| unskilled manual | 8.2 |

*Source*: Clinic data

planning, foresight, and desire to control family size at an earlier stage in marriage. This is similar to other findings,[16] which show that contraceptive efficiency increases after a couple attains their desired family size, and suggests that different social sectors had different ideals of family size and thus also different patterns of contraceptive use and efficiency.

This is further corroborated by examining the number of pregnancies women had had by the time of their first visit (see Table 44). This leaves little doubt that women married to unskilled workers tended not only to marry earlier and have a greater number of pregnancies, but also did not seek means of controlling fertility until much later in married life than other sectors of the population. Why was this the case?

One obvious reason could be less security. Those in unskilled jobs, particularly during this period, were undoubtedly less secure in employment and more apt to be underemployed and unemployed (see Table 45). Even if employed, there was a higher probability of becoming unemployed among the unskilled sector, and this situation of uncertainty and insecurity could have resulted in a belief that it made little sense to plan. Those in more secure positions could plan their future with greater certainty. Insecurity of employment

**Table 42**   *Age at marriage by social class, mothers' clinic*

| Social class | 16–20 (%) | 21–25 (%) | 26–30 (%) | 31 or over (%) |
| --- | --- | --- | --- | --- |
| routine non-manual | 14 | 55 | 26 | 5 |
| skilled manual | 20 | 61 | 16 | 3 |
| semi-skilled manual | 27 | 56 | 16 | 1 |
| unskilled manual | 31 | 49 | 14 | 6 |

*Source*: Clinic data

**Table 43** *Percentage of women coming to the clinic in the first three years of marriage and after eleven years or more of marriage, by social class*

| Social class | Married 0–3 years (%) | Married 11 years or more (%) |
|---|---|---|
| routine non-manual | 31 | 19 |
| skilled manual | 22 | 22 |
| semi-skilled manual | 19 | 18 |
| unskilled manual | 21 | 34 |

*Source*: Clinic data

for the husband may also have resulted in a higher desire and need to employ children as soon as possible – as noted earlier, truancy was still common at this time, particularly among the unskilled sector. These families may, therefore have wanted – or at least not minded – larger families.

Another possibility is that women with several unplanned children, who would therefore tend to be close in age, had less time and opportunity to communicate much with people who might have provided information. When looking at how women found out about the clinic, the differences were striking (see Table 46). The fact that fewer women married to unskilled workers obtained information from personal contacts could reflect less rootedness in a community, and relatively greater isolation from social networks.

The question arises as to whether use, non-use and type of contraception can in any way be employed as general indicators of family organization and marital role-relationships, as mentioned earlier. Table 47 shows a breakdown of these variables for the

**Table 44** *Mean number of pregnancies, and percentage of women having six or more pregnancies at first visit, by social class*

| Social class | Mean pregnancies | Having 6 pregnancies or more (%) |
|---|---|---|
| routine non-manual | 2.3 | 3 |
| skilled manual | 2.9 | 12 |
| semi-skilled manual | 3.2 | 13 |
| unskilled manual | 3.9 | 21 |

*Source*: Clinic data

**Table 45**   *Employment status of husbands, by social class*

| Social class | Unemployed (%) | Part-time (%) |
|---|---|---|
| routine non-manual | 7 | – |
| skilled manual | 15 | 2 |
| semi-skilled manual | 16 | 2 |
| unskilled manual | 22 | 5 |

*Source*: Clinic data

Manchester and Salford data. It is important to remember here that women from the unskilled sector tended to come to the clinic later in marriage, and after more pregnancies, than the other sectors, and that therefore usage among the other sectors would have been generally higher at the same stage in marriage. It is interesting to note that the highest percentage of couples using male methods was in the skilled and semi-skilled sectors, and the lowest among the unskilled. Further, if the sheath, pessaries and cap are taken as being more reliable methods, it is clear that the lower the social position, the less effective the methods used. What inferences can be drawn from these data?

First let us consider the routine non-manual sector. As these women came to the clinic on average earlier than others, one can assume that they wished to control childbearing sooner and probably had lower ideals of family size than the other sectors. The fact that there was a high proportion of female methods of contraception in this sector suggests two possibilities regarding their family organization and marital role-relationships: on the one hand, it could be indicative of a segregated role-relationship with the female taking a large degree of responsibility for the family and for birth control, while the male regarded such matters as of little

**Table 46**   *How women found out about the clinic, by social class*

| | Personal (%) | Institutional (%) | Media (%) | Other (%) |
|---|---|---|---|---|
| routine non-manual | 57 | 21 | 18 | 4 |
| skilled manual | 60 | 31 | 7 | 2 |
| semi-skilled manual | 67 | 25 | 8 | – |
| unskilled manual | 49 | 38 | 7 | 6 |

*Source*: Clinic data

**Table 47**  *Use, non-use and type of contraceptive by sex of user and by social class*

| | Male methods | | | |
| | none | coitus interruptus | sheath | total |
| | (%) | (%) | (%) | (%) |
|---|---|---|---|---|
| routine non-manual | 35 | 24 | 9 | 33 |
| skilled manual | 29 | 22 | 18 | 40 |
| semi-skilled manual | 22 | 33 | 10 | 43 |
| unskilled manual | 50 | 15 | 12 | 27 |

| | Female methods | | | | | | |
| | pessaries (%) | douche (%) | sponge (%) | pills (%) | cap (%) | other* (%) | total (%) |
|---|---|---|---|---|---|---|---|
| routine non-manual | 12 | – | 2 | 4 | 9 | 7 | 27 |
| skilled manual | 13 | 4 | 2 | 2 | 3 | 7 | 24 |
| semi-skilled manual | 14 | 6 | 1 | 1 | 1 | 12 | 23 |
| unskilled manual | 5 | 5 | 2 | 2 | 1 | 8 | 15 |

*abstinence, safe period

*Source*: Clinic data

concern to himself. On the other hand, it could indicate a relatively joint role-relationship where both partners took a certain, if not equal, amount of responsibility regarding family organization and size, and where they decided that the female methods were safer and more satisfactory to both partners. As the principal female methods in this group are the most reliable ones, and in view of previous discussions of the socio-economic situation and marital relations of this group and the likelihood that these women would have had greater exposure to information and new ideals through work experience prior to marriage as well as through the media, then it seems most likely that the pattern of contraceptive use could be taken as a broad indicator of a joint role-relationship and joint decision-making process concerning family size and contraceptive use. The socio-economic situation of the routine non-manual sector, their tendency to isolate themselves from social groups, their precarious economic position at the time, and a greater emphasis on home and family life all suggest that family size and contraceptive use would be issues which were considered important and relevant to both partners.

Second, in the skilled manual sector, the use of the sheath was higher than among any other social sector. The higher percentage of men using contraception and the fact that there were fewer pregnancies on average than in the other manual groups suggest that the men in this sector were taking more responsibility, and with more success, than among the unskilled. The greater differential between male and female methods could indicate a greater power differential between partners, as had been the case with the middle classes in the nineteenth century. In other words, while it would seem that marital role-relationships were in one way becoming more joint, with more participation on behalf of the male in family life and responsibilities, one effect of this was to give the husband greater power within the family and home than had previously been the case, when such matters had been regarded primarily as the wife's concern.

It is probable that this development was partly a result of national trends, partly a result of a more secure economic situation for the men, and of a tendency for fewer married women to work in this sector. Unfortunately there are no data on the participation of these women in the labour market, but the census data for 1911 showed that only 7.6 per cent of all married women in Manchester and Salford were employed, which although above the national average was much lower than that of the textile towns, Bethnal Green or Stoke-on-Trent, and it is reasonable to conclude that few of the women in this sector would have been employed. The fact that nearly two-thirds of them found out about the clinic through personal contact is indicative of the presence and influence of some sort of local social network; this would tend to suggest a more segregated type of role-relationship than that of the routine non-manual sector. Some of these trends might appear contradictory; it is suggested that what these data indicate is a process of change occurring where marital role-relationships were becoming somewhat more joint (perhaps also less equal) among this group; social groups and networks were obviously still important for these women, but probably less so than previously. The skilled worker's family was becoming somewhat more isolated and the marital role-relationships within it less segregated.

Third, the characteristics of the semi-skilled sector are very similar to those of the skilled sector. The exceptions to this are that *coitus interruptus* was more widely used, and the sheath less so, while the more reliable female methods were also used less. In other words, while use of some form of contraception is similar to that of the skilled sector – indeed, greater – the methods used were less reliable. It is therefore not surprising that women from this group had had a greater number of pregnancies. The fact that there was actually a greater percentage of men using contraception in this sector than in all others – *coitus interruptus* was used by a third – suggests either a less responsible and rational attitude towards control of family size and/or a greater degree of ignorance. Certainly the high proportion of men taking the initiative on contraception would seem to indicate a greater power of the men within marriage in this group. The data do not provide any ready answers or clues as to why this might be so; it is possible that their motivation to control fertility was as great, perhaps even greater, than that of the skilled and routine non-manual sectors, but that their socio-economic situation was such (less security economically, possibly, less rootedness) that they had less access to information networks, etc.

The relatively high incidence of abstinence and the safe period does suggest both a mutual agreement and sharing of decision-making concerning contraception, as well as a lack of knowledge of reliable means of doing so. This would support the contention that in this group, motivation was not lacking, but for various social and economic reasons, adequate knowledge of and access to reliable means of birth control was. As far as it is possible to gauge, contraceptive use would suggest a pattern of marital role-relationships similar to that in the skilled sector, with the important exception of weaker social group formation and social networks, and also therefore a tendency for somewhat greater isolation.

The unskilled sector is quite markedly different from all others; a relatively high level of fertility has persisted here over time, as has the tendency to marry younger – the two are obviously linked. Why has this been the case? Is it a reflection of a fatalistic attitude towards the potential of controlling one's environment, as Rainwater and Askham maintain? What causes such an attitude in the first place?

The low proportion of men using contraception suggests that marital role-relationships tended to be far more segregated here than in the other sectors, and that the family was regarded as being primarily the woman's concern and responsibility. The reasons for this were varied; first of all, employment opportunities for men tended to be poor and irregular and the nature of their jobs (when they had them) more isolated; more frequent changing from job to job would mean they had less chance of becoming part of a social group through shared work experience, thereby having less access to information networks or new values and norms concerning the family. They would thus have been more likely to retain beliefs and norms developed during childhood experience of the parental home. Second, women in this sector were less likely to have had work experience prior to marriage which would have been conducive to the exchange of information and exposure to new values; their employment was likely to have been as domestic servants, laundry workers, outworkers etc., jobs which tended to be isolated. Frequent childbearing from an early age and the likelihood of moving frequently as the husband changed job (or as the bailiffs called, if he were unemployed) both meant less likelihood of having access to local social groups after marriage. In addition, children in these families may well have still been considered as something of an asset economically, given that truancy and illegal work before school-leaving were still quite common among this sector in the first few decades of the century.

Less exposure to new values, beliefs, norms and information for such couples meant a greater likelihood of their retaining parental values, which were likely to entail notions of a segregated role-relationship, female responsibility for the family and a higher ideal of family size. These people, too, were likely to have been least affected by national trends in the realm of education (many of them probably worked before school-leaving age), the media (they were less likely to be able to afford the cinema, a radio, even newspapers and magazines, and moreover, were far less likely to have the *time* available to enjoy them) and suburbanization, improvements in housing (council houses were too expensive for a great many of this sector) and improvements in the standard of living generally. Thus the unskilled sector was in many ways the most isolated sector, but their isolation tended not to be isolation resulting in more joint marital relations as it was for many in the other sectors, but was characterized by segregated marital role-

**Table 48** *Number of miscarriages, by social class*

| Social class | 1 (%) | 2 (%) | 3 or more (%) | Total (%) |
|---|---|---|---|---|
| routine non-manual | 15 | 5 | – | 20 |
| skilled manual | 11 | 4 | 4 | 19 |
| semi-skilled manual | 16 | 6 | 3 | 25 |
| unskilled manual | 22 | 7 | 1 | 30 |

*Source*: Clinic data

relationships where the men tended to dismiss family affairs as being matters concerning the woman alone, while the women were not in a situation to have ready access to alternative information through social networks. Because of their relations to the socio-economic system, these couples tended to be more isolated from national trends, from local social groups, and also from one another.

What about the incidence of abortion among these women? Of course there is no reliable data, but it is none the less worthwhile considering the figures on miscarriages (shown in Table 48), bearing in mind that the Inter-Departmental Committee on Abortion estimated that *at least* 40 per cent of all miscarriages were as a result of induced abortion. The high incidence of miscarriages among the unskilled and semi-skilled sectors suggests that abortion was a more common form of fertility control among these groups. This would certainly fit with the theory that marital role-relationships, particularly among the unskilled, tended to be more segregated, and family matters left largely in the wife's hands. While the high incidence of abortion does indicate the existence of social groups and networks among these sectors, I would suggest that in view of their relations to the socio-economic system, these groups would tend to transmit values, norms and information of a more traditional nature, and would not necessarily entail exposure to *new* belief-systems or information, as might well have been the case for the skilled workers' wives.

Considering the place of residence of clinic attendants, the data suggest that there may well have been social interaction between women married to men from different social classes, but that there was a tendency for wives of unskilled and semi-skilled workers to form a social group separate from wives of skilled workers. Certainly the fact that a higher proportion of the unskilled sector obtained information about the clinic from institutional sources (welfare centres, health visitors, midwives, etc.) is interesting. The low proportion obtaining information from personal contacts substantiates the theory of weaker social group formation; the reference from institutional sources indicates that this was the group most affected by middle-class and state efforts at promoting use of preventive methods of birth control. The unskilled and semi-skilled sectors also constituted the greatest proportion of attendants at other clinics (apart from Wolverhampton and Birmingham), as shown in Table 49. Making allowances for differences in occupational structure between the areas, and also for Himes's system of classification (e.g. he classifies *all* miners as unskilled in the case of Cannock, which is certainly open to criticism), it seems apparent none the less that the birth control clinics were having more appeal to, and more impact on, the unskilled sector of the population. Given the paucity of clinics, their concentration in large urban areas, and the fact that women from this sector apparently spread, and received, less information between themselves, it is doubtful whether the impact of the clinics on this sector throughout society as a whole can have been more than slight. Nevertheless, the large proportion of unskilled workers' wives seeking advice from the clinics does indicate a real demand for more explicit and reliable information on contraception from these women.

**The role of birth control**

The question still remains, however, as to why there was an increase in working-class use of mechanical means of contraception during the early twentieth century, whether this was usually linked to the decline in family size, and whether or not it was a result of middle-class diffusion of ideals and information to the working class.

The debate as to whether the increased availability of more reliable birth control methods created an increased demand for them among the working class, or whether the demand stimulated the supply, is difficult to disentangle. Nonetheless, as birth control and abortion, in some form or another, were both known and practised among what would seem to have been a fairly sizeable proportion of the working class during the nineteenth century (if not earlier), it would seem that both the increased commercialization

**Table 49** *Summary of occupational status of husbands at various birth control clinics (data collected 1927)*

| Location of clinic | Unskilled (%) | Semi-skilled (%) | Skilled (%) |
| --- | --- | --- | --- |
| North Kensington | 37.9 | 32.8 | |
| Manchester | 32.6 | 11.1 | 31.0 |
| Wolverhampton | 12.6 | 5.6 | 77.9 |
| Cambridge | 32.0 | 17.0 | 25.2 |
| Liverpool | 46.8 | 16.2 | 19.6 |
| Birmingham | 24.2 | 13.9 | 40.0 |
| Glasgow | 34.6 | 18.0 | 24.6 |
| Aberdeen | 38.5 | 7.3 | 20.2 |
| Cannock | 100.0 | | |

*Source*: Himes (1931)

of contraceptives and abortifacients and middle-class efforts to promote preventive means as opposed to abortion were responses to – and exploitation of – an already existing demand. As Peel comments: 'the increased popular demand for contraceptives during the first quarter of the twentieth century brought about a multiplication of retail outlets, an abundance of variations in the basic established products, but few significant innovations in technique or improvements in manufacture'.[17] Increased commercialization, however, coupled with the rapid expansion of the media and discussion of the issue therein, cannot but have resulted in a greater awareness of the *possibility* of controlling fertility with preventive means among a large section of the population. Awareness of such a possibility, of course, is by no manner of means equivalent to *motivation*.

The reasons for changing motivations towards smaller families have already been discussed at length. But if the motivation was already there, and if knowledge of traditional means of birth control/abortion was fairly prevalent, why the increase in use of mechanical means? Obviously increased awareness of these methods, and the realization that they were safer and more reliable, played an important part. More important is the fact that the changing relations of certain sectors of the working class to the socio-economic system led to an increased *privatization* of the family and of married life. An integral part of this trend was the tendency for marital role-relationships to become more joint, for a weakening of community-based social groups, and for an increasing emphasis on the importance of family life and leisure. It was pointed out earlier that contraception, as opposed to abortion, is essentially a private act between marriage partners. Thus one important result of the increasing privatization of the family among the working classes at this time was also a tendency to resort to the use of more private means of birth control. The differentials between working-class sectors, regarding contraceptive use, sex of user and recourse to abortion, are all, in a sense, important indicators of the extent to which various sectors had been affected by these trends.

Is this, then, evidence of diffusion of middle-class ideals and ideology of the family, evidence of the *embourgeoisement* of the working-class family? If *embourgeoisement* is interpreted as 'aping the middle classes' and their ideals and values, then the answer is certainly no. Privatization of the working-class family, increasing emphasis on ideals of domesticity and shared family life came about primarily as a result of the changing relations of all members, but particularly of women and children, to the socio-economic system and, in particular, their changing patterns of participation, and experience, in the labour market. Their new domestic/family ideology was essentially a reaction to, an interpretation of, and a glorification of, these new relations. Further, although many working-class women and children, through increased dependence on working-class men as sole breadwinners, were in an apparently similar position to middle-class women and children, the similarity stopped there. Working-class children were expected, on the whole, to find employment by the age of 14 and to contribute to the family income until marriage; this was not the case for most middle-class children. Educational facilities and career prospects were radically different for the two classes. Many middle-class women were still able to hire domestic servants/ charwomen to perform the bulk of their domestic drudgery, thus freeing themselves for a greater participation in activities outside the home. Working-class women were expected to, and expected, to perform all domestic duties in their own home, and relatively little time or money was left for other activities besides simple leisure pursuits such as walking or occasional visits to the pub or cinema: 'The wife's social life outside her immediate family is found over the washing-line, at the corner-shop, visiting relatives at a moderate distance occasionally, and perhaps, now and again, going with her husband to his pub or club.'[18] In other words, the position of working-class women and children within the family was, in many ways, different to that of their middle-class counterparts, and thus the *meanings* attached to them and to their roles in society also differed; there was not an identical, universal domestic ideology shared by both the middle classes and the working classes. The fact that family size and contraceptive use among the working classes was becoming similar to that of the middle classes did not necessarily mean that their reasons for limiting family size were identical.

On the other hand, it could also be argued that these new relations of the working class to the socio-economic system were a direct result of middle-class intervention and influence through state action and policy. Through middle-class beliefs that child labour was immoral and 'inhuman' (or in other words, it conflicted with their definition of children and their role in the family and in society), ideals which were in direct opposition to those held by most of the working class, the middle classes were able to enforce a longer period of dependence and compulsory education on all working-class children. Once the actual relations of children to the economic system had thus been radically changed, it was inevitable that children would take on a different *meaning* to working-class parents, and that their ideals of children, the family and family size would also be significantly altered. A similar process occurred in areas/occupations where the employment of married women was either discouraged or expressly forbidden. Distinct separation of home from work in state policies concerning council housing, planning and New Towns are similar examples.

Thus, privatization of the working-class family, the development of a domestic ideology, and changing motivations for smaller families were not direct results of middle-class ideals and practices 'filtering down' the class system, but were rather a result of the changing economic and social position of working-class individuals achieved as a result of parliamentary legislation in response to middle-class political pressure. In this sense, it can certainly be said that middle-class ideology *did* affect the working classes, but that the effect was achieved through political action and superior political power which altered the relations of working-class women and children to the economic system, and also, through Education Acts, Housing Acts and so on, to the social system. It should be pointed out, however, that many of these changes were also a result of increasing pressure from the male-dominated trade unions

– much of which was pressure for a 'family wage', that is for men to be sole breadwinners with an adequate wage to keep women and children as dependants. These changes resulted in turn in a redefinition of values, norms and beliefs concerning women, children, the family and family size among the working classes.

It cannot be denied, however, that in the first half of the twentieth century, when variables such as family size and contraceptive use are examined in conjunction with class variables, there is a definite pattern whereby the 'highest' social classes have smaller families and use contraception more, decreasing down the social scale to the 'lowest' class manifesting the largest families and the lowest proportion of contraception use. This pattern, at first glance, does seem to suggest some process akin to diffusion.[19] However, such patterns depended to a great extent on the relations of those sectors to the socio-economic system and considerable variations based on geographical area and occupation existed, i.e. considerable variations existed *within* the class category, and these classifications often mask important variations based on other criteria besides that of social class.

To illustrate this further, the data for the Manchester and Salford Mothers' Clinic showed quite definitely that the most prevalent means whereby women coming to the clinic obtained information was from personal contacts; this indicated the importance of information networks and social groups based on local community. Lella Secor Florence, on the other hand, made the following comments in a discussion of her work with the birth control clinic in Cambridge during the same period:

A great many patients come to the Clinic quite secretly, determined to conceal their visit from their mother-in-law or their grandmother who disapproves of birth control, or from their neighbour, who would be likely to broadcast the news. It has not been our experience, as it seems to have been at other clinics, that women discuss birth control with their neighbours and send their friends to the Clinic after they have been themselves.... We made a practice of always asking the patient how she heard about us. Apart from a considerable number who are sent by medical men, the great majority read the advertisement, which appears every week in the newspaper, and come alone on their errand.... 'I keeps myself to myself', they say.[20]

Now the *class* structure of the husbands of women attending this clinic was in no way unusual; it was in fact very similar to that of the Manchester clinic. Social group formation, however, would seem to have been extremely weak in Cambridge in comparison with Manchester and Salford. This seems to substantiate the contention made earlier that the processes of centralization and privatization tended to be far more pronounced in the South-East than in the rest of the country. Similarly, the occupational structures for both men and women were very different in these two areas, and this affected social group formation, work experience prior to marriage, marital role-relationships and social networks.

The findings of Secor Florence are, in fact, very similar to those from the interviews carried out in North-East Essex, particularly that of much weaker social group formation and isolation/ privatization of the family. For the interview data in Burnley and South Wales, however, just the opposite was the case. These differences cannot be explained in terms solely of social class as defined by the male's occupation, and point again to the difficulties, as well as the potentially misleading nature, inherent in both use of social class as defined by the male's economic situation and of national data which give no idea of the extent of differentials and variations between areas and occupations.

To conclude, the increased use of mechanical means of birth control by the working classes can be seen, at one and the same time, as a reflection of their changing ideals, or 'targets' of family size, brought about primarily by the changing nature of their relations to the socio-economic system, and as a response to the national trends of centralization and privatization of the family. Differentials in contraceptive use between social sectors can, in a very broad sense, be regarded as indicators of the extent to which various sectors were affected or not affected by these trends. In particular, different patterns of contraceptive use according to the sex of the user throw an interesting light on changing patterns of, and variations in, marital role-relationships and power relationships.

It must also be remembered, however, that an increasing use of birth control at this time by the working classes was by no means their only response to their changing socio-economic situation and their new ideals and beliefs concerning family size; the increased use of birth control was also paralleled with an increasing number of induced abortions and a tendency to defer marriage. This latter trend is completely invisible if national statistics alone are consulted. In other words, the working classes' response to both national and local trends affecting their relations to the social and economic systems, and their ideals of family size, was highly varied.[21]

Had preventative means of birth control *not* been available on a large scale at this time through commercial outlets, and to a much lesser extent clinics, there would still have been a decline in family size among the working classes. It would have been achieved, however, through the generally less reliable traditional methods of *coitus interruptus* and abortion. The fact that these methods were less reliable would have meant that the decline might have been somewhat less rapid and less pronounced. Nevertheless, use of mechanical methods was not *that* extensive, although it was increasing. Moreover, age at marriage might then have been even further delayed and the result would have been much the same. There can be little doubt that the escalation of the birth control movement, the establishment of birth control clinics, the efflorescence and expansion of commercial contraceptive firms and their advertising, the rapid growth of the media in which these issues were increasingly discussed and advertised, as well as the eventual, if reluctant, endorsement of birth control by both the state[22] and the church,[23] affected the awareness and knowledge of contraception among the working classes. Equally, there can be little doubt that the *motivation* to restrict family size was already present; in many sectors and groups, achievement of smaller family size preceded these developments (for example, textile workers in the nineteenth century). Knowledge of birth control without motivation to restrict fertility is essentially useless, witness the dismal failure of the birth control campaign in recent years in India.[24] The motivation was present, albeit in varying degrees, among the working classes during this period, indeed for many prior to 1900, and therefore it is only possible to conclude that the birth control movement was in no way a *cause* of the decline of family size among the working classes. It did, however, make the means by which the desired family size could be achieved safer, more reliable and, for some, also more accessible.

# Conclusion

The structural changes occurring in the socio-economic, political and cultural spheres between 1900 and 1939 significantly altered the relations of all working-class individuals to these systems, albeit in different ways and degrees. These changes in turn led to new meanings and values among the working class, to new interpretations of their situations and, in particular, to the meanings ascribed to the family, work, women, children and family size.

These changes affected everyone in one way or another, but it has been shown that those affecting women were of much greater significance than has often been supposed. Arguably the most important changes were in the economic and occupational spheres. While there was a gradual 'opening-up' of new occupations to women, there was a decline in residential domestic service and an increase in the proportion of women in the clerical, semi-skilled and unskilled sectors. Parallel to this was a decline in the number of married women working and an increase of single women working. This change in the relation of working-class women to the economic system according to marital status was important. As we have seen, it was partly a result of the changing nature of the economy and industry, but was also very much a result of changes in working-class men's relation to the economic system and, in particular, the increasingly widespread assumption that a man's wages should be sufficient to maintain a wife and children as dependants. This concept of the wife and children as dependants was increasingly reinforced by state policies, which had earlier been influenced by middle-class ideologies of domesticity and childhood. The result for working-class wives was that, although many enjoyed a higher standard of living than had earlier generations and few experienced the 'double burden' of paid work outside the home and unpaid work within it, they were nevertheless dependants and as such were more subject to a status of subordination to the husband. While their comforts increased, to a great extent their power decreased.

On the other hand, these factors must be considered in conjunction with the changes that occurred for single women. The increasing proportion of single women in clerical work, semi-skilled and unskilled factory work and the decline of residential domestic service meant that many more women were experiencing greater exposure to new values and information as well as greater independence before marriage. This was, to a great extent, reinforced by the rapidly expanding media and mass literacy. Many women were therefore less isolated, more educated and more exposed to information and wider values concerning marriage, the family and reproduction. The overwhelming emphasis in these new values, however, was on women's place within the home and the fulfilment of their 'natural' roles of mother and wife.

More women were experiencing greater independence prior to marriage and, paradoxically, less after marriage. Nevertheless, the interview data has shown how their pre-marital experience affected their attitudes to, and subsequent behaviour in, marriage. The result of this generally was to increase communication and sharing of responsibility between marriage partners. Thus, questions relating to childbirth and family size were becoming more of a shared issue between husband and wife. Shared responsibility in turn meant more responsibility, and this generally meant smaller families. This correlation between joint marital role-relationships, contra-ceptive effectiveness and smaller families has also been noted in contemporary studies.[1] Thus, one of the crucial developments during this period among the working classes was an increase in joint marital role-relationships, but a decrease in equal relationships.

The changing position of children also had important effects on family structure and, in particular, on women within the family. State policy, through the education system, prolonged the period of dependency for children; it also increased the possibility for higher education and individual social mobility for working-class children. These developments coupled with the dramatic decline in infant mortality, meant not only that working-class parents could assume all their children would reach maturity, but that all their children would be more of an economic liability for a longer period of time than previously.[2] It also put additional pressure on women in particular to be 'good' mothers and to give them a better chance of achieving success.

The development of psychological theories related to the impor-tance of childhood, of medical opinion emphasizing the need for better standards of nutrition, health and hygiene during childhood all contributed to an increasingly elaborate 'ideology of childhood'. Central to this ideology was the concept of a happy, clean home environment; the responsibility for creating and maintaining this environment was invariably seen as the married woman's principal role. The ability to achieve it, however, was directly related to the husband's capacity to earn an adequate and regular wage as well as to the couple's ability to control childbearing. A large family both weakened the economic basis and put too many demands on time and space for the mother. Implicit in both ideologies of childhood and domesticity was the importance of a small family.

Social changes that had important effects on working-class families were also numerous. The increasing growth of suburbanization, increased mobility and the revolution in transportation led to a weakening of social groups and networks for men, women and children. Better housing facilities, the provision of council houses, the growth of home ownership and the gradual rise in the standard of living generally meant that working-class housing was increasingly more spacious, comfortable and hygienic. These trends, coupled with more state intervention in employment, health and so on led to an increasing privatization of many families. Some of the functions previously performed by, and within, the community were now controlled by the state,[3] while others were consolidated within the family unit. Leisure pursuits (the cinema, the radio, the seaside holiday) became noticeably more family- or couple-oriented, rather than based on social groups within the community. This, too, had crucial implications for family size; the ability of a working-class family to enjoy home-centred leisure pursuits together, to be able to afford a mortgage or rent for a council house to a great extent precluded the possibility of a large family.

Political developments were also important. The incorporation of the Labour Party into the political system, the decline of trade union membership and the various defeats suffered by the radical working-class movement (epitomized by the General Strike of 1926) led to a decline in working-class hope for radical change through political action, and an increasing belief in the possibility of *individual* social mobility for their children through the education system. For those who held such aspirations there were serious financial problems: in particular the need to prolong a child's period of dependency. This, too, was a strong motive to restrict family size.

These changes did not apply equally to all sectors of the working class, nor to all families within a sector. Variations can be seen primarily as a result of different relations of the family to the socio-economic system and, in particular, variations in occupational experience, job security and community structure. These criteria resulted in different belief-systems, marital role-relationships and power relationships.

Thus, women whose pre-marital occupational experience had been isolated, with little exposure to information networks (the prime example being domestic service), were likely to enter marriage with little knowledge of what it entailed, or indeed, the possibility of a means for controlling reproduction. They were apt to regard topics relating to sex as taboo and to see their role in marriage solely as one of continued, but unpaid, domestic work. Many of these women married men from the unskilled or semi-skilled sectors, with low job security and a liability to unemployment, underemployment and the frequent necessity to move in search for work. This, in conjunction with the probability of frequent pregnancies and the taboo on discussing sex, made their chances of becoming part of a community-based social group of married women with its networks of information less likely. They were more isolated both from community and husband, less secure financially, and more apt to have segregated unequal role-relationships. Knowledge of, and responsibility for, birth control was apt to be ill defined between partners. Relative lack of exposure to the ideologies of domesticity and childhood all meant that, unless the husband was highly motivated to control reproduction (and this was exceptional), they were the group most prone to uncontrolled, or poorly controlled, reproduction, and their family size tended to be larger than that of other working-class groups. Family size among this group, however, did decline and, on the basis of the clinic data, one of the most salient factors in the decline must have been the intervention of, and information provided through, state health agencies, ante-natal clinics and, where available, birth control clinics.

Areas and groups characterized by high unemployment during the 1920s and 1930s did not correlate as closely with fertility as has often been assumed, particularly when demographic factors were considered. Fertility and family size in mining areas, for instance, dropped quite dramatically, while fertility in areas such as Liverpool remained relatively high. The census data has suggested that the cessation of in-migration into South Wales after 1911 led to a general consolidation of community; that the second and third generation male immigrants were less likely to see large families as essential economically, as their fathers and grandfathers had. Community-based social groups for women were strong and there was a widespread knowledge of, and access to, abortions and abortifacients. More important, perhaps, was that male unemployment often resulted in a shift in power relations within marriage; male economic supremacy was weakened, many men staying at home, doing some or most of the domestic work while their wives and children tried to supplement the dole through part-time work. Furthermore, the ideology of childhood tended to be strong within this group; many thought it of utmost importance that their children should not suffer the hardships and uncertainties which they were suffering themselves, and consequently put great emphasis on the importance of social mobility for their children through the education system. This can also be seen as a reaction to their political defeat, an acknowledgement that group mobility was impossible and that the only chance was for individual mobility – for their children. The importance of the family and home, but in particular of small family size, was therefore crucial to these beliefs.

The low fertility of textile areas since the nineteenth century has long puzzled demographers, as has the association between married women working and low fertility. The interview data has indicated that the relation of married women and their husbands to the socio-economic system, the nature of their occupations, resulted in a marital role-relationship quite distinct from that of other groups. Where both partners did similar work in the same, or similar, workplace, they tended to have a joint and equal role-relationship. Domestic chores were seen as tasks to be shared and not simply as the woman's role. Because these couples spent relatively little time at home, there was no evidence of a glorification of the home and domesticity: a domestic ideology was absent. Similarly, there was an evident lack of an ideology of childhood or the belief that the woman's primary task was childrearing, the latter often being left to nearby kin or neighbours. Children conflicted with the mother's work, they were an economic liability and as a potential threat to the mother's health, also posed a threat to the mother's earning capacity, which was seen by both partners as essential. Textile workers therefore wanted small families. Their ability to control reproduction successfully can be seen partly as a result of more open' knowledge of and discussion of sexual matters in both family and workplace, between men and women, the married and the single, and as a result of the relatively equal marital power relationships prevailing. Family size and successful control of reproduction was an issue of crucial and equal importance to both partners.

The decline in family size among the working class can thus be seen as a result of the changing relations of working-class men, women and children to the socio-economic, political and cultural systems. These changes led to a new interpretation of their situation, their roles, their families and children. Many of these changes came about as a result of state legislation which, while not necessarily designed to reduce working-class family size, nevertheless created the conditions for this as a response. State policies restricting child and female labour, instituting compulsory education, improvements in health and hygiene were a result of combined pressures from various middle-class groups, the trade unions and general economic changes. While both pressure and ensuing policies were often well imbued with middle-class domestic ideology, it is not viable to see all of these changes as a direct attempt to diffuse middle-class values to the working class. The male-dominated trade union movement played an important part in pressing for many of the changes increasing women's and children's dependency. Variations were primarily a result of the different impact of these trends at a local and occupational level.

Crucial to all these developments was the changing nature of women's relations to the socio-economic system. While the association between married women working and low fertility has been noted and analysed elsewhere, the findings of this research indicate that the association is less clear-cut. The data have suggested that a woman's reproductive behaviour is primarily a result of several factors. First, it depends on her occupational experience before marriage and the type and nature of her work. This period in a woman's life-cycle seems to be the most important one for her formation of ideals and knowledge of marriage, family life and family size. Second it depends on whether or not she works after marriage and childbirth, and the nature of that work. During the early part of this century, marriage was the dividing-line between participation or non-participation in the labour market for women; the contemporary pattern tends to be the birth of the first child.[4] During this period of a woman's life cycle, this research has indicated that it is the nature, and above all, location of women's work that affects fertility. Agricultural work, outwork etc. are not associated with low fertility because they do not conflict with a woman's role as childbearer and childrearer. Only when work is distinctly separate from the home does it become associated with low fertility. This supports the findings of other recent research on women's work and fertility.[5] Third, it depends also on her husband's relation to the socio-economic system, his occupational experience, job security and so on. Fourth, it depends on the relation of children to the socio-economic system, their period of dependency, chances of survival, education opportunities and emotional value. All these factors affect marital role-relationships and power relationships, the extent of knowledge of reproduction and birth control, and the degree of communication between marriage partners. These in turn determine both the desire and the ability to limit family size effectively.

To conclude, while this pattern seems to explain much of the decline of family size among the working class between 1900 and 1939, there are also indications that it would apply to other time periods. Further research is needed to explore in greater depth the influence of pre-marital occupational experience on women's ideals and subsequent reproductive behaviour. Research of a detailed nature following women's life cycles to explore in greater detail the effects of participation in the labour market at different points in time is also needed to understand better how this affects the timing and spacing of children, as well as completed family size. More work analysing the effects of marital role-relationships and power relationships on reproductive behaviour is also needed. Much of this research has been merely suggestive; a great deal still remains to be done in this field. Hopefully further research will begin to move away from the usual narrow economic approach to fertility and begin to see questions of fertility and family size as central issues affecting, and affected by, broader social, political and ideological trends, and subject in turn to *interpretation* by individuals. More than this, it is time to consider problems of this nature in terms of the relations of *all* individuals to society; the usefulness of social class as determined by the male's relation to the labour market is very limited indeed.

# Appendix 1
## The population structure

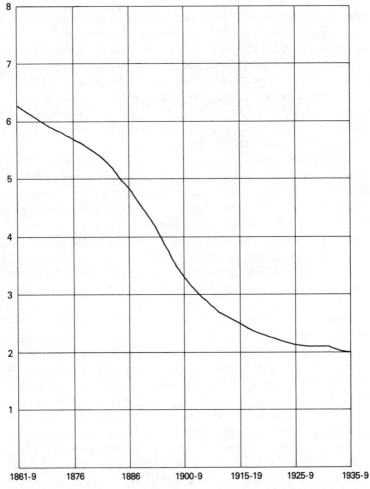

Figure 1  *The decline in family size by marriage cohorts, 1861–1939, England and Wales*

*Source*: Royal Commission on Population (1949)

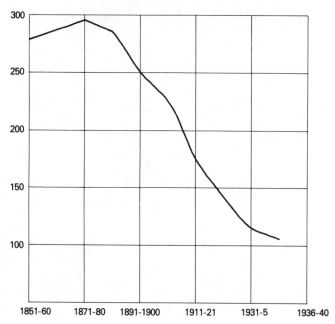

Figure 2   *Marital fertility rate, 1851–1940, England and Wales*

*Source*: Royal Commission on Population (1949)

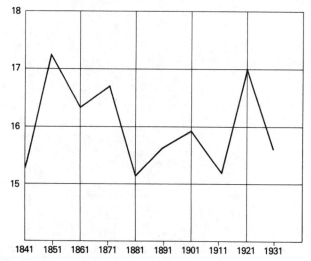

Figure 3   *Decennial marriage rates, 1841–1931*

*Source*: Royal Commission on Population (1949)

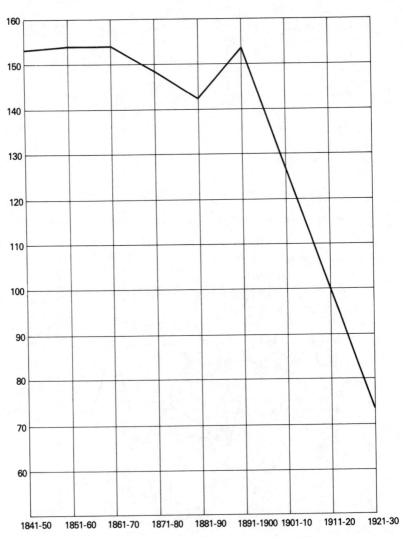

Figure 4   *Deaths under 1 year per 1000 births, 1841–1930*

*Source*: Royal Commission on Population (1949)

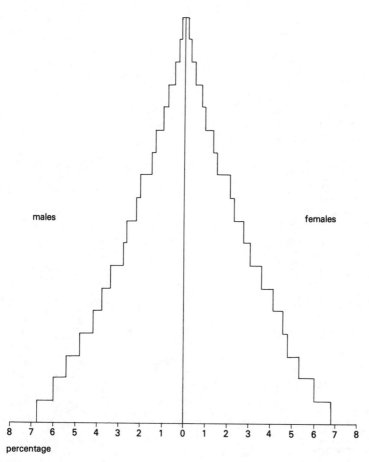

Figure 5 *Population structure of the UK by quinquennial age groups, 1871*

*Source*: Census (1911 and 1931)

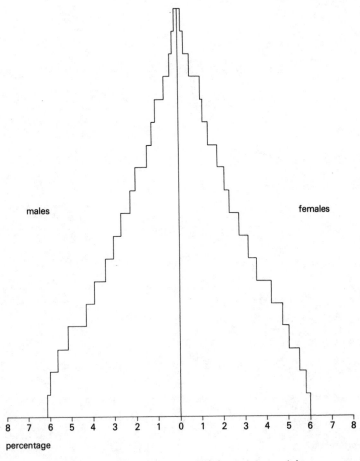

males                    females

8  7  6  5  4  3  2  1  0  1  2  3  4  5  6  7  8
percentage

Figure 6  *Population structure of the UK by quinquennial age groups, 1891*

*Source*: Census (1911 and 1931)

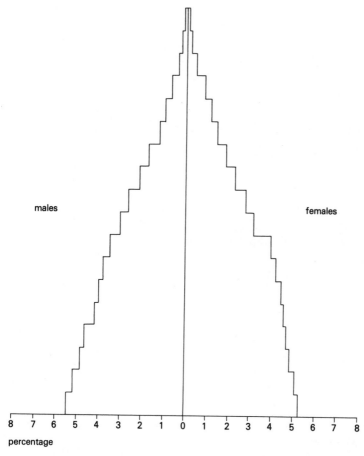

males females

percentage

Figure 7 *Population structure of the UK by quinquennial age groups, 1911*

*Source*: Census (1911 and 1931)

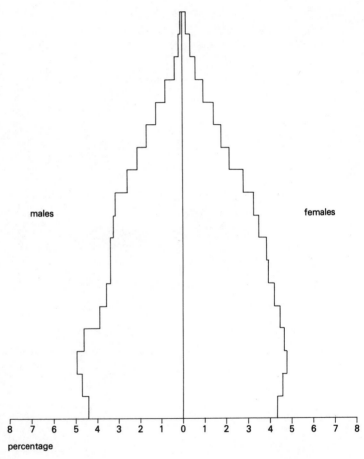

Figure 8 *Population structure of the UK by quinquennial age groups, 1921*

*Source*: Census (1911 and 1931)

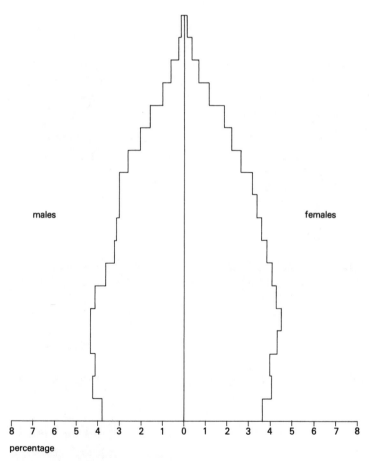

males          females

8  7  6  5  4  3  2  1  0  1  2  3  4  5  6  7  8

percentage

Figure 9  *Population structure of the UK by quinquennial age groups, 1931*

*Source*: Census (1911 and 1931)

**Table 50**   *Percentage distribution of social class in the Family Census, the 1931 Census and the Manchester and Salford Mothers' Clinic records*

| Social class | Family Census (%) | 1931 Census (%) | Clinic records (%) |
|---|---|---|---|
| 1 professional, etc. | 2.9 | 2.7 | 0.2 |
| 2 intermediate between 1 and 2 | 5.3 | 16.2 | 17.8 |
| 3 skilled workers | 53.8 | 48.5 | 41.2 |
| 4 semi-skilled workers | 26.8 | 16.9 | 12.6 |
| 5 unskilled workers | 10.7 | 15.7 | 25.0 |
| 6 unoccupied or no information | 0.5 | – | 3.2 |

**Table 51**   *Birth control use (any type) by social class, for the Family Census (marriage cohorts 1920–34) and the clinic records (use of birth control prior to coming to the clinic)*

| Social class | Family Census (%) | Clinic records (%) |
|---|---|---|
| 1 professional, administrative and routine non-manual | 59 | 65 |
| 2 skilled working class | 61 | 71 |
| 3 semi-skilled and unskilled working class | 60 | 64 |

**Table 52**   *Average family size, manual and non-manual, for the Family Census (cohorts 1910–29) and the clinic records*

| Social class | Family Census | Clinic records |
|---|---|---|
| non-manual | 2.0 | 2.3 |
| manual | 2.9 | 3.4 |

**Table 53**   *Percentage using appliance methods, by social class, for the family census (all cohorts) and the clinic records (prior to coming to the clinic)*

| Social class | Family Census (%) | Mothers' clinic (%) |
|---|---|---|
| 1 | 66 | 35 |
| 2 | 43 | 43 |
| 3 | 34 | 34 |

# Appendix 2
## The interviews

Respondents were contacted initially through wardens of sheltered accommodation in the relevant areas. I gave the wardens detailed information as to age groups, occupational experience and so on, and left them to select appropriate respondents who were willing to be interviewed.

Although I never used an interview schedule in the interview itself (I found this tended to inhibit a good relationship between myself and the respondent), nevertheless I had designed a schedule and always covered all the topics in it. As some respondents, however, were less willing to talk about personal and intimate questions than others, in some cases certain questions were phrased differently or omitted. The interview schedule is therefore more of a guide to the *type* of questions and the general subjects covered than a precise description of every question asked.

While thirty interviews were carried out, one provided very scanty data as the tape recorder had not recorded properly. Thus in many of the tables in previous chapters calculations are made on the basis of twenty-nine respondents.

### The interview schedule

1   *General information*

Respondent's name, address, marital status, year of birth, birthplace.
Year of marriage; place of marriage.
Husband's year of birth, birthplace.
Mother's date of birth, birthplace, occupation.
Father's date of birth, birthplace, occupation.
Number of children, sex, dates of birth, birthplaces.

2   *Family life during childhood*

How many brothers and sisters did you have? Can you remember how many years there were between them. Where did you come?

Can you remember any of your brothers and sisters being born? If so, were you at home? Was your father at home? Who was there? What exactly do you remember about it?

Did either your mother or father ever explain anything about birth or sex to you? Your periods? If not, who did?

Did your father do any jobs in the house? What were they?

What jobs did you do in the house? Your brothers? Your sisters?

Do you remember if your mother and father went out together? About how often? Where would they go?

Did your father go out by himself? About how often? Where? Your mother?

Do you remember if your mother worked when you were young? What did she do?

If she went out to work, who looked after the children?

Was your father ever unemployed? If so, what do you remember about that time?

Did you or your brothers or sisters ever work before you left school? What did you do? About how much did you earn? Was the money yours to keep?

Did you ever wish you had fewer brothers and sisters? More? How many would you have liked to have had? Why?

How did you get on with your brothers and sisters?

Was your mother an easy person to talk to? Your father?

Would you say that your parents were strict?

Did either of your parents cuddle you much as a child? Did they play with you? Read to you?

[If the family was larger than three children] What would you say were the advantages of being part of a large family? The disadvantages? [Repeat for small family if less than three children]


## 3   *Kinship and leisure during childhood*

Do you know where your mother's parents came from? Their occupations? What about your father's parents?

Did any of your grandparents live near you when you were young? If so, how often would you see them? Do you think they ever helped your parents in any way? Did you ever stay with them? Did they ever stay with you?

Do you know how many brothers and sisters your mother had?

Your father? Did any of them live nearby? How often would you see them? Do you know if they ever helped your parents in any way? Did your parents ever help them?

If your mother was at home in the evening, what would she do? Your father?

What did you usually do in the evening? Your brothers and sisters? Were you allowed out in the evening? Did you have to be back at a certain time?

Who would you play with? Where did you usually play? Did your parents let you play with whomever you wished?

Did the whole family ever take a day's outing? How often? Where? What about a holiday?

4   *Education, religion and politics during childhood*

How old were you when you started school? Did you like it?

How old were you when you left? Why did you leave? Have you got any qualifications or certificates?

Did the other children at school come from a similar sort of home as yours?

Did your parents go to church? What denomination were they? Did you go?

Did you go to Sunday School? Until what age?

When you were older, did you stop going to church? Why?

Could you work or play on Sundays if you wished?

Was your father interested in politics? Your mother? Did they ever discuss politics? Do you know if your father or mother belonged to a trade union?

Can you remember if your father was ever on strike? For how long?

Were you interested in politics when you were young?

What class or group would you say your family belonged to? Did most of your friends belong to the same group?

Were there any families that were particularly popular? Why do you think this was so? Were there any particular unpopular ones? Why?

5   *Occupational experience before marriage*

When you left school, did you get a job? What was it? Did you choose the job yourself? If not, who did? Why?

What sort of work did you have to do? What hours did you work? Did you like it? How did you get on with your employer? Did you belong to a union?

Did you work on Saturdays? Sundays? Did you have a holiday?

Did you give any of your wages to your parents? How much? Do you remember what your wages were?

Did you have many friends at work? Were they about the same age as you?

Were any of your friends boys? Were any of them married? Can you remember what sort of thing you talked about together? Did you ever talk about getting married? Having babies?

Did you and your friend(s) go out together? Where would you go? What would you do?

For how long did you work in your first job? Why did you leave?

What jobs did you have after that? Description, dates.

Were you ever without a job? For how long?


## 6    *Courtship and marriage*

When did you start going out with boys? Where did you usually go? When did you have to be home?

For how long did you know the man you married? Were you engaged? For how long? What did your parents think of him?

Would you have liked to have married sooner or later than you did? Why?

How old were you when you got married? Your husband? Did you have a church wedding?

At the time, what did you see as the advantages of getting married? And the disadvantages?

Before you got married, did you and your husband ever talk about having children? How many would you have liked to have had? And what about your husband? Did you want to wait a while before having any? Why?

Did either of you save any money before you got married?

Did you want to work after you got married? What did your husband think?

What was his occupation when you married? Had he had other jobs? What were they?

Can you remember how much he was earning when you got married? And you?

Was he ever unemployed? When? For how long? How did you manage?

Were you ever unemployed? When? For how long?

Did your husband belong to a union? Was he ever on strike? When?

Did you belong to a union? Were you ever on strike? When?

Which of you paid the bills?

## 7   Housing

Where did you live when you got married? For how long?

How many rooms were there in the house/flat? Was there an inside lavatory? A bathroom? What sort of heating was there? Lighting? Garden? Did you have an allotment?

Did you ever own a house before 1939? If so, did you ever have trouble with mortgage payments? When? Do you remember how much they were?

[If lived in rented accommodation] How much rent did you pay?

Why did you move from the first house/flat?

Could you give me an account of all the houses or flats you lived in up until 1939?

Did you live near any of your relatives? Which ones? How often would you see them?

Did they ever help you in any way? How? When? Did you ever help them? In what way? When?

## 8   Married life

Did your husband ever help with any of the housework? Exactly what jobs would he do? What *wouldn't* he do?

How did you manage if you were ill? What would your husband do?

Did you go out together much? Where would you go? How often?

Did you go out by yourself? What would you do? How often? Your husband?

Did you enjoy housework? What parts of it did you like especially? And what parts did you dislike?

If you were at home in the evening, what would you usually do? Your husband?

Did you ever have a radio? Can you remember when you first had one? Did you listen to it much?

Did you get a daily paper? Which one? Any magazines? Which
ones?

Did you or your husband belong to any clubs? What were they?


9    *Children and family life*

Did you enjoy being pregnant? For all of your pregnancies?

Did you have any difficulties with childbirth? Was it painful?
How long were you in labour? Did the midwife/doctor use
forceps?

Did you have your children at home? Was your husband there?
What about the other children? Was anybody else there?

How did you feed your baby/babies? When were they weaned?

What did you like best about looking after a baby? And least?

What jobs would your husband do with the baby when it was
small? And what wouldn't he do?

Would you have liked to have had more children? Fewer? What
about your husband?

Did you talk about how many you wanted after you were married?

Did you or your husband ever use any kind of birth control? What
did you use?

Did you use anything before your first child was born? Afterwards?

Did anyone ever advise you not to have any more children? Your
doctor? Your parents? Friends? Neighbours?

Did you ever know anybody who tried to get rid of a pregnancy?
How?

Would you have liked more boys? More girls? Fewer of either?

What do you think is the perfect family size? Why?

Do you think it is a good or bad idea to have children close
together? Why? And how close?

How did the birth of your first baby affect your household routine?
The others?

Did you do any work, full-time or part-time, after you were
married? After you'd had children? What sort of work? When?

Who looked after the child/children when you worked?

What would you say were your ambitions for your children?

Did any of them stay at school? What qualifications did they get?

Would you say you were close to your children? Closer than your
parents were with you? Why do you think this was so?

Did you cuddle your children? Read to them? Play with them?
Would your husband?

[If more than one] How did they get on together?

Would the whole family ever do things together? Such as? Did you go on any day's outings? Holidays?

Did you mind who your children played with? Where did they usually play?

Did any of them work before leaving school? What sort of work?

Did they give you any of the money?

Did you give them any pocket money? How much?

Do you think you were strict with your children? As strict as your parents?

Did they go to Sunday school? When did they stop?

Did you talk to your children about how babies are born? Did you explain about periods?


## 10   Community life

How did you get on with your neighbours?

Did you see them often? How often?

Did you 'pop in' to one another's houses much?

What sort of things would you talk about?

Did any friends or neighbours ever give you any advice on child-birth? Birth control? How to get rid of a pregnancy? Did you take their advice seriously?

[If worked] Did any of your friends at work talk about things like birth control or how to get rid of a pregnancy?

Did your husband have any friends from work? Would he go out with them when he wasn't working? Where would they go? How did you feel about this?

Did he have any friends among your neighbours? Did they go out? Where would they go?

Did you ever go to an ante-natal or post-natal clinic? Were they helpful? Did they ever give you any advice about how many children you should have?

If you were upset about something, who would you usually talk to about it?

If you needed help, who would you go to?

If you were ill, did you usually go to the doctor? What if the children were ill?

**Table 54**  *The respondents*

| Date of birth | Siblings | Occupation before marriage | Occupation after marriage | Husband's occupation | Family size |
|---|---|---|---|---|---|
| 1913 | 1 | (1) domestic servant (2) barmaid | – | decorator | 4 |
| 1907 | 1 | domestic servant | – | policeman | 3 |
| 1904 | 1 | book-keeper | – | tram driver | 2 |
| 1900 | 7 | (1) laundress (2) shop assistant | – | nurse | 4 |
| 1905 | 1 | domestic servant | – | decorator | 2 |
| 1899 | 3 | secretary | – | businessman | 1 |
| 1893 | 4 | tailoress | – | (1) baker (2) labourer | 1 |
| 1898 | 8 | domestic servant | seasonal farm work | fisherman | 9 |
| 1904 | 3 | clerk | clerk | engineer | 1 |
| 1902 | 2 | typist | | clerk | 1 |
| 1907 | 10 | assistant teacher | outwork/lacemaking | agricultural worker | 1 |
| 1894 | 7 | at home | outwork/sewing | miner | 4 |
| 1896 | 5 | shop assistant | – | miner | 4 |
| 1911 | 8 | domestic servant | – | miner | 3 |
| 1897 | 3 | delivered milk | – | miner | 3 |
| 1915 | 15 | domestic servant | – | miner | 3 |
| 1900 | 3 | at home | – | railwayman | 1 |
| 1899 | 6 | shop assistant | – | miner | 2 |
| 1895 | 6 | spinner | – | miner | 2 |
| 1899 | 6 | at home | – | miner | 2 |

| Date of birth | Siblings | Occupation before marriage | Occupation after marriage | Husband's occupation | Family size |
|---|---|---|---|---|---|
| 1902 | 9 | shop assistant | charring laundry | miner | 2 |
| 1899 | 4 | (1) domestic servant (2) barmaid | charring laundry | miner | 2 |
| 1908 | 10 | weaver | weaver | glass blower | 1 |
| 1908 | 5 | weaver | weaver | textiles/haulage | 1 |
| 1895 | 1 | weaver | weaver | weaver | 4 |
| 1896 | 10 | weaver | weaver | weaver | 1 |
| 1894 | 5 | weaver | weaver | joiner | 3 |
| 1901 | 9 | weaver | weaver | weaver | 2 |
| 1894 | 8 | weaver | weaver | bus conductor | 1 |
| 1899 | 4 | machinist/textiles | – | miner | 2 |

# Appendix 3
## The husband's occupational and employment status

Tables 55 and 56 show the numerical and percentage distribution of the husband's occupational and employment status for the women analysed in the Manchester and Salford Mothers' Clinic data.

**Table 55** *Husband's occupational status*

| Occupation | Number | (%) |
|---|---|---|
| professional | (1) | 0.2 |
| managerial | (4) | 0.8 |
| higher inspectorate | (8) | 1.6 |
| lower inspectorate | (19) | 3.8 |
| routine non-manual | (58) | 11.6 |
| skilled manual | (206) | 41.2 |
| semi-skilled manual | (63) | 12.6 |
| unskilled manual | (125) | 25.0 |
| no information | (16) | 3.2 |
| total | (500) | 100.0 |

*Source*: Clinic data

**Table 56** *Husband's employment status*

| Employment status | Number | (%) |
|---|---|---|
| unemployed | (89) | 17.8 |
| part-time employees | (11) | 2.2 |
| full-time employees | (339) | 67.8 |
| employer | (5) | 1.0 |
| no information | (56) | 11.2 |
| total | (500) | 100.0 |

*Source*: Clinic data

# Notes and references

## Chapter 1: Theories of fertility and the family

1  See, for instance, Goode (1969); Parsons and Bales (1956).
2  Wrigley (1966); Habakkuk (1971); Clarke (1949).
3  Hajnal (1947–8).
4  As was the case in England and Wales in the 1970s.
5  Parkin (1971), p. 82.
6  Malthus (1966), p. 13.
7  Eversley (1959), p. 268.
8  Engels (1972), p. 119.
9  Sacks (1974), p. 211.
10  Becker (1960).
11  Leibenstein (1957).
12  Okun (1958).
13  See, in particular, Blake (1968); Easterlin (1969).
14  Such as that of Schultz (1973).
15  Birdsall (1976), p. 705.
16  Cain and Weininger (1973).
17  Levine (1965–6), p. 152.
18  Macintyre (1976), p. 152.
19  Banks (1954).
20  Although, in fact, the decline began earlier.
21  Banks (1954), p. 30.
22  Young and Wilmott (1973), p. 20.
23  Banks (1968).
24  Carlsson (1966–7), p. 152.
25  ibid., p. 155.
26  Wrigley (1966).
27  Rainwater (1965).
28  ibid., p. 15.
29  ibid., p. 193.
30  Bott (1968), p. 59.
31  Turner (1971), p. 240.
32  See Parsons (1964); Parsons and Bales (1956). As Leonard (1980) remarks when discussing functionalist theories of the family:

the 'spouses' are treated as inter-changeable and marriage is seen as having the same 'meaning' for both – as being their principle *nomos*-creating institution. This totally ignores the work the two sexes do – the different ways in which they make their living – and the consequent disparity, and indeed antagonism, of their life situations, and it has made it impossible to integrate the study of kinship or the family, or indeed women, children, and the old, into the study of the rest of society (which is taken to be *the whole* of society): the world of adult men. (p. 261)

33   Families vary, and have varied, not only in terms of size and the relations of various members to the economic system, but also in terms of inheritance patterns and descent (matrilineal, patrilineal, etc.) and numbers of spouses (androgynous and polygynous). The very word 'family' has had a variety of definitions, sometimes referring solely to kin regardless of place of residence, sometimes to a household and all its residents, whether or not related by blood. For instance:

> it was still the case in the second half of the eighteenth century, both in France and England, and whatever the social milieu concerned, that the members of the family were held to include both the kinsfolk residing in the house and the domestic servants, in so far as they were all subject to the same head of the family. (Flandrin, 1979, p. 5)

34   Flandrin has shown how *both* nuclear and extended families existed in pre-industrial Europe: 'British historians and those of the Paris Basin attempt to relegate the extended family to the museum of sociological myths, in complete ignorance of the censuses held in Southern France which confirm its existence.' (ibid, p. 3.) Similarly, Anderson (1971) has suggested that, if anything, industrialization in the nineteenth century resulted in an increased number of, and reliance on, extended family networks. The work of Wilmott and Young in Bethnal Green in the 1950s indicated the persistent importance of extended kinship networks, particularly among women, in the working class (Wilmott and Young 1962).

35   Macfarlane (1970), for instance, provides interesting insight into seventeenth century family life indicating that psychological and personality factors certainly *were* important.

36   Parsons and Bales (1956), pp. 309 and 313.

37   Goode (1969).

38   See, for instance, Anderson (1971). It was very unusual for young women to live independently, as their wages were seldom more than half those of young men. This phenomenon is, to a slightly less extent, still with us today.

39   Harris (1972), p. 109.

40   Laing (1971); Laing (1960); Laing and Esterson (1970); Cooper (1972).

41   In particular, the work of the Cambridge Group and French demo-

graphers such as Flandrin (1979) and Louis Henry (1965).

42   There is now a wide range of literature relating to this problem, but see Barker and Allen (1976a and 1976b); Delphy (1977); Firestone (1970); Kuhn and Wolpe (1978); Garnsey (1978).

43   See Secombe (1973).

44   Such as that of Dalla Costa and James (1972).

45   Gardiner (1976).

46   Delphy (1977).

47   See, in particular, Smith-Rosenberg (1975); Cott (1977).

48   Gittins (1974).

49   ibid.

50   The main problem when using aggregate data is that of the 'ecological fallacy': 'in an *ecological correlation* the statistical object is a group of persons . . . . The thing described is the population of a state, and not a single individual. The variables are percentages, descriptive properties of groups, and not descriptive properties of individuals' (Robinson, 1950, p. 351). In this study, the problem was overcome as far as possible by control of the variables and going back to the original data. For instance, where it seemed likely that an association was affected by demographic factors such as an unbalanced sex ratio, then areas were selected with a balanced sex ratio to see if the association still held. The most useful data, not surprisingly, came from the most homogeneous areas.

51   Caplow (1954), p. 124.

52   But see Bell and Newby (1976) for a discussion of power relations within marriage.

53   The principal variables analysed were as follows: (1) age structure and sex ratio, by quinquennial age groups; (2) proportions of men and women married by quinquennial age groups; (3) proportions of men and women in various occupations (this was divided by marital status for women in 1911, but not in 1931); (4) various fertility measures: the marital fertility rate, the crude birth rate, the general fertility rate, child/woman ratio and female child/woman ratio (the marital fertility rate was generally used, as this is the most accurate for the purposes here, of the above measurements); (5) measurements of illegitimacy, infant mortality and the crude death rate.

54   The first birth control clinic was set up in London in 1921; by 1930 there were twenty such clinics, and by 1939, sixty-five.

55   For a full discussion of these problems, see Thompson (1978) and Gittins (1979).

## Chapter 2: A period of contradictions, 1900–39

1    **Table A**    *The size of family by marriage cohorts, 1861–9 to 1930–4, England and Wales*

| Marriages celebrated | Family size |
| --- | --- |
| 1861–9 | 6.16 |
| 1876 | 5.62 |
| 1886 | 4.81 |
| 1890–9 | 4.13 |
| 1900–9 | 3.30 |
| 1915–19 | 2.46 |
| 1925–9 | 2.11 |
| 1930–4 | 2.07 |

*Source*: Wrigley (1969)

See Banks (1954) for analysis of the decline of family size among the Victorian middle class.

2    Royal Commission on Population (1949), p. 26.

3    See, for example, Banks (1954); Young and Wilmott (1973).

4    The first birth control clinic was set up by Marie Stopes in London in 1921. In 1930 the National Birth Control Council (later to become the Family Planning Association) was founded, and ran twenty clinics. By 1939 the FPA was running sixty-five clinics – all in urban areas.

5    The percentage of all women working in 1901 was 29.1 per cent, in 1931, 29.7 per cent, while the percentage of married women working was 6.3 per cent in 1901 and 4.8 per cent in 1931. (Census for England and Wales, 1911 and 1931.)

6    Such as Pilgrim Trust (1938); Caradog Jones (1934); Llewellyn Smith (1934); Tout (1938).

7    Compare that with the rate of maternal mortality, for instance, in France in 1935, which was just half that of England and Wales, that is: 2.3 (Mervyn Herbert, 1939).

8    'Males and females born between 1838 and 1854 could expect to live on average 39.9 and 41.9 years respectively. For those born in the period 1901–12 average life expectancy at birth had risen to 51.5 and 55.4 years, and for the cohort born between 1930 and 1932 to 58.7 and 62.9 years.' (Tranter, 1973, p. 57)

9    See Hollingsworth (1964).

10    See the Royal Commission on Population (1949) for a discussion of this.

11    Foster (1976).

12    Sayers (1973), p. 147.

13    Lewis (1970), p. 77.

14    Stevenson (1977), p. 15.
15    ibid., p. 17.
16    Sayers (1973), p. 7.
17    Spring Rice (1939), p. 132.
18    Stevenson (1977), p. 177.
19    Spring Rice (1939), p. 194.
20    Stevenson (1977), p. 17.
21    ibid., p. 127.
22    Spring Rice (1939), p. viii.
23    Mervyn Herbert (1939), p. 99.
24    Spring Rice (1939).
25    ibid., p. 46.
26    See, for instance, Stopes (1925 and 1929).
27    Many people, of course, had more to spend, but note how they spent it:

**Table B**  *Selected items of consumer expenditure as percentages of total consumer expenditure, selected years.*

| Year | Food (%) | Alcoholic drink (%) | Furniture electrical and other durables (%) | Cars and motorcycles (%) |
|------|------|------|------|------|
| 1900 | 27.3 | 20.8 | 2.5 | 0.00 |
| 1905 | 28.5 | 18.7 | 2.6 | 0.07 |
| 1910 | 28.7 | 16.0 | 2.5 | 0.15 |
| 1921 | 29.9 | 12.4 | 3.4 | 0.02 |
| 1925 | 30.2 | 10.3 | 4.0 | 0.09 |
| 1930 | 30.2 | 8.4 | 4.7 | 0.08 |
| 1935 | 29.6 | 7.0 | 5.5 | 1.02 |

*Source*: Halsey (1972), p. 89

28    Pilgrim Trust (1938), p. 247.
29    ibid., p. 258.
30    Roberts (1974), p. 147.
31    Mowat (1968), p. 284.
32    Davidoff (1956).
33    Stevenson (1977), p. 22.
34    Spring Rice (1939), p. 52.
35    ibid., p. 52.
36    Mowat (1968), p. 16.
37    Although this could simply be seen as a result of what the government defined as typical.
38    Brown (1978), p. 135.
39    McCleary (1933), p. 2.

40  ibid., p. 143.
41  Quoted in Stevenson (1977), p. 143.
42  Lowndes (1969), p. 177.
43  See Donnison (1977).
44  Sayers, (1973).
45  Lewis (1979).
46  Richards (1974), p. 54.
47  Lowndes (1969), p. 81.
48  Halsey (1972), p. 558.
49  ibid., p. 89.
50  Mowat (1968), p. 240.
51  White (1970).
52  Mowat (1968).
53  ibid., p. 98.
54  Sayers (1973), p. 137.
55  There was also an increase in paid holidays during this period. In the 1920s approximately 1.5 million wage-earners were entitled to a week's paid holiday each year; by 1938 the number was 3 million, and by 1939 (mostly as a result of the Holidays with Pay Act of 1938), about 11 million (Mowat, 1968).
56  Sayers (1973)
57  McGregor (1957), p. 90.
58  Richards (1974), p. 59.
59  Pilgrim Trust (1938).
60  Hutt (1933), p. 184.
61  Pilgrim Trust (1938), pp. 108 and 110.
62  Liddington and Norris (1978), p. 20.
63  Stevenson (1977), p. 189.
64  **Table C**  *Means and standard deviations of proportions of women married, aged 15–34, and correlations with marital fertility rate, 1911 and 1931*

| Women married | 1911 | | | 1931 | | |
|---|---|---|---|---|---|---|
| | Mean | Standard deviation | $R^2$ | Mean | Standard deviation | $R^2$ |
| aged 15–19 | 1.2 | 0.8 | 18.7 | 1.8 | 0.6 | 9.9 |
| aged 20–24 | 23.7 | 6.9 | 33.7 | 25.9 | 6.1 | 21.0 |
| aged 25–29 | 55.0 | 9.9 | 25.3 | 57.9 | 7.3 | 18.1 |
| aged 30–34 | 70.4 | 9.1 | 21.8 | 72.3 | 7.0 | 20.3 |

*Source*: Census (1911 and 1931)

65  M. Abrams (1945).

## Chapter 3: Work before marriage

1  This does not include one woman who delivered milk and one who worked as an assistant teacher before marriage.
2  See McBride (1976).
3  Glass (1938b).
4  See Royal Commission on Population (1949).
5  McBride (1976), p. 11.
6  ibid., p. 82.
7  Halsey (1972), p. 114.
8  Lockwood (1958), p. 57.
9  ibid., p. 63.
10  This does not include one woman who delivered milk, one who worked as an assistant teacher and three who stayed at home before marriage.
11  This has, of course, been noted and analysed in other research. See the earlier discussion on theory, Birdsall (1976); Hawthorn (1970); Hawthorn and Paddon (1970).

## Chapter 4: Work after marriage

1  See Birdsall (1976); Hawthorn (1970); Hawthorn and Paddon (1970).
2  The 1931 Census does not give data on marital status by area.
3  See Busfield and Paddon (1977); Birdsall (1976).
4  There were 3632 women outworkers in the tailoring trade alone in London in 1911, almost entirely in the East End. This was the largest proportion of women outworkers anywhere at the time. It was estimated that of these outworkers in London, 68.1 per cent were married. See Tawney (1915).
5  'They are predominantly the wives and daughters, usually the wives, of men whose employment is casual or whose wages are low, and who are described as 'labourers' of one kind or another.' (Tawney, 1915, pp. 194–5)
6  Westover (1977), p. 16.
7  See, for instance, Jaffe and Azumi (1960); Gendell, Maraviglia and Kreitner (1970); Bindary and Baxter (1973).
8  'There is some evidence – though the statistical information on the subject is scanty – that the trend of family size has differed between people of different religious affiliation. The decline has been slower among Roman Catholics than among Protestants.' (Royal Commission on Population, 1949, p. 29)
9  While the figures shown in Table D are for 1938 (and the textile

industry experienced considerable depression during the inter-war period, mainly as a result of the loss of the export market) they are a useful indicator of wage differentials among men.

**Table D**    *Average earnings of adult male wage-earners in the last pay-week of October 1938*

| Occupational groups | Average earnings |
| --- | --- |
| motor vehicles, cycles and aircraft | £4  3s.  3d. |
| general engineering | £3 13s.  7d. |
| shipbuilding and ship-repairing | £3 10s.  1d. |
| pottery, earthenware, etc. | £3      11d. |
| Wool | £2 17s.  6d. |
| jute | £2 11s.  1d. |
| cotton | £2 10s.  9d. |

*Source*: Fogarty (1945)

For women in 1911, however, the average income per week was £1 8s. 10¾d. for a cotton weaver, compared with 10s. 7½d. for a tailoring machinist doing outwork (Tawney, 1915).

10   In 1931, 23 per cent of all men aged 15–64 were unemployed in Burnley; the percentage of men employed in textiles declined from 41 per cent in 1911 to 28 per cent in 1931, while the percentage of women employed in textiles there only declined from 53 per cent to 48.5 per cent (Census, 1911 and 1931).

11   Royal Commission on Population (1949), p. 24.

12   ibid., p. 25.

13   See Davis (1970) on the multiphasic response to fertility.

14   See Inter-Departmental Committee on Abortion (1939).

15   But see Davis (1970), who rightly points out that 'in all of the industrializing countries rural–urban migration removed not only the farmers' natural increase but also a substantial portion of the base population as well' (p. 34). See also Eisenstadt (1970).

16   See Jenkins (1971) and also Birdsall (1976).

17   See Davis (1970).

18   See, for instance, Hajnal (1948).

19   This is discussed in Birdsall (1976).

20   **Table E**    *Total fertility rate, selected social classes, 1931*

| Social class | Fertility rate |
| --- | --- |
| skilled | 2.103 |
| semi-skilled | 2.425 |
| unskilled | 2.733 |
| miners | 2.765 |
| agricultural labourers | 2.316 |

*Source*: Hopkin and Hajnal (1948)

### Chapter 5: Family life: organization and domestic ideology

1  The analysis of a couple's role-relationship was carried out by extracting information from each interview to complete a brief questionnaire summarizing the respondent's life history. Each partner's responsibilities in the areas of housework (specifying chores, approximate frequency of help), childcare, financial responsibilities and contributions, and leisure pursuits (what they were, frequency, whether or not they were shared with the partner and/or children), discussion of and responsibility for birth control were all noted. In most cases analysis was then quite straightforward. Husbands who performed some household chores also tended to help with childcare and share some, or all, of their leisure pursuits with their families; such couples were therefore classified as having a joint role-relationship. In less clear-cut cases, the role-relationship was assessed using three main areas: housework, childcare and leisure. If the husband participated in two of the three areas, the role-relationship was classified as joint, if in only one (or none) it was classified as segregated. Financial contributions, responsibility for bills and payments, responsibility for birth control and participation in the labour market were used in a similar way to analyse power relationships. While role-relationships and power relationships obviously varied (some were more joint, or more equal than others), it was felt that the four categories of joint, segregated, equal and unequal were adequate for the data used.

2  The methods I define as reliable include: sterilization, the sheath, abstinence and the diaphragm. Those defined as unreliable include: *coitus interruptus* (withdrawal), the safe period, the douche and lactation.

3  Corroboration of this would depend on interviewing *both* husband and wife, and not just the wife.

4  It is difficult to say exactly why this was so. It seems likely that given the more isolated situation of women at home, they would be more easily influenced by, and more apt to seek advice from, welfare and similar institutions, as well as from the media – all of which would emphasize the importance of professional medical advice. Women who had frequent and easy access to work colleagues, friends, neighbours and kin, on the other hand, would be more apt to seek advice from them, advice which would often consist of folk remedies, 'old wives' tales' and so on.

5  Few of the women interviewed who did not work during their early married life ever worked later, even after their children left home. Several did do war work during the Second World War, and one took in lodgers when her husband was unemployed. Generally, however,

among women of this generation – in contrast with recent trends – if she did not work after marriage and childbirth, it was unusual for her ever to seek employment except in times of real emergency.

## Chapter 6: Birth control: clinics and communication

1 See, for instance, Himes (1936); Fryer (1965); Gordon (1975); McLaren (1978); Russell (1975).
2 Peel (1963–4), p. 116.
3 Wrigley (1966).
4 Although there is anthropological evidence from other societies suggesting that it is, and has been, a public issue among various 'primitive groups'. See Douglas (1966).
5 McLaren (1978).
6 ibid.
7 See, for instance, Banks (1954); Carlsson (1966–7).
8 Hoggart (1959), p. 41.
9 McLaren (1976).
10 Florence (1930), p. 105.
11 Stopes (1929), p. 183.
12 Such as those of Beckwith, Whitehouse, Pindar; see Inter-Departmental Committee on Abortion (1939).
13 This may have been a result of their way of *classifying* reasons.
14 Inter-Departmental Committee on Abortion (1939), p. 15.
15 For comparison of these data with national data, see Appendix 1.
16 See, in particular, Sagi, Potter and Westoff (1961–2).
17 Peel (1963–4), p. 119.
18 Hoggart (1959), p. 34.
19 Although, of course, detailed data over time would also be needed to indicate diffusion.
20 Florence (1930), p. 49.
21 This supports Kingsley Davis's theory of change and response to economic changes.
22 Ministry of Health (1930 and 1934).
23 The Lambeth Conference, 1930.
24 See, for example, M. Marndani (1972).

## Conclusion

1 Ann Cartwright (1976), for example, concludes

this study supports the findings from other inquiries that husbands and wives who discuss their problems and decisions have smaller families than those who do not. They also share more of the household tasks and care of children . . . they are more effective in their use of contraception. (p. 164)

2 But it is likely they were increasingly regarded as an important means of *emotional* security in old age.
3 A prime example of this is midwifery.
4 See Busfield and Paddon (1977).
5 As, for example, described in Birdsall (1976).

# Bibliography

Abrams, M. (1945), *The Condition of the British People 1911–1945*, London: Gollancz

Alford, B. W. E. (1972), *Depression and Recovery? British Economic Growth 1918–1939*, London: Macmillan

Allardt, E. (1969), 'Aggregate analysis: the problem of its informative value', in Dogan and Rokkan (eds.)

Aluko, S. A. (1971), 'Population growth and the level of income', *The Journal of Modern African Studies*, vol. 9, no. 4

Ambrose, P. (1974), *The Quiet Revolution*, London: Chatto and Windus

Anderson, M. (1971), *Family Structure in Nineteenth Century Lancashire*, London: Cambridge University Press

Anderson, M. (ed.) (1971), *Sociology of the Family*, Harmondsworth: Penguin

Anderson, M. (1976), 'Sociological history and the working class family: Smelser revisited', *Social History*, no. 3

Anshen, R. N. (ed.) (1959), *The Family: Its Function and Destiny*, New York: Harper

Ariès, P. (1973), *Centuries of Childhood*, trans. R. Baldick, London: Peregrine Books

Askham, J. (1975), *Fertility and Deprivation*, London: Cambridge University Press

Banks, J. A. (1968), 'Population change and the Victorian city', *Victorian Studies*, vol. II

Banks, J. A. and Banks, O. (1968), 'The Bradlaugh–Besant trial and the English newspapers', *Population Studies*, vol. 8

Banks, J. (1954), *Prosperity and Parenthood*, London: Routledge and Kegan Paul

Baran, P. A. and Sweezy P. M. (1970), *Monopoly Capitalism*, Harmondsworth: Penguin

Barker, D. L. and Allen, S. (eds.) (1976a), *Dependence and Exploitation in Work and Marriage*, London: Longman

Barker, D. L. and Allen, S. (eds.) (1976b), *Sexual Divisions and Society: Process and Change*, London: Tavistock

Bartlett, F. C. (1965), *Remembering*, London: Cambridge University Press

Becker, G. (1960), 'An economic analysis of fertility', in National Bureau of Economic Research, *Demographic and Economic Change in Developed Countries*, Princeton, NJ: Princeton University Press

Behrman, S. J., Corsa, L., and Freedman, R. (eds.) (1969), *Fertility and Family Planning: A World View*, Michigan: University of Michigan Press

Bell, C. and Newby, H. (1976), 'Husbands and wives: the dynamics of the deferential dialectic', in Barker and Allen (eds.) (1976a)

Bell, Lady (1911), *At the Works*, London: Nelson

Benjamin, B. (1963–4), 'The urban background to public health changes in England and Wales 1900–1950', *Population Studies*, vol. 17

Benjamin, B. (1968), *Demographic Analysis*, London: Allen and Unwin

Berent, Jerzy (1952), 'Fertility and social mobility', *Population Studies*, vol. 5

Berger, P. and Kellner, H. (1974), 'Marriage and the construction of reality' in Coser (ed.)

Berger, P. and Luckmann, T. (1976), *The Social Construction of Reality*, Harmondsworth: Penguin

Bernard, J. (1973), *The Future of Marriage*, London: Souvenir Press

Beshers, J. M. (1967), *Population Processes in Social Systems*, New York: Free Press

Bindary, A. and Baxter, C. (1973), 'Urban–rural differences in the relationship between women's employment and fertility: a preliminary study', *Journal of Biosocial Science*, vol. 5

Birdsall, N. (1976), 'Women and population studies', *Signs: Journal of Women in Culture and Society*, vol. 1

*The Birth Control Movement in England* (1930), London: Bale, Sons and Danielsson

Blacker, C. P. (1926), *Birth Control and The State*, London: Kegan Paul, Tench, Trubner and Co.

Blake, J. (1967), 'Parental control, delayed marriage and population policy', in *Proceedings of the World Population Conference*, vol. 2

Blake, J. (1968), 'Are babies consumer durables?', *Population Studies*, vol. 22

Blumberg, F. (1931), 'The Manchester, Salford and District Mother's Clinic', in Sanger and Stone (eds.)

Bott, E. (1968), *Family and Social Network*, London: Tavistock

Bourne, A. (1962), *A Doctor's Creed*, London: Gollancz

Brackett, J. W. (1968), 'The evolution of Marxist theories of population', *Demography*, vol. 5

Branca, P. (1975), *Silent Sisterhood: Middle Class Women in the Victorian Home*, London: Croom Helm

Branson, N. and Heinemann, M. (1971), *Britain in the 1930s*, London: Weidenfeld and Nicolson

Bruce, M. (1961), *The Coming of the Welfare State*, London: Batsford

Bulmer, M. (1975), *Working-Class Images of Society*, London: Routledge and Kegan Paul

Busfield, J. and Paddon, M. (1977), *Thinking about Children*, London: Cambridge University Press


Cadbury, E. Matheson, M. C. and Shann, G. (1906), *Women's Work and Wages*, London: T. Fisher Unwin

Cain, G. G. and Weininger, A. (1973), 'Economic determinants of fertility', *Demography*, vol. 10

Campbell, J. M. (1924), *Maternal Mortality*, London: HMSO

Caplow, T. (1954), *The Sociology of Work*, Minneapolis: University of Minnesota Press

Caradog Jones, D. (1934), *The Social Survey of Merseyside*, London: University Press of Liverpool

Carlsson, G. (1966–7), 'The decline of fertility: innovation or adjustment process', *Population Studies*, vol. 20

Cartwright, A. (1976), *How Many Children?*, London: Routledge and Kegan Paul

Census for England and Wales, 1911 (1914), *Occupations and Industries*, pts 1 and 2, London: HMSO

Census for England and Wales, 1931 (1934), *Occupation Tables*, London: HMSO

Chambers, J. S. (1965), 'Three essays on the population and economy of the Midlands', in Glass and Eversley (eds.)

Charles, E. (1932), *The Practice of Birth Control: Experiences of 900 Women* London: Williams and Norgate

Charles, E. (1938), 'The effect of present trends in fertility and mortality upon the future population of Great Britain and upon its age composition', in Hogben (ed.)

Charles, E. and Mashinsky, O. (1938), 'Differential fertility in England and Wales during the past two decades', in Hogben (ed.)

Chessler, E. S. (1928), *Youth*, London: Methuen

Clark, C. (1949), 'Age at marriage and marital fertility', *Population Studies*, vol. 2

Coale, A. J. (1965), 'Factors associated with the development of low fertility: an historic summary', *Proceedings of the World Population Conference*, vol. 2

Cochrane, S. H. (1975), 'Children as by-products, investment goods and consumer goods: a review of some micro-economic models of fertility', *Population Studies*, vol. 29

Cockburn, C. (1973), *The Devil's Decade*, London: Sidgwick and Jackson

Cohen, M. (1945), *I Was One of the Unemployed*, London: Gollancz/ Left Book Club

Cole, G. D. H. (1915), *Labour in War-Time*, London: G. Bell and Sons

Cole, G. D. H. and Postgate, R. (1971), *The Common People*, London: Metheun

Committee on Holidays with Pay (1938), *Report*, Cmnd 5724, London: HMSO

Connell, K. H. (1950), *The Population of Ireland 1750–1845*, Oxford: Clarendon Press

Cooper, D. (1971), *The Death of the Family*, Harmondsworth: Penguin

Corfield, W. F. (1929–39) *Annual Report of the Medical Officer of Health*, Colchester: Wiles and Son

Coser, R. L. (ed.) (1974), *The Family: Its Structures and Functions*, London: Macmillan

Cott, N. (1977), *The Bonds of Womanhood, Woman's Sphere in New England 1780–1835*, New Haven, Conn: Yale University Press

Coulson, M. Magas, B. and Wainwright, H. (1975), 'The housewife and her labour under capitalism – a critique', *New Left Review*, no. 89

Cox, P. R. (1952), 'Studies in the recent marriage and fertility data of England and Wales', *Population Studies*, vol. 5

Cox, P. R. (1965), 'Patterns and trends in recent British population developments', in *Biological Aspects of Social Problems*, London: Oliver and Boyd

Craig, A. (1934), *Sex and Revolution*, London: Allen and Unwin

Crosswick, G. (1976), 'The Labour aristocracy and its values: a study of mid-Victorian Kentish London', *Victorian Studies*, vol. 19

Dalla Costa, M. and James, S. (1972), *The Power of Women and the Subversion of the Community*, Bristol: Falling Wall Press

Daly, H. E. (1971), 'A Marxian-Malthusian view of poverty and development, *Population Studies*, vol. 25

Davidoff, L. (1956), 'The employment of married women in England 1850–1950', unpubl. MA thesis, London School of Economics

Davidoff, L. (1976), 'The rationalization of housework', in Barker and Allen (eds.) (1976a)

Davidoff, L., L'Esperance, J. and Newby, H. (1976), 'Landscape with figures: home and community in English society', in Oakley and Mitchell (eds.)

Davies, R. (1975), *Women and Work*, London: Arrow Books

Davis, K. (1967), 'Population policy: will current programs succeed?', *Science*, vol. 158

Davis, K. (1975), The theory of change and response in modern demographic history', in Ford and De Jong (eds.)

Delisle Burns, C. (1932), *Leisure in the Modern World*, London: Allen and Unwin

Delphy, C. (1977), *The Main Enemy: A Materialist Analysis of Women's Oppression*, no. 3, London: WRRC Explorations in Feminism

Demos, J. (1970), *A Little Commonwealth: Family Life in Plymouth Colony*, New York: Oxford University Press

Dennis, N. *et al.* (1969), *Coal is Our Life*, London: Tavistock

de Tray, D. N. (1973), 'Child quality and the demand for children', *Journal of Political Economics*, vol. 81

Deutsch, K. (1969), 'On methodological problems of quantitative research', in Dogan and Rokkan (eds.)

Dogan, M. and Rokkan, S. (eds.) (1969), *Social Ecology*, Cambridge, Mass: MIT Press

Donnison, J. (1977), *Midwives and Medical Men*, London: Heinemann

Douglas, M. (1966), 'Population control in primitive groups', *British Journal of Sociology*, vol. 17

Draper, E. (1972), *Birth Control in the Modern World*, Harmondsworth: Penguin


Easterlin, R. A. (1969), 'Towards a socio-economic theory of fertility', in Behrman, Corsa and Freedman (eds.)

Eaton, J. W. and Mayer, A. J. (1954), *Man's Capacity to Reproduce*, Glencoe, Ill.: Free Press

Ebery, M. and Preston, B. (1976), *Domestic Service in Late Victorian and Edwardian England 1871–1914*, Reading: Reading Geographical Papers

Edwards, J. N. (ed.) (1969), *The Family and Change*, New York: Knopf

Eisenstadt, S. N. (1970), 'Analysis of patterns of immigration and absorption of immigrants', in Ford and De Jong (eds.)

Elder, G. and Bowerman, C. (1970), 'Family structure and child-rearing patterns: the effect of family size and sex composition', in Ford and De Jong (eds.)

Engels, F. (1972), *The Origin of the Family, Private Property and the State*, London: Lawrence and Wishart

Enke, S. and Zind, R. G. (1969), 'Effects of fewer births on average Income', *Journal of Biosocial Science*, vol. 1

Eversley, D. E. C. (1959), *Social Theories of Fertility and the Malthusian Debate*, Oxford: Oxford University Press


Farrag, A. M. (1964–5), 'The occupational structure of the labour force', *Population Studies*, vol. 18

Filstead, W. J. (1970), *Quantitative Methodology: First-Hand Involvement with the Social World*, Chicago: Markham Publishing Co.

Firestone, S. (1970), *The Dialectic of Sex*, New York: Morrow

Flandrin, J. L. (1979), *Families in Former Times*, Cambridge: Cambridge University Press

Fletcher, R. (1966), *Family and Marriage in Britain*, Harmondsworth: Penguin

Flinn, M. W. and Smout, T. C. (eds.) (1974), *Essays in Social History*, London: Oxford University Press

Florence, L. S. (1930), *Birth Control on Trial*, London: Allen and Unwin

Floud, R. (1973), *An Introduction to Quantitative Methods for Historians*, London: Metheun

Fogarty, M. P. (1945), *Prospects of the Industrial Areas of Great Britain*, London: Metheun

Foley, A. (1973), *A Bolton Childhood*, Manchester

Ford, P. (1939), *Incomes, Means Tests and Personal Responsibility*, London: P. S. King

Ford, T. R. and De Jong, G. F. (eds.) (1970), *Social Demography*, New York: Prentice Hall

Foster, J. (1976), 'British imperialism and the labour aristocracy', in Skelley (ed.)

Fremlin, C. (1940), *The Seven Chars of Chelsea*, London: Metheun

Freund, J. (1970), *The Sociology of Max Weber*, Harmondsworth: Penguin

Friedlander, D. (1970), 'The spread of urbanization in England and Wales, 1851–1951', *Population Studies*, vol. 24

Friedlander, D. and Roshier, J. R. (1965–6), 'A study of internal migration in England and Wales', *Population Studies*, vol. 19

Fryer, P, (1965), *The Birth Controllers*, London: Secker and Warburg

Fyfe, H. (1933), *Revolt of Women*, London: Rich and Cowan


Gardiner, J. (1975), 'Women's domestic labour', *New Left Review*, no. 89

Gardiner, J. (1976), 'Political economy of domestic labour in capitalist society', in Barker and Allen (eds.) (1976a)

Garnsey, E. (1978), 'Women's work and theories of class stratification', *Sociology*, vol. 12 (May)

Gendell, M. *et al.* (1970), 'Fertility and economic activity of women in Guatemala city, 1964', *Demography*, vol. 7

Giddens, A. (1976), *New Rules of Sociological Method*, London: Hutchinson

Gillis, J. R. (1974), *Youth and History*, New York: Academic Press

Gittins, D. (1974), 'The decline of family size and differential fertility in the 1930s', unpubl. MA thesis, University of Essex

Gittins, D. (1979), 'Oral history, reliability and recollection', in Moss and Goldstein (eds.)

Glaser, B. and Strauss, A. (1967), *The Discovery of Grounded Theory: Strategies for Qualitative Research*, Chicago: Aldine

Glass D. V. (1938a), 'Changes in fertility in England and Wales 1851–1931', in Hogben (ed.)

Glass, D. V. (1938b), 'Marriage frequency and economic fluctuations in England and Wales, 1851 to 1934', in Hogben (ed.)

Glass, D. V. (1954), *Social Mobility in Britain*, London: Routledge and Kegan Paul

Glass, D. V. and Eversley, D. E. C. (eds.) (1965), *Population in History: Essays in Historical Demography*, London: Edward Arnold

Glass, D. V. and Grebenik, E. (1954), 'The trend and pattern of fertility in Great Britain', *Papers of the Royal Commission on Population*, vol. 6

Glass, R. and Davidson, F. (1951), 'Household structure and housing needs', *Population Studies*, vol. 4

Goode, W. J. (1969), 'Changes in family patterns', in Edwards (ed.)

Goodman, L. A. (1953), 'Ecological regressions and behaviour of individuals', *American Sociological Review*, vol. 18

Goody, J. (1974), 'The evolution of the family', in Laslett (ed.)

Gordon, L. (1975), 'The politics of birth control, 1920–1940: the impact of professionals', *International Journal of Health Services*, vol. 5

Gordon, L. (1976), *Woman's Body, Woman's Right: A Social History of Birth Control*, New York: Grossman

Graves, R. and Hodge, A. (1940), *The Long Week-end: A Social History of Great Britain, 1918–1939*, London: Faber

Greenwood, W. (1972), *Love on the Dole*, Harmondsworth: Penguin

Gregg, P. (1976), *Black Death to Industrial Revolution*, London: Harrap

Greven, P. (1970), *Four Generations*, Ithaca, NY: Cornell University Press

Griffith, E. R. (1937), *Modern Marriage and Birth Control*, London: Gollancz


Habakkuk, H. J. (1971), *Population Growth and Economic Development Since 1750*, Leicester: Leicester University Press

Habakkuk, H. J. (1974), 'Family structure and economic change in nineteenth-century Europe', in Coser (ed.)

Hajnal, D. (1947–8), 'Aspects of recent trends in marriage in England and Wales', *Population Studies*, vol. 1

Hajnal, J. and Henderson, A. (1950), 'The economic position of the family', *Papers of the Royal Commission on Population*, vol. 5

Halsey, A. H. (ed.) (1972), *Trends in British Society Since 1900*, London: Macmillan

Hardin, G. (1964), *Population, Evolution and Birth Control*, San Francisco: Freeman

Harris, C. C. (1972), *The Family*, London: Allen and Unwin

Hauser, P. M. (1960), *Population Perspectives*, New Brunswick, NJ: Rutgers University Press

Hawthorn, G. (1970), *The Sociology of Fertility*, London: Collier-Macmillan

Hawthorn, G. and Paddon, M. (1970), 'Work, family and fertility: an interpretation of data for four industries', paper given at eleventh International Family Research Seminar, London

Heer, D. M. (1970), 'Economic development and fertility', in Ford and De Jong (eds.)

Henderson, A. (1950), 'The cost of children', pts 1, 2 and 3, *Population Studies*, vol. 3

Henry, L. (1965), 'The population of France in the eighteenth century', in Glass and Eversley (eds.)

Hiller, E. T. (1956), 'A culture theory of population trends', in Spengler and Duncan (eds.)

Himes, N. E. (1931), *A Guide to Birth Control Literature*, London: Noel Douglas

Himes, N. E. (1936), *A Medical History of Contraception*, Baltimore, Md: Williams and Wilkins

Hindell, K. and Simms, M. (1971), *Abortion Law Reformed*, London: Peter Owen

Hobsbawm, E. J. (1974), 'From social history to the history of society', in Flinn and Smout (eds.)

Hogben, L. (ed.) (1938), *Political Arithmetic*, London: Allen and Unwin

Hoggart, R. (1959), *The Uses of Literacy*, London: Chatto and Windus

Hollingsworth, T. H. (1964–5), 'The demography of the British peerage', supplement to *Population Studies*, vol. 18

Hollingsworth, T. H. (1976), *Historical Demography*, Cambridge: Cambridge University Press

Hopkin, W. and Hajnal, D. (1948), 'Analysis of the births in England and Wales, 1939, by father's occupation', pts 1 and 2, *Population Studies*, vol. 1

Hutt, A. (1933), *The Condition of the Working Class in Britain*, London: Martin Lawrence

Innes, J. W. (1938), *Class Fertility Trends in England and Wales, 1876–1934*, Princeton, NJ: Princeton University Press

Inter-Departmental Committee on Abortion (1939), *Report*, London: HMSO

Investigation into Maternal Mortality (1937), *Report*, Cmnd 5422, London: HMSO

Jackson, A. (1973), *Semi-Detached London*, London: Allen and Unwin

Jaffe, A. J. and Azumi, K. (1960), 'The birth rate and cottage industries in underdeveloped countries', *Economic Development and Culture Change*, vol. 4

Jenkins, D. (1971), *The Agricultural Community in South-West Wales at the Turn of the Twentieth Century*, Cardiff: University of Wales Press

Kammeyer, K. (1969), *Population Studies*, Chicago: Rand McNally

Keat, R. and Urry, J. (1975), *Social Theory as Science*, London: Routledge and Kegan Paul

Kelsall, R. K. and Mitchell, S. (1959–60), 'Married women and employment in England and Wales', *Population Studies*, vol. 13

Kiser, C. V. and Whelperton, P. K. (1954), 'Resumé of the Indianapolis study of social and psychological factors affecting fertility', *Population Studies*, vol. 7

Klingender, F. D. (1935), *The Condition of Clerical Labour in Britain*, London: Martin Lawrence

Krishman Namboodiri, N. (1972), 'Economic framework for fertility analysis', *Population Studies*, vol. 26

Kuczynski, J. (1938a), *Hunger and Work: Statistical Studies*, New York: International Publishers

Kuczynski, J. (1938b), 'The international decline of fertility', in Hogben (ed.)

Kuhn, A. and Wolpe, A. (1978), *Feminism and Materialism*, London: Routledge and Kegan Paul

Laing, R. D. (1960), *The Divided Self*, Harmondsworth: Penguin

Laing, R. D. (1971), *The Politics of the Family and Other Essays*, London: Tavistock

Lane, T. (1974), *The Union Makes Us Strong*, London: Arrow Books

Laslett, P. (1965), *The World We Have Lost*, London: Methuen

Laslett, P. (1969), 'Historical and regional variations in Great Britain', in Dogan and Rokkan (eds.)

Laslett, P. (ed.) (1974a), *Household and Family in Past Time*, Cambridge: Cambridge University Press

Laslett, P. (1974b), 'Mean household size in England since the sixteenth century', in Laslett (ed.)

Lehrman, R. (1936), *The Weather in the Streets*, London: Collins

Leibenstein, H. (1957), *Economic Backwardness and Economic Growth*, New York: John Wiley

Leonard, D. (1980), *Sex and Generation*, London: Tavistock

Lesser, C. E. V. (1958–9), 'Trends in women's work participation', *Population Studies*, vol. 12

Levine, A. 'L. (1965–6), 'Economic science and population theory', *Population Studies*, vol. 19

Lewis, J. (1981), *The Politics of Motherhood*, London: Croom Helm

Lewis, W. A. (1970), *Economic Survey 1919–1939*, London: Allen and Unwin

Lewis-Faning, E. (1949), 'Report on an enquiry into family limitation and its influence on human fertility during the past fifty years', *Papers on the Royal Commission on Population*, London: HMSO

Leybourne, G. G. and White, K. (1940), *Education and the Birth-Rate*, London: Jonathan Cape

Lichtheim, G. (1974), *Europe in the Twentieth Century*, London: Sphere Books

Liddington, J. and Norris, J. (1978), *One Hand Tied Behind Us: The Rise of the Suffrage Movement*, London: Virago

Llewellyn Smith, H. (ed.) (1934), *The New Survey of London Life and Labour*, London: P. S. King

Lockwood, D. (1958), *The Blackcoated Worker*, London: Unwin

Lockwood, D. (1966), 'Sources of variation in working class images of society', *The Sociological Review*, vol. 14, pp. 249–67

Logan, W. P. D. (1951), 'Mortality in England and Wales from 1848 to 1947', *Population Studies*, vol. 4

Lorimer, F. (1956a), 'Culture and human fertility: conclusions', in Spengler and Duncan (eds.)

Lorimer, F. (1956b), 'The differentiation of logical levels in social inquiry', in Spengler and Duncan (eds.)

Losch, A. (1956), 'Population cycles as a cause of business cycles', in Spengler and Duncan (eds.)

Lowndes, G. (1969), *The Silent Social Revolution*, London: Oxford University Press


McBride, T. M. (1976), *The Domestic Revolution*, London: Croom Helm

McCleary, G. F. (1933), *The Early History of the Infant Welfare Movement*, London: H. K. Lewis

Macfarlane, A. (1970), *The Family Life of Ralph Josselin: A Seventeenth-Century Clergyman*, Cambridge: Cambridge University Press

McGregor, O. R. (1957), *Divorce in England*, London: Heinemann

Macintyre, S. (1976), 'Who wants babies? The social construction of "instincts"', in Barker and Allen (eds.) (1976b)

McKeown, T., Brown, R.G. and Record, R.G. (1972), 'The modern rise of population in Europe', *Population Studies*, vol. 26

McLaren, A. (1976), 'Abortion in England: 1890–1914', unpubl. paper, University of Victoria

McLaren, A. (1977), 'Women's work and regulation of family size', *History Workshop Journal*, vol. 4

McLaren, A. (1978), *Public Debates and Private Practices: Birth Control in England 1800–1914*, London: Croom Helm

Malthus, T. (1966), *First Essay on Population*, London: Macmillan (first published 1798)

Mandani, M. (1972), *The Myth of Population Control*, New York: Monthly Review Press

Marchant, Sir J. (ed.) (1926), *Medical Views on Birth Control*, London: Martin Hopkinson

Marsden, D. and Duff, E. (1975), *Workless: Some Unemployed Men and their Families*, Harmondsworth: Penguin

Marsh, D. C. (1958), *The Changing Social Structure of England and Wales*, London: Routledge and Kegan Paul

Marshall, T. H. (1938), *The Population Problem: The Experts and the Public*, London: Allen and Unwin

Martin, G. (1959), *The Story of Colchester from Roman Times to the Present Day*, Colchester: Benham Newspapers

Marwick, A. (1965), *The Deluge: British Society and the First World War*, London: Macmillan

Mass Observation (1945), *Britain and Her Birth Rate*, London: John Murray

Matras, J. (1973), *Populations and Societies*, New Jersey: Prentice-Hall

Meade, J. *et al.* (1970), 'Demography and economics', *Population Studies*, vol. 24

Medick, H. (1976), 'The proto-industrial family economy: the structural function of household and family during the transition from peasant society to industrial capitalism', *Social History*, no. 3

Meek, R. L. (1953), *Marx and Engels on Malthus*, London: Lawrence and Wishart

Melvyn Howe, G. (1976), *Man, Environment and Disease in Britain*, Harmondsworth: Penguin

Mervyn Herbert, S. (1939), *Britain's Health*, Harmondsworth: Penguin

Michael, R. T. (1973), 'Education and the derived demand for children', *Journal of Political Economics*, vol. 81

Ministry of Health (1930), Memo 153MCW

Ministry of Health (1934), *Birth Control: To Maternity and Child Welfare Officers*, Circular 1408 (31 May)

Mitchell, B. R. and Deane, P. (1971), *Abstract of British Historical Statistics*, Cambridge: Cambridge University Press

Mitchell, J. (1971), *Woman's Estate*, Harmondsworth: Penguin

Mitchinson, N. (1934), *The Home and a Changing Civilisation*, London: Bodley Head

*More Secret Remedies* (1912), London: British Medical Association

Morgan, D. H. J. (1975), *Social Theory and the Family*, London: Routledge and Kegan Paul

Moser, C. A. and Kalton, G. (1971), *Survey Methods in Social Investigation*, London: Heinemann

Moss, L. and Goldstein, H. (eds.) (1979), *The Recall Method in Social Surveys*, London: Institute of Education

Moss, W. W. (1975), *Oral History Program Manual*, New York: Praeger

Mostyn Bird, M. (1911), *Women at Work*, London: Chapman and Hall

Mowat, C. L. (1968), *Britain Between the Wars*, London: Metheun

Musgrove, F. (1970), 'Population changes and the status of the young', in Musgrove (ed.)

Musgrove, P. W. (ed.) (1970), *Sociology, History and Education*, London: Metheun

Myrdal, A. and Klein, V. (1968), *Women's Two Roles: Home and Work*, London: Routledge and Kegan Paul

Nag, M. (1968), *Factors Affecting Human Fertility in Non-Industrial Societies*, Human Relations Area Files Press

Nemilow, A. (1932), *The Biological Tragedy of Women*, London: Allen and Unwin

Newman, G. (1906), *Infant Mortality*, London: Methuen

Newson, J. and Newson, E. (1963), *Infant Care in an Urban Community*, London: Allen and Unwin

Newson, J. and Newson, E. (1974), 'Cultural aspects of childrearing', in Richards (ed.)

Nisbet, R. A. (1972), *The Sociological Tradition*, London: Heinemann

Oakley, A. (1974a), *Housewife*, London: Allen Lane

Oakley, A. (1974b), *The Sociology of Housework*, London: Martin Robertson

Oakley, A. and Mitchell, J. (eds.) (1976), *The Rights and Wrongs of Women*, Harmondsworth: Penguin

Okun, B. (1958), *Trends in Birth Rates in the United States Since 1870*, Baltimore, Md: Johns Hopkins Press

Orwell, G. (1972), *The Road to Wigan Pier*, Harmondsworth: Penguin

Orwell, G. (1974), *A Clergyman's Daughter*, Harmondsworth: Penguin

Osterud, N. and Fulton, J. (1978), 'Family limitation and age at marriage: fertility decline in Sturbridge, Massachusetts, 1730–1850', *Population Studies*, vol. 30

Parker, S. (1976), *The Sociology of Leisure*, London: Allen and Unwin

Parkin, F. (1971), *Class Inequality and Political Order*, St Albans: Paladin

Parkin, F. (ed.) (1974), *The Social Analysis of Class Structure*, London: Tavistock

Parsons, T. (1964), *The Social System*, London: Routledge and Kegan Paul

Parsons, T. and Bales, R. F. (1956), *Family Socialization and Interaction Process*, London: Routledge and Kegan Paul

Peel, J. (1963–4), 'The manufacture and retailing of contraceptives in England', *Population Studies*, vol. 17

Peel, J. (1964–5), 'Contraception and the medical profession', *Population Studies*, vol. 18

Pember Reeves, M. S. (1914), *Round About a Pound a Week*, London: G. Bell and Sons

Petersen, W. (1964), *The Politics of Population*, London: Gollancz

Pilgrim Trust (1938), *Men Without Work*, London: Cambridge University Press

Pinchbeck, I. (1969), *Women Workers and the Industrial Revolution 1750–1850*, London: Frank Cass

Poynter, F. N. L. (1961), *The Evolution of Medical Practice in Britain*, London: Pitman Medical Publishing

Rainwater, L. (1960), *And the Poor Get Children*, Chicago: Quadrangle Books

Rainwater, L. (1965), *Family Design*, Chicago: Aldine

Rainwater, L. and Weinstein, K. (1970), 'A qualitative exploration of family planning and contraception in the working class', in Ford and De Jong (eds.)

Ranum, O. and Ranum, P. (eds.) (1972), *Popular Attitudes Towards Birth Control in Pre-Industrial France and England*, London: Harper and Row

Richards, M. P. M. (ed.) (1974), *The Integration of a Child into a Social World*, London: Cambridge University Press

Ridley, J. C. (1959), 'Number of children expected in relation to non-familial activities of the wife', *Milbank Memorial Fund Quarterly*, vol. 37

Roberts, R. (1974), *The Classic Slum*, Harmondsworth: Penguin

Robinson, J. (1975), *The Life and Times of Francie Nichol of South Shields*, London: Allen and Unwin

Robinson, W. S. (1950), 'Ecological correlations and the behaviour of individuals', *American Sociological Review*, vol. 15

Rosaldo, M. and Lamphere, L. (eds.) (1974), *Woman Culture and Society*, Stanford: Stanford University Press

Rowbotham, S. (1973a), *Hidden From History*, London: Pluto Press

Rowbotham, S. (1973b), *Woman's Consciousness, Man's World*, Harmondsworth: Penguin

Rowntree, G. and Carrier, N. H. (1957–8), 'The resort to divorce in England and Wales, 1858–1957', *Population Studies*, vol. 11

Rowntree, G. and Pierce, R. M. (1961–2), 'Birth control in Britain', *Population Studies*, vol. 15

Royal Commission on the Distribution of the Industrial Population (1940), *Report*, Cmnd 6153, London: HMSO

Royal Commission on Population (1949), *Report*, Cmnd 7695, London: HMSO

Runciman, W. G. (1972), *Relative Deprivation and Social Justice*, Harmondsworth: Penguin

Russell, D. (1975), *The Tamarisk Tree*, London: Virago

Russell, J. C. (1948), 'Demographic patterns in history', *Population Studies*, vol. 1

Ryder, N. B. (1973), 'Comment', *Journal of Political Economy*, vol. 81

Sacks, K. (1974), 'Engels revisited: women, the organisation of production and private property', in Rosaldo and Lamphere (eds.)

Sagi, P. C., Potter, R. G. and Westoff, L. F. (1961–2), 'Contraceptive effectiveness as a function of desired family size', *Population Studies*, vol. 15

Samuels, R. (1977), 'The workshop of the world', in *History Workshop Journal*, Spring, no. 3

Sanger, M. (1932), *My Fight for Birth Control*, London: Faber

Sanger, M. and Stone, H. (eds.) (1931), *The Practice of Contraception*, London: Bai Uiere, Tindall and Co.

Sauvy, A. (1969), *General Theory of Population*, London: Weidenfeld and Nicolson

Saville, J. (1957), *Rural Depopulation in England and Wales, 1851–1951*, London: Routledge and Kegan Paul

Sayers, R. S. (1973), *A History of Economic Change in England 1880–1939*, London: Oxford University Press

Schnaiberg, A. (1973), 'The concept and measurement of child dependency: an approach to family formation analysis', *Population Studies*, vol. 27

Schofield, A. S. (1970), 'Age specific mobility in an eighteenth century rural English parish', *Annals de Demographic Historique*

Schorr, A. (1970), 'Income maintenance and the birth rate', in Ford and De Jong (eds.)

Shultz, T. W. (1973), 'The value of children: an economic perspective', *Journal of Political Economy*, vol. 81

Scott, W. (1957–8), 'The fertility of teachers in England and Wales', *Population Studies*, vol. 11

Secombe, W. (1973), 'The housewife and her labour under capitalism', *New Left Review*, no. 83

Seebohm Rowntree, B. (1941), *Poverty and Progress (A Second Social Survey of York)*, London: Longman, Green and Co.

Segal, C. S. (1939), *Penn'orth of Chips*, London: Gollancz

Shannon, H. A. and Grebenik, E. (1943), *The Population of Bristol*, Cambridge: Cambridge University Press

Shorter, E. (1975), *The Making of the Modern Family*, London: Fontana/ Collins

Simms, M. (1974), 'Midwives and abortion in the 1930's', *Midwife and Health Visitor*, vol. 10

Skelley, J. (ed.) (1976), *The General Strike*, London: Lawrence and Wishart

Slater, E. and Woodside, M. (1951), *Patterns of Marriage: A Study of Marriage Relationships in the Urban Working Classes*, London: Cassel

Smelser, N. J. (1974), 'Sociological history: the industrial revolution and the British working-class', in Flinn and Smout (eds.)

Smith-Rosenberg, C. (1975), 'The female world of love and ritual: relations between women in nineteenth century America', *Signs*, vol. 1

Spengler, J. J. and Duncan, O. D. (eds.) (1956), *Population Theory and Policy*, Glencoe, Ill.: Free Press

Spring Rice, M. (1939), *Working-Class Wives*, Harmondsworth: Penguin

Stearns, P. N. (1975), *European Society in Upheaval*, London: Collier Macmillan

Stella Browne, F., Ludovici, A. and Roberts, H. (1935), *Abortion*, London: Allen and Unwin

Stenton, D. M. (1957), *The English Woman in History*, London: Allen and Unwin

Stinchcombe, A. L. (1968), *Constructing Social Theories*, New York: Harcourt, Brace and World, Inc.

Stone, L. (1977), *The Family, Sex and Marriage in England, 1500–1800*, London: Weidenfeld and Nicolson

Stopes, M. (1919), *Married Love*, London: G. P. Putnam's Sons Ltd

Stopes, M. (1925), *The First Five Thousand*, London: Bale, Sons and Danielsson

Stopes, M. (1929), *Mother England*, London: Bale, Sons and Danielsson

Storm-Clark, C. (1971), 'The miners 1870–1970: a test case for oral history', *Victorian Studies*, vol. 15

Stycos, J. M. and Weller, R. (1967), 'Female working roles and fertility', *Demography*, vol. 4

Sullerot, E. (1971), *Woman, Society and Change*, London: World Universal Library


Tawney, R. H. (1915), *The Establishment of Minimum Rates in the Tailoring Industry under the Trade Boards Act of 1909*, London

Terkel, Studs (1970), *Hard Times: An Oral History of the Great Depression*, London: Allen Lane/Penguin

Terry, G. B. (1975), 'Rival explanations in the work–fertility relationship', *Population Studies*, vol. 29

Thane, P. (ed.) (1978), *The Origins of Social Policy*, London: Croom Helm

Thompson, E. P. (1974), 'Time, work-discipline and industrial capitalism', in Flinn and Smout (eds.)

Thompson, P. (1977), *The Edwardians: The Remaking of British Society*, St Albans: Paladin

Thompson, P. (1978), *The Voice of the Past: Oral History*, London: Oxford University Press

Thurtle, D. (1940), *Abortion: Right or Wrong?*, London: C. A. Watts

Titmuss, R. (1938), *Poverty and Population*, London: Macmillan

Titmuss, R. (1943), *Birth, Poverty and Wealth*, London: Hamilton Medical Books

Titmuss, R. and Titmuss, K. (1942), *Parents Revolt*, London: Secker and Warburg

Tout, H. (1938), *The Standard of Living in Bristol*, Bristol University Press

Tranter, N. (1973), *Population Since the Industrial Revolution: The Case of England and Wales*, London: Croom Helm

Turchi, B. A. (1975), *The Demand for Children*, Cambridge, Mass.: Ballinger Publishing Co.

Turner, C. (1971), 'Conjugal roles and social networks re-examined', in Anderson (ed.)

United Nations (1970), *Demographic Yearbook*, New York: United Nations

United Nations (1971), *Human Fertility and National Development*, New York: United Nations

United Nations, Population Division (1956), 'History of population theories', in Spengler and Duncan (eds.)

United Nations, Population Division (1967), *Proceedings of the World Population Conference*, vol. 2, New York: United Nations

Westoff, C. F. (1956), 'The changing focus of differential fertility research: the social mobility hypothesis', in Spengler and Duncan (eds.)

Westoff, C. F. and Potvin, R. H. (1967), *College Women and Fertility Values*, Princeton, NJ: Princeton University Press

Westover, B. (1976), 'Military tailoring in Colchester 1890–1925', unpubl. BA thesis, University of Essex

Whelpton, P. K., Campbell, A. A. and Patterson, J. E. (1966), *Fertility and Family Planning in the United States*, Princeton, NJ: Princeton University Press

White, C. L. (1970), *Women's Magazines 1693–1968*, London: Michael Joseph

Williams, G. (1958), *The Sanctity of Life and the Criminal Law*, London: Faber

Willis, R. J. (1973), 'A new approach to the economic theory of fertility behaviour', *Journal of Political Economy*, vol. 81, no. 2

Wilmott, P. and Young, M. (1962), *Family and Kinship in East London*, Harmondsworth: Penguin

Women's Co-operative Guild (1915), *Maternity: Letters from Working Women*, London: G. Bell and Sons

Wrigley, E. A. (1966), 'Family limitation in pre-industrial England', *Economic History Review*, no. 19

Wrigley, E. A. (1969), *Population and History*, London: World University Library

Young, M. and Wilmott, P. (1973), *The Symmetrical Family*, London: Routledge and Kegan Paul

Yaan Tien, H. and Bean, F. D. (eds.) (1974), *Comparative Family and Fertility Research*, Leiden: E. J. Brill

Zweig, F. (1952), *Women's Life and Labour*, London: Gollancz

# Index